D0913931

# The Parnell Myth and Irish Politics 1891–1956

# American University Studies

Series IX

History

Vol. 21

PETER LANG

New York · Berne · Frankfurt am Main

William Michael Murphy

# THE PARNELL MYTH AND IRISH POLITICS 1891–1956

PETER LANG
New York · Berne · Frankfurt am Main

**Library of Congress Cataloging-in-Publication Data**

Murphy, William Michael
The Parnell myth and Irish politics, 1891–1956.

(American University Studies. Series IX,
History ; vol. 21)
Revision of thesis (Ph. D.) – University of Chicago, 1981.
Bibliography: p.
Includes index.
1. Parnell, Charles Stewart, 1846–1891 – Influence.
2. Ireland – Politics and government – 20th century.
3. Ireland – Politics and government – 19th century.
4. Politicians – Ireland – Biography. 5. Nationalists – Ireland – Biography. 6. Ireland – Historiography.
I. Title. II. Series.
DA958.P2M87 1986 41.5081'092'5 86-20176
ISBN 0-8204-0351-2



CIP-Kurztitelaufnahme der Deutschen Bibliothek

**Murphy, William Michael:**
The Parnell Myth and Irish Politics 1891 – 1956 / William Michael Murphy. – New York ; Berne ; Frankfurt am Main : Lang, 1986.
(American University Studies : Ser. 9, History ; Vol. 21)
ISBN 0-8204-0351-2

NE: American University Studies / 09



Printed by Weihert-Druck GmbH, Darmstadt (West Germany)

**for Lamar**

## TABLE OF CONTENTS

## TABLES

## ACKNOWLEDGMENTS

Most of the research for this study was done in the National Library of Ireland, the Library of Trinity College, Dublin, and the Joseph Regenstein Library of the University of Chicago. I wish to thank the staff members of those institutions for their unfailing kindness as well as their professional help. I am also grateful to staff members of the Royal Irish Academy, the Dublin Public Library, the Central Catholic Library of Dublin, the New York Public Library, and the Harvard University Library for their assistance.

Emmet Larkin served for many years as my graduate adviser. This study owes much to his painstaking instruction in how to think historically and to his deep understanding of Irish nationalist politics. William McNeill read every chapter more than once and challenged me to think broadly about the meaning of the Parnell Myth. A number of others have offered valuable insights at critical times, including Charles Gray, David Grene, Michael Murrin, Carol Eck, Michael Hazel, Mary Druke, Rebecca McCauley, Bethel House, Lawrence McBride, and George Bernstein.

My hosts in Dublin during my research were Mrs. Maureen Moran and her family. Ray, Brenda, Fiona, and their friends--especially Mick Moore--not only made me feel welcome but taught me much of what I learned about Ireland.

Laura Koenig, a student at the University of Chicago, not only typed the manuscript but made many helpful corrections and suggestions.

History is a very rewarding pursuit. For that reason, a historian may owe debts of gratitude that far exceed the products of his abilities. He can never thank adequately the individuals who have brought history alive for him and given him a gift that will enrich his life as long as it lasts. Among the professional educators to whom I owe much are the Rev. Christian Ceplecha, O.S.B., Robert E. Burns, Francis Phelan, Boleslaw Szczesniak, Thomas Meehan, Jack Nelson, Sr. M. Faith, C.S.C., Sr. M. Thomas More, C.S.C., and Edna Brown.

I owe special debts to my family. From the time I was a little boy, my aunts Edna and Doris McGlynn took me in tow to numerous historical sites and monuments, gave me books, answered my questions about the past, especially the past of their beloved New England, and ultimately took me to Ireland. My parents somehow got us all educated; both parents and siblings have been generous with their good-humored encouragement and moral support.

My wife Lamar read and commented on the entire manuscript and assisted with the tedious tasks of proofing and indexing. Her contribution went far beyond her insightful editorial comments; she encouraged me every step of the way, making considerable sacrifices as she did so. This book represents merely one more reason to be grateful I ever met her.

# CHAPTER 1

# INTRODUCTION

The subject of this study is the writing about Charles Stewart Parnell by politicians, journalists and historians published between his death in 1891 and the year 1956. It constituted a single phenomenon, the Parnell Myth, held together by a central theme (independence and dignity) and a central symbol (Parnell's public attitude,[1] projecting those qualities). In the course of this study, I will delineate the Parnell Myth's principal characteristics, describe the historical context within which it developed, and analyze the relationship between Myth and context. The Myth played a significant historical role (because its central symbol partially filled the vacuum in leadership left after Parnell's death), and examination of it leads to a better understanding of the dynamics of Irish nationalism.

One of the chief purposes of this introduction is to delineate the scope of this study by indicating what it does not include. The definition of the Parnell Myth in my opening sentence actually excludes more material than it includes. It does not include the oral traditions about Parnell, the representations of him in literature, or the political material written about him before his death or after 1956. The reason for excluding the oral traditions is that the manner of their transmission was so different from that of the printed matter. These stories were passed down by word of mouth until they were recorded in the Irish Folklore Collection in the years between the World Wars. Because they were transmitted differently from the stories in print, they acquired different characteristics and therefore merit a separate analysis.

The aspect of this study which will probably surprise readers the most is the exclusion of serious literature from its scope. It is, after all, the writing of James Joyce and William Butler Yeats that first come to mind at the mention of a "Parnell myth." Like the oral traditions, however, the literary material about Parnell exhibits different characteristics from the political writing and so requires a separate analysis. Once I had reached this conclusion--which surprised me, too--it became clear that the political material had to be analyzed first: it provided the background for the artists' work. In the event, of course, that decision brought its own rewards, as the political writing turned out to be historically important in its own right.

The period covered by this study begins with Parnell's death on October 6, 1891, and closes at the end of the year 1956. The decision to take Parnell's death as the starting point deserves some comment. After all, Thomas Sherlock's Charles Stewart Parnell,[2] published in 1881, and T. P. O'Connor's The Parnell Movement,[3] which appeared five years later, were heavily relied upon, directly or indirectly, by most subsequent writers. Why exclude these books and the newspaper accounts published during Parnell's lifetime? They, or memories of them, continued to shape people's perceptions of Parnell long after his death. The answer is that it is necessary to distinguish between two fundamentally distinct, if similar, phenomena. One was Parnell's public image, manipulated in part by himself, and the other was the Parnell Myth, the portrayal of him by others independent of his direct influence. To be understood properly, these phenomena have to be analyzed separately.

I chose 1956 as the terminal point of this study for two reasons. First, the sixty-five year period 1891-1956 was long enough to span several different phases of Irish political history, so the Myth could be observed against a changing political background. This meant that its enduring characteristics could be isolated and the interactions of Myth and context could be traced. Second, the terminal point came just before the Myth could have been expected to be affected by the revolution in modern Irish historiography. (Conor Cruise O'Brien's pioneering Parnell and His Party[4] was published in 1957.) Taking 1956 as the end point, therefore, ensured that the external forces shaping the Myth in the years under study came from culture and politics, not scientific scholarship.

Having described the boundaries of this study, I should also offer a few words of caution about terminology. Preconceptions about the meanings of three terms, Irish nationalism, Parnell myth, and myth, can be very misleading. Irish nationalism is markedly different from the nationalism spawned in world powers such as Britain and the United States. This point was brought home to me by two experiences during a trip to Ireland in 1972. One evening, at a cinema in a small country town, I was startled by the applause which erupted when a character in the film mentioned Irish whiskey. Then it occurred to me that, for Irishmen, virtually all cinema is foreign. Only rarely does it portray the sights and sounds of everyday life in Ireland. A few days later I explored the Woolworth's store in Galway. The boys' toys were much like those at home: cowboy pistols, toy soldiers, trucks and planes and cars. The toy soldiers were British, German and American; the warplanes bore British and American markings. There were also some police patrol cars, black and white, with red lights, marked "POLICE." Irish patrol cars at the time were white, with blue lights, and carried the legend, "GARDA." Like the cinema--and television, with its British, American and Australian programs--the children's toys represented daily life as it existed in larger, wealthier, more powerful countries. The applause I heard in the country cinema was as much an assertion of pride in Irish nationality as the singing of the national anthem before a hurling match in Dublin's Croke Park.

We are used to conceiving of the nationalism of the great powers as a kind of overweening chauvinism, at its worst in wartime. Irish nationalism, though it has its own ugly side, is a different thing. Ireland is a small nation whose size, poverty and long-time colonial status have made it easy to dismiss as unimportant. Irish nationalism resembles nothing so much as a response to that kind of dismissal. Its message might be articulated this way: "Ireland is important, worthy of respect. It is an ancient nation with a culture centuries in the making. It represents something to be cherished rather than to be contemptuously, or indifferently, dismissed." In the Parnell Myth, this meaning emerges unmistakably in the motif of contempt/disdain/scorn, which I discuss in Chapters 4 and 5.

The expression Parnell Myth is a convenient label for the phenomenon under discussion because it is familiar to students of Irish history and literature. Its very familiarity can, however, lead to misconceptions, so a few words of caution are in order. In the first place, the term myth should not be taken in any technical sense. Myth theory is still in the early stages of its development, and there is no consensus among the specialists of the various concerned disciplines about what myths are or what characteristics they share. The phenomenon under study here is the political writing about Parnell. It says nothing to call it a myth, because myth has no commonly accepted meaning. I discuss the relationship between the Parnell Myth and various theoretical propositions about myth in Chapter 6. The point to be stressed here is that questions about whether the Parnell Myth is a "true myth," or what kind of myth it is, are inappropriate because myth is not a true generic term.

I have capitalized Parnell Myth to distinguish the object of this study from the meaning of "Parnell myth" as the expression has traditionally been used by historians. Some have concluded, after examining the work of the best known literary artists and certain political writers, that the "Parnell myth" is essentially a Parnellite interpretation of the Split married to a republican interpretation of Parnell's career. In Chapter 6, I discuss the differences between their conclusions--a result of their discussing what is really a different body of material--and my findings. In fact, the Parnell Myth of this study has a focus different from the arguments of the Split or the traditional disagreements between constitutional and republican politicians in Ireland. It centers, rather, on Parnell's public posture, his attitude, which projects independence and dignity.

So far from being a Parnellite creation, the Parnell Myth is composed of writing by authors of three different nationalities (Irish, English, and American) and of a variety of political points of view. It also reflects the changing political context within which it developed. While the Split was extremely bitter--some say much more bitter that the Civil War of 1922-23--it dominated politics only until the Irish Parliamentary Party reunited in 1900. After that, the renewed struggle for Home Rule, the rapid succession of crises which followed the onset of the first World War, and the struggle to establish the new state absorbed public attention. Still, people continued to write about Parnell, and politicians continued to claim his legacy. The reason for this was more basic than the rancor of the Split, the tragedy of Parnell's fall, or the poignancy of the love story. The Myth's appeal was based on qualities with a compelling attraction for the people of an emerging nation. I discuss this point at length in Chapters 7 and 8.

The Parnell Myth had its roots in the real career of Parnell, in his actual words and deeds, rather than in fanciful stories. It remains, however, very different from an historical account. First of all, it is an amalgam of many different books and articles, not a single work. Many incidents are described several times, with differing interpretations. Its basic unity, instead of resting on consistency of interpretation, is based upon the central theme and central symbol, a shared perception of qualities in Parnell's attitude which the Myth's diverse authors did not fully recognize. Would a straight-through reading of the entire body of evidence, as if it were a single, giant text, yield an historically "true" picture of what happened? The chronicle of events would be quite accurate--though, of course, very repetitive--but the interpretations of the meaning of those events, as well as the aims of the actors who shaped them, would be bewildering in their variety. At the level of interpretation, the Parnell Myth tells many stories, not one. Its essential unity and coherence lies deeper, at the level of theme and symbol.

I gathered the evidence for this study by taking notes on the items listed as sources in the chronological bibliography. In order to discover whether there were patterns in the evidence, I compiled two indexes to the notes I had taken. The first covered material from the years 1891-99, and it formed the basis of my analysis in Chapters 3 and 4. The analysis is recounted in some detail so that the reader can understand how I used the evidence to arrive at my conclusions. Chapter 4 is based on the second index, covering material published between 1900 and 1956. It consists of a much briefer analysis and of a comparison of the characteristics of the material from 1900-56 with those of the material from 1891-99. My purpose in using the indexes was to uncover patterns which already existed in the evidence rather than to impose patterns myself or to arrive at them impressionistically. In Chapter 5, I also discuss the importance of this inductive approach.

Chapter 2 traces the ways in which Parnell was commemorated in the years after his death. It is meant to capture something of the emotional climate in which the Parnell Myth was born. In addition, the sketches which I offer of a few of the most important contributors to the Myth will acquaint the reader with their individual contributions while demonstrating, by example, that the Parnell Myth was not some kind of group project but rather the unintentional product of many authors pursuing diverse aims.

**Biographical Sketch of Parnell**

Charles Stewart Parnell was born June 27, 1846, the second son of Delia Tudor Stewart and John Henry Parnell, at Avondale, near Rathdrum, Co. Wicklow. His mother was the daughter of United States Navy Commodore Charles Stewart, "Old Ironsides," a hero of the War of 1812. His paternal grandfather, William Parnell, was noted for pamphlets he had written supporting Catholics' and tenants' rights. William's father, Sir John Parnell, was famous as a patriot who had been an incorruptible Chancellor of the Irish Exchequer and who had been dismissed from office for opposing the Act of Union (1800), which abolished the Irish Parliament.

Parnell's education took place largely in England, including four undistinguished years at Magdalen College, Cambridge. This experience was notable chiefly for its effect on his sense of Irish nationality. "These English," he said to his brother John, "despise us because we are Irish; but we must stand up to them. That's the way to treat the Englishman--stand up to him."[5]

Parnell left Cambridge in 1869--suspended after fighting with a local--and took up residence at Avondale, which he had inherited, along with a substantial annual income, from his father. He travelled in the United States in 1872-73; when he returned home, he served as a member of the Synod of the Church of Ireland and as High Sheriff of Wicklow. He was a progressive landlord, interested in agricultural improvements and especially in exploiting the timber and mineral resources on his estates.

In 1874, Parnell decided to enter politics. Prevented by his position as High Sheriff from standing for his native Wicklow in that year's general election, he fought and lost a by-election for County Dublin later in the year. He won a seat for Meath in 1875, pledged to support Home Rule (a separate Irish government and parliament with control over purely Irish affairs).

Parnell took a strong nationalist line from the first. His maiden speech, delivered on his fifth day in the House of Commons, included the rhetorical question:

> Why should Ireland be treated as a geograhical fragment of England, as I heard an

> ex-Chancellor of the Exchequer call her some time ago? Ireland is not a geographical fragment. She is a nation.[6]

It was a remark Parnell made in the House the following year, however, that brought him to public attention. The Chief Secretary for Ireland referred in passing to three Fenians as murderers who had accidentally shot a policeman while trying to free one of their compatriots. Parnell interrupted him and, explaining his outburst, said that he would never believe that the incident had been a murder. The Fenians, advocates of complete separation from Great Britain by means of physical force, immediately took notice. Their interest increased when Parnell joined an association pressing for amnesty for Fenian prisoners.

In 1877, a few Irish M.P.s, including Parnell, began obstructing the business of the House of Commons to force it to pay more attention to Irish grievances. Their actions slowed the business of the House, and, when the government pressed bills forward, resulted in long sittings, punctuated by tedious points of order, motions to report progress, motions to adjourn, and the like. On July 31-August 1, the Irish nationalists held the House in continuous session for a then-record twenty-six hours. This provoked severe criticism, not just from English members, but from more moderate Irish members, who charged that the obstructionists were undermining the dignity of the greatest representative body in the world. Through the remaining years of the decade, Parnell and his colleagues doggedly persisted, drawing the ire of the British press and public but winning the admiration of Irish nationalists and the grudging good will of many Fenians.

While the obstructionists waged their campaign in Parliament, the Fenians made a significant change in policy. Hitherto firmly opposed to both constitutional politics and every cause except separation from Britain, they decided on a "New Departure." They would support the agitation for agrarian reform and would cooperate with sufficiently vigorous constitutional politicians. The New Departure was the creation of American Fenian leader John Devoy and of Michael Davitt, a convicted Fenian gun-runner recently released from a British prison. Devoy offered their support to Parnell, who met with Davitt but cautiously declined to reply.

Shortly afterwards Davitt began a movement among tenants in the impoverished West of Ireland to agitate against rack rents and evictions. Parnell agreed to speak at an early meeting, doing so in the face of episcopal warning and urging his listeners to "keep a firm grip of your homesteads."[7] By October 1879, Parnell had been elected President of the National Land League of Ireland. That winter he visited North America, addressing the U.S. House of Representatives on Irish conditions and raising funds to assist the tenants. It was on this journey, in Montreal, that Parnell was first hailed as the "uncrowned King of Ireland."

He had to cut his trip short to return to Ireland for the general election of 1880. Parnell campaigned vigorously for advanced nationalist candidates and enjoyed remarkable success. When the Irish Parliamentary Party met, he was voted chairman by twenty-three votes to eighteen over the incumbent, moderate Home Ruler William Shaw. In 1879, the obstructionists had numbered only four or five.

It was just after the 1880 general election that Parnell met Katharine O'Shea, the wife of new Irish M.P. William O'Shea. The O'Sheas had already been living apart for some time when Katharine and Parnell met. They very quickly became lovers. Between 1882 and 1884 Katharine bore their three children.

The agrarian agitation continued to increase in intensity. The Land League aggressively expanded the scope of its operations, and Parnell remained in the lead. In September, in Ennis, he told his audience that anyone who took a farm from which a tenant had been evicted, should be put "into a moral Coventry, by isolating him from the rest of his kind as if he was a leper of old--you must show him your detestation of the crime he has committed."[8] The practice of refusing to buy from or sell to--or even speak to--such people spread quickly, taking its name, boycotting, from an early victim, a Captain Boycott.

As the agitation increased, so did agrarian crimes, from 301 in 1878 to 2,590 in 1880.[9] In January 1881, William E. Gladstone's new government brought in a coercion bill suspending certain civil rights in Ireland. The Irish Parliamentary Party fought it fiercely, obstructing its passage clause by clause. After one debate that lasted forty-one hours, and was ended only by the Speaker's extraordinary action, the government introduced new rules of procedure limiting debate. The Party fought the new rules, too, but they eventually passed, with Parnell and twenty-six followers being suspended for their disorderly protests. The coercion bill passed eventually as well.

Gladstone followed coercion with concession, offering a land bill that established principles known in Ireland as the three Fs: fair rents (to be fixed, if need be, by a land court), fixity of tenure, and free sale of the tenant's interest in his holding. Parnell responded that the bill was alright as far as it went but did not go far enough. The Party gave it qualified support, offering extensive amendments in committee.

Actually, the Land Act of 1881 posed a significant problem for Parnell. It was not radical enough for the Land League's left wing, but the tenants were bound to flood the new land court with petitions for lower rents. Unable therefore wholeheartedly to endorse or condemn the new law, Parnell instead recommended that its operation be tested using cases selected by the Land League. And, with a wary eye on the left wing, he continued to make inflammatory speeches in the countryside. He also launched a weekly newspaper, United Ireland, edited by William O'Brien, to support the League's activities. Finally, he secured passage by a meeting of the Land League of a resolution that tenants should not utilize the land court until after the League's test cases had been decided.

It was too much for Gladstone. In a famous speech at Leeds on October 7, 1881, the Prime Minister denounced Parnell's approach and warned him that the "resources of civilisation were not exhausted." Parnell replied two days later by calling Gladstone a "masquerading knight-errant" and "pretending champion of the rights of every other nation except those of the Irish nation.... who, by his own utterances, is proud to carry fire and sword into your homesteads, unless you humbly abase yourselves before him and before the landlords of this country."[10] Three days later Parnell was arrested and detained in Kilmainham Jail under the Coercion Act. A number of his Party and Land League colleagues were also detained over the next few days. Davitt had already had his parole revoked and was back in prison. On October 18 the nationalists in Kilmainham issued a manifesto urging the tenants to withhold their rents "until the Government relinquishes the existing system of terrorism and restores the constitutional rights of the people."[11] The government responded by proclaiming the Land League an illegal organization. Parnell had foreseen this difficulty and had already established the Ladies' Land League under the effective leadership of his sister Anna. The Ladies' League surprised him, however, by advocating measures more extreme than he was willing to countenance.

Parnell's imprisonment and the government's proclamation of the Land League extricated him from the political predicament the Land Act had created If he stayed in prison too long, however, he would lose control of the movement--as the Ladies' Land League was demonstrating. He also felt some personal pressure, since Katharine O'Shea was expecting their first child. The government, too, wanted a settlement. The eventual agreement, negotiated partly through the agency of William O'Shea, was called the Kilmainham Treaty. It provided for the prisoners' release, amendment of the Land Act in the tenants' favor, and Parnell's promise to help quell agrarian violence.

Parnell was released from Kilmainham on May 2, 1882. That same day, W. E. Forster, the Chief Secretary for Ireland, resigned from Gladstone's government in protest. Four days later, the new Chief Secretary and his principal civil servant were assassinated by extreme nationalists while walking in Dublin's Phoenix Park. The shock was felt in both countries. Parnell offered to Gladstone to resign his seat; Gladstone declined the offer. He was obliged, however, to bring in a new, tougher coercion bill, which the Irish naturally opposed at every stage.

Released from detention, Parnell responded to the Ladies' Land League's adventurism by cutting off its funds. He then moved to replace both defunct tenants' organizations by a new body, the Irish National League, dominated by himself and his lieutenants. During the next few years, the National League became a formidable political organization. The National League, and the local conventions it sponsored, laid the basis for Parnell's triumph in the 1885 general election. The conventions selected strong nationalists, and--crucial to Party discipline in later years--began requiring a pledge that they would "sit, act and vote" with the Party or resign.

The years between the Kilmainham Treaty and the 1885 general election, while less dramatic than the half decade that preceded them, were noteworthy nevertheless. The land agitation continued. American Fenians dissatisfied with the New Departure began a dynamite campaign against British bridges and railway stations, culminating in an attempt to blow up the Houses of Parliament and the Tower of London in January 1885. And W. E. Forster, the former Chief Secretary, accused Parnell in a famous House of Commons speech of encouraging crime in Ireland. Forster's indictment and Parnell's icy reply that he owed no explanations to an English assembly captured many imaginations; they are discussed at length in Chapters 4 and 5.

By 1885, Parnell was in a very strong position. The Irish Parliamentary Party's growing moderation--in nationalist terms, at least--and its advocacy of Catholic causes in Parliament won over the clergy. Most New Departure Fenians remained loyal to Parnell, and so did the economic classes that counted in nationalist Ireland, the tenant farmers and shopkeepers. The general election, brought about when the Irish and Tories combined to defeat Gladstone's government, proved a remarkable triumph. The Party swept all sixty-eight seats outside Ulster, lost the two university seats, and took seventeen of Ulster's thirty-three. In addition, one of Parnell's lieutenants, T. P. O'Connor, carried a predominantly Irish Liverpool constituency, so the Party won a total of eighty-six seats.

One ominous event occurred during the 1885 election. William O'Shea tried and failed to win a seat in Liverpool. Since T. P. O'Connor had been returned for both Galway city and Liverpool, and he chose to represent Liverpool, the Galway seat became vacant. Parnell then endorsed O'Shea, well known as at best a lukewarm nationalist, for the vacancy in Galway. This provoked a revolt among Party members J. G. Biggar, Timothy Healy and--briefly--O'Connor. In the end, Parnell won over all but his friend Biggar, and O'Shea won the seat, but Parnell's liaison with Katharine O'Shea received brief public notice for the first time. (The blunt Biggar alluded to it publicly, but the nationalist

Freeman's Journal did not report his remarks.)

The final election results gave the Liberals 335 seats, the Tories 249 and the Irish 86. If the Irish cast their lot with the Tories, the result would be a tie; with Irish support, the Liberals had a majority of 172. Shortly after the election results were known, Gladstone hinted his support for Home Rule. When Parliament met in January, the Tories, who had been flirting cautiously with Parnell, announced their intention to bring in another coercion bill, and the Liberals and Irish combined to defeat their caretaker government. Gladstone again became Prime Minister and introduced the first Home Rule bill. It provided for a separate parliament for Ireland with modest powers of self-government in domestic matters. This measure split the Liberal Party. The Home Rule bill was defeated; Gladstone obtained a dissolution and took his case to the country, where he was defeated again. The results of the 1886 general election put the Conservatives in government supported by the anti-Home Rule Liberals, called Liberal Unionists, with the Liberals and Irish in opposition.

Parnell largely disappeared from public view for the next few years. He had bouts of ill health, notably in the winter of 1886-87, and, since the Irish-Liberal alliance held out the promise of another Home Rule bill after the next general election, it was not necessary for him to play so conspicuous a role.

All was not quiet in the Irish countryside, however. The tenant farmers' plight continued to worsen. Even the rents fixed by the land court in 1881 were increasingly beyond the tenants' shrinking resources as overseas competition drove down agricultural prices. Parnell's lieutenants responded with the Plan of Campaign. The Plan, essentially an attempt to combine the tenants into estate-wide bargaining units, provided that, if a landlord refused to grant the reduction they demanded, the tenants should withhold their rents and pool them to support any families that were subsequently evicted. If the pooled rents could not sustain the evicted tenants, the National League would provide support. The Plan was pushed by William O'Brien and John Dillon; Parnell, ill when it was first announced, eventually gave it qualified approval. He was concerned about its effects on English Liberal and Irish episcopal opinion as well as on the coffers of the National League. But the Plan enjoyed considerable popular support in Ireland.

Parnell's reclusiveness contributed to the prominence of his "lieutenants," the Party's elite. They included the deputy chairman, Justin McCarthy, a popular novelist and historian; Timothy Healy, a journalist, barrister and brilliant parliamentary tactician; Thomas Sexton, the Party's expert on public finance; William O'Brien, editor of United Ireland; O'Brien's close friend, John Dillon, admired in Ireland and feared in England as an agrarian agitator; Timothy Harrington, political operative in charge of National League patronage; T. P. O'Connor, another gifted journalist; and, in the late 1880s, John Redmond, future leader of the Parnellites.

The Conservative government met the challenge of the Plan of Campaign with yet another coercion bill, more objectionable than its predecessors because it was "perpetual"; it would not have to be renewed each year. While the debate raged in the Commons, the Times began on March 7, 1887, a series of articles entitled "Parnellism and Crime,"attempting to link Parnell to the violence that attended the land agitation. The most sensational of the stories featured a letter apparently written by Parnell apologizing to Fenian leaders for condemning the Phoenix Park murders. Parnell denied authorship in Parliament, and, when a court case brought more letters and charges to light, asked for a select committee of the House to investigate the authenticity of the letters. The government responded by appointing a special commission charged to examine all the charges brought by the Times against Parnell and the nationalist movement. The denouement was highly dramatic: in February 1889, Richard Pigott, the Dublin journalist who had forged the letters, broke down under cross-examination, escaped abroad, and shortly after shot himself. Even before the special commission reported its verdict clearing Parnell and his followers of criminal charges, English public opinion had exonerated him. Parnell was at the peak of his influence.

It was in December 1889 that William O'Shea filed for divorce, citing Parnell as co-respondent. When the case came to trial in November of the following year, Parnell and Katharine O'Shea elected not to defend it--it was the only way they could marry--and, after offering, uncontradicted, some very damaging testimony, O'Shea was granted his divorce.

At first the Party appeared to unite behind Parnell. Expressions of support were offered from hastily convened local meetings, and Parnell was reelected chairman of the Party. But the situation quickly changed. The day before the Party met, Gladstone had written a letter for John Morley to show Parnell--that he was unable to show him before the Party met--saying that Parnell's continued leadership would render his own, based as it was on the issue of Home Rule, "almost a nullity." After Parnell was reelected, Gladstone allowed his letter to be published. The Irish Party met again to discuss the leadership, but Parnell was adamant. The members agreed to reconvene in a week. Parnell, determined to regain the initiative from Gladstone, published a manifesto questioning Gladstone's and the Liberals' soundness on Home Rule. This last move, seen as treachery to allies, cost Parnell the support of Dillon and O'Brien, then in America raising funds for the tenants. This set the stage for the famous debate in Committee Room 15 of the House of Commons.

It was there that the Party met on December 1-6, 1890 to reconsider Parnell's chairmanship. Dillon, O'Brien, and Harrington (a Parnellite) were still in America. McCarthy, Sexton, O'Connor, and Healy (soon called Antiparnellites) opposed Parnell; John Redmond and the ex-Fenian J. J. O'Kelly supported him. For the most part, the debate was conducted on a high plane. The Antiparnellites, in the majority, argued that, especially after his manifesto, Parnell had become a threat to the Liberal alliance and thus to Home Rule. The Parnellites warned that Parnell was the only leader who could deliver Home Rule and accused the Antiparnellites of submitting to English dictation. Parnell, in the chair, used his authority arbitrarily to prevent his leadership from coming to a vote. Healy made a few famous, tasteless remarks. During a wrangle about who was to be master of the Party, for example, he asked rhetorically who was to be its mistress. Healy's words here and later on the hustings added significantly to the personal bitterness of the Split. Unable to force a vote, the Antiparnellites finally withdrew from Committee Room 15 under McCarthy's leadership.

The debate continued in the country as the two factions fought three by-elections in the first half of 1891. Parnell lost all three. He pushed himself mercilessly, crossing from England to Ireland every weekend to address public gatherings. When he married Katharine in July, the Freeman's Journal deserted him, and he set about establishing a new national daily newspaper, the Irish Independent. The exertions of this last campaign proved too much for a constitution that had never been robust, and he succumbed to a fever on October 6, 1891.

The Split left a legacy of division and bitterness in the nationalist ranks. The Fenians supported Parnell; the Roman Catholic clergy denounced him. This led to charges that Parnell deliberately flirted with separation and physical force in his rhetoric, and to counter-charges that the Antiparnellites were open to clerical as well as English dictation. The Parnellites were called placemen (that is, financially dependent on Parnell-controlled Party funds); the Antiparnellites were accused of being envious of their former chief, who had made them what they were. It was a very long time before those wounds were healed and an even longer time before the bitter disillusion disappeared.

## Notes to Chapter 1

[1]Throughout this study, attitude appears in italics when it refers to Parnell's public posture, the central symbol of the Myth.

[2]Thomas Sherlock, The Life of Charles Stewart Parnell: With An Account of His Ancestry (Boston: Murphy & McCarthy, 1881).

[3]T. P. O'Connor, The Parnell Movement: With a Sketch of Irish Parties from 1843 (London: Kegan Paul & Co., 1886).

[4]Conor Cruise O'Brien, Parnell and His Party 1880-1890 (Oxford: Clarendon Press, 1957).

[5]Quoted in R. Barry O'Brien, The Life of Charles Stewart Parnell 1846-1891 3rd ed., 2 vols. (London: Smith, Elder & Co., 1899), 1:41. Hereinafter referred to as RBOB. This biographical sketch follows O'Brien and the Dictionary of National Biography (1895 ed.), s.v. "Parnell, Charles Stewart."

[6]Quoted in RBOB, 1:85.

[7]Quoted in Dictionary of National Biography, s.v. "Parnell, Charles Stewart," p. 325.

[8]Ibid., p. 327.

[9]Dictionary of National Biography, s.v. "Parnell, Charles Stewart," p. 328.

[10]RBOB, 1:307-8.

[11]Quoted in F. S. L. Lyons, Parnell, Irish History Series, no. 3 (Dublin: Dublin Historical Association, 1970), p. 11.

# CHAPTER 2

# PARNELL REMEMBERED

## Commemorations of Parnell in Ceremony and Stone

Parnell's death resulted in a flurry of memorial activity. The funeral, which took place in Dublin, was huge. Hundreds of thousands of people looked on as the procession moved along its winding route from City Hall to Glasnevin Cemetery. Those marching in the cortege included representatives of athletic, social and labor organizations, led by the Parnellite M.P.s and a host of other Parnellite politicians from around the country. The Antiparnellites, however, stayed away: Dublin had always been a Parnellite city, and feelings were running high against them. (Placards were distributed which read, "Murdered to satisfy Englishmen," and the wreath sent by the Belfast Parnell Leadership Committee carried the menacing inscription, "Murdered--Avenge.")[1] The tone of the funeral, however, was sad and dignified rather than vengeful. As one of the organizers reported,

> The one thought that animated all was a desire to honour the remains of him whom they had loved so well; and so throughout the day a spirit of unselfishness spread itself over the mighty crowd, and brought orderly arrangement and solemn bearing where no power of man could have enforced it...Here, too, we at the head of the procession are passing into a narrow street apparently too full already. Yet a quiet word to the crowd 'Help us to honour him by making room'--at once the passage is cleared, some of the people moving to the front, others making their ways into doorways of houses, others pressing up against the walls; anywhere so that they make room for <u>him</u>. That was how the great crowds were organized.[2]

Parnell was buried in Glasnevin Cemetery, not far from the round tower which marked Daniel O'Connell's grave. For the next several weeks, the grave was visited by large crowds. They came to see the Chief's last resting-place and the multitude of wreaths, bouquets and immortelles which covered it. A few also came to pay debts of thanks. James Stephens, the old Fenian, brought an immortelle with a card incribed "to the revered memory of my sincere friend."[3] Shortly before his death, Parnell had endorsed a public subscription to purchase a home for Stephens.[4] A week after Stephens's visit to the grave, he was followed by Prince George of Wales and the Prince's uncle, the Duke of

Clarence and Avondale.[5] It is likely that this pilgrimmage, too, was prompted by feelings of gratitude. In July 1889, Parnell had joined Gladstone in supporting an additional Parliamentary grant of support to the Prince of Wales. In Gladstone's opinion,

> Nothing could be better than Parnell's conduct on that occasion. He showed the greatest skill, tact, and ability, and gave me the most efficient help at every turn.[6]

Even though the princes' visit was the result of personal gratitude, Irishmen must have found it particularly gratifying that the royalty should honor the memory of their "uncrowned King," as Parnell was often called.

Parnell's grave underwent may changes in subsequent years. In the late autumn of 1891, a women's committee was formed to tend the grave, but this group must not always have been effective. Mrs. Parnell wrote in her memoir that she had been informed by a friend "a few short years" after Parnell's death that "your husband's grave is the most neglected spot in the whole cemetery." In response to this disquieting news, she had sent a servant over to Dublin with some flowers for the grave. His report, she sadly related, had been even worse:

> Fragments of glass from the broken artificial wreaths, placed there years before; trampled, neglected grass, and little of that but weeds; and the bare untidy backings and wires of the wreaths I had been sending for the greeting of so many days marked only in the calendar of our love.[7]

In time, conditions improved. Early in this century, the grave was covered in shrubbery which spelled out <u>Parnell</u> in Irish letters. Later still, the shrubbery was replaced by a granite boulder from Parnell's own quarries. It sits now on a slightly raised circular mound which is surrounded by a low iron railing. In the boulder's side is carved the single word, <u>PARNELL</u>.

Each October during the 1890s, the anniversary of Parnell's death was observed with massive demonstrations. Increasingly, these became platforms for Parnellite Party rhetoric rather than occasions for commemorating Parnell personally. The tone changed significantly after the Irish Parliamentary Party reunited in 1900, but the demonstrations also declined in size and enthusiasm after that time. The two anniversary celebrations most worthy of note took place in 1911 and 1941. The Parnell monument was dedicated in 1911. It consisted of a large pedestal surmounted by a statue of Parnell created by the American sculptor, Augustus Saint-Gaudens, and behind the statue, an obelisk. The obelisk carried the most famous of Parnell's political pronouncements, his dictum that

> No man has a right to fix the boundary of the march of a nation. No man has a right to say, 'Thus far shalt thou go, and no further'; and we have never attempted to fix the <u>ne plus ultra</u> to the progress of Ireland's nationhood, and we never shall.[8]

The principal speaker at the dedication was the Party leader, John Redmond. In his speech, he inquired where were the opponents of Parnell that day. "Some were beside him on the platform," Sinn Féin commented, somewhat unfairly, with pointed reference to John Dillon.[9] The reason why no opponents of Parnell were visible on Sunday, October 1, 1911, was not that Parnellite arguments had finally carried the day but that the Antiparnellite position had been eroded by events and that Parnell had come to stand for more than just orthodox Parnellism. As the structure of the Parnell Myth indicates, he had become identified with the very qualities, independence and dignity, which the emerging nation valued most highly.

The anniversary celebration took on an international flavor in 1941. Present at the ceremonies in that year were the diplomatic representatives of Germany, Italy, Japan, the United States, France and the United Kingdom, among others. And the reason underlying this substantial diplomatic attendance would have gratified Parnell more than the fact of it. The diplomats were there because Ireland was a neutral state in the World War, and their presence was testimony that the daring gamble of that ultimate exercise of independence, neutrality, was being won. It was fitting that the diplomatic representative of the great powers should be present at the commemoration of the fiftieth anniversary of Parnell's death. Their very attendance was further evidence that Ireland was achieving the independence and dignity for which Parnell had stood.

When Parnell died, his estate, Avondale, passed to his older brother John. (Parnell died technically intestate because he had neglected to change his will after he had married Katharine. John therefore became his heir under Irish law.) John Parnell held the place for several years, but he was unable to make headway with the considerable burden of debt his brother had left behind. There was some desultory talk about the Parnellite Party buying the house and demesne as a monument to Parnell, but nothing came of it. In the end, John sold Avondale to a wealthy Irishman. After a few years more, it passed into the hands of the Department of Forestry, and there it has remained. At present, part of the house is used for the Department's school but three rooms are open to the public as an exhibit.

During his lifetime, Parnell had maintained a hunting lodge (actually, a converted British barracks dating from the eighteenth century) at Aughavannah, in Co. Wicklow not too far from Avondale. Aughavannah probably had more sentimental value for Parnellites than Avondale. While few of them had ever visited Avondale, Parnell had sometimes invited intimates along on his shooting trips to Aughavannah, and it was from Aughavannah that he had sent braces of birds to friends like Justin McCarthy. In the nineties, John Redmond purchased Aughavannah. He may have wished to preserve a memento of the Chief, or just to identify himself more clearly in the public mind as Parnell's successor. Whatever Redmond's reasons, he remodeled the lodge, and he and his family occupied it for a number of years. After his death, Aughavannah was again abandoned, and it is now a ruin.

The other place especially identified with Parnell is "his" room in Kilmainham Jail. William O'Brien once called it "the room which, so long as a stone stands upon a stone of Kilmainham, will be known as 'Mr. Parnell's room.'"[10] This room, which Parnell occupied during his detention in Kilmainham (1881-82), has been set aside as a small museum. It contains documents and mementos of Parnell--more, indeed, than Avondale--and it is the most frequently visited of the places connected with his memory.

Since 1892, the symbol of adherence to Parnell's memory has been the ivy leaf. In its description of the Parnell Anniversary demonstration of 1892, the Dublin Evening Mail reported that "several groups of boys, in most cases decorated with ivy,...proceeded through the streets, cheering for Parnell and groaning for T M Healy."[11] The ivy leaves the boys wore were not the result of spontaneous inspiration but rather of a successful publicity campaign by the Irish Daily Independent. The campaign had been, apparently, the Independent's cause alone. The other national Parnellite paper, United Ireland, had not participated, and the Parnell Anniversary Organising Committee had selected an official commemorative badge in no way evocative of the ivy motif. The badge had consisted of "a handsome vignette portrait of the dead Chief lithographed in white satin between two black bars, underneath the portrait being the words 'Died October 6th, 1891.'"[12] If, however, the Independent's campaign had been a lonely one, it had nevertheless been quite successful.

The Parnell Anniversary was commemorated on October 6th in 1892. The Independent had run this advertisement on October 4th and 5th:

> Ivy Day
>
> The Parnell Anniversary Committee earnestly invite all supporters of the policy and the Dead Leader, in town and country, to wear an ivy leaf on next Thursday, 6th October, in token of their fidelity to his Independent principles.
>
> City Residents can obtain Ivy Leaves from the Ladies' Parnell Grave Committee, 43 Upper O'Connell street, or at the Irish Daily Independent and Evening Herald Offices, 23 College Green, on Wednesday afternoon or Thursday morning.
>
> Friends in the country would confer a great favour on the Committee by sending in packages of Ivy Leaves, small or large, to either of the offices mentioned above, on Wednesday.[13]

Then, on the 6th, it ran a leading article entitled "Ivy Day." "Ivy Day" made it quite clear that the ivy leaf was being worn that day, not only as a badge of mourning, but also as a political party ribbon. The editorial concluded:

> In town and country to-day the ivy worn in the button-hole will be regarded not merely as a token of sorrow for the loss the nation has sustained through his decease, but also as plain and determined evidence of devotion to the Independent principles which must always be associated with the name of "the Chief." To give such evidence, quietly but impressively, is now every man's duty, and the display of that meaningful sprig of ivy is simply a confession of political faith in the face of the enemy. To-day will be inaugurated an annual custom as significant as it is pretty, and it is to be hoped that every Parnellite in the country will support it and that its initiation will be successful.[14]

The innovation was a triumph. Women passed sprigs of ivy out free at street corners. The men wore ivy in their lapels or hats, and the women--more women that men, it was said, wore the leaf--wore sprigs of it attached to their dresses. Some of the leaves had been specially stamped with the letters "CSP" in gold.[15] The Independent celebrated the birth of this new institution, as "Ivy Day" had instantly become, by publishing a poem, "The Green Ivy," by Katharine Tynan, on October 7th. Here is a substantial excerpt:

The Green Ivy

O'er many an Irish castle, great and hoary
The Irish ivy trails;
And o'er grey fanes that catch the sun's last gilding,
See the last sails.

And o'er the Round Towers that forget their building,
The Irish ivy trails;
.....................

And because you were our Tower, our Castle,
Tall in the landscape grey,
Though all the lights were out, and over wassail,
And night usurps the day,

And since--our sorrow!--in the grave you're sleeping,

The ivy you shall have,
Wrapping your towering height in tender keeping,
Kissing your grave.
..................

All your splendour shall the ivy cover
With dew and rain-drops wet,
And ever greener as the years go over,
Closer and greener yet.[16]

Katharine Tynan's imagery made the symbol's meaning clear: ivy stood for Parnellite fidelity.

Use of the new badge spread rapidly. The very next year, the Independent was able to quote the London Daily Chronicle's observation that "yesterday throughout London the ivy leaf was in strong evidence in button-holes and, perhaps, even more in bonnets."[17] It had taken the custom but a single year to cross the Irish Sea and take hold in London, and the momentum continued. In 1895, the Lord Mayor of Cork told a gathering of his fellow citizens that

> He would impress on every man and every woman to wear, tomorrow, the National emblem--the Ivy Leaf--which represented fidelity, and which would be worn on Sunday throughout the length and breadth of Ireland.[18]

By 1896, the official Parnell Anniversary badge, approved by the Organising Committee, had ivy worked into its border design--the badge remained a portrait of Parnell on a white satin ribbon. A second, unofficial badge, "Mounted on Brass, and Richly Enamelled," consisted of a portrait of Parnell encircled with his "last words" (which had been invented by the Parnellite leadership), "Give my love to my colleagues and to the Irish people," in the center of a large green ivy leaf.[19] The ivy leaf continued popular in 1896. "The wearers of the ivy," the Independent exulted next day after the celebration, "were confined to no one class, and nearly as many ladies as gentlemen were to be found showing the leaf."[20]

Ivy certainly was an excellent choice for the symbol of Parnellism. As a clinging vine, it represented fidelity to the Chief. As a green plant, it showed the natural color, yet it was not so likely to remind people of Parnell's superstitious aversion for green as a cloth badge might have been. And, as the leaf of a common plant, it made a cheap and easily available badge. For the many years that have passed since 1892, those who have wished to honor Parnell's memory have followed the custom instituted by the Independent by donning the ivy leaf each October. By doing it, they have followed this injunction, uttered by an Irish-American poet of the nineties:

Then, take Glasnevin's ivy leaf
O'er Parnell's grave that's seen,
And twine it with your shamrock
When you're wearing of the green.[21]

## Commemorations of Parnell in Print

There was an explosion of writing about Parnell at his death. The newspapers carried biographical sketches, personal reminiscences, interviews with those who had known him, and critical assessments of his career. There were, in addition, magazine articles and even a book hurried into print by T. P. O'Connor. While these writings repeated much that was already known about Parnell--and drew heavily on the books written by O'Connor and Thomas Sherlock in the eighties--they also disclosed much that was new, especially in little anecdotes which revealed his political attitudes or illustrated facets of his character. The explosion was over by the end of the year, but it was repeated, on a smaller scale, each succeeding October during the 1890s.

Since that great outpouring of material, there have really been only two significant additions to the body of public knowledge about Parnell. The first was Barry O'Brien's The Life of Charles Stewart Parnell,[22] published in 1898. O'Brien was comprehensive. He discussed the background of each of the major events of Parnell's career--except that he avoided all but the briefest description of Parnell's affair with Katharine O'Shea--and he made very successful use of the interviews he had obtained with many of the principals in the story, from American Fenians to British cabinet ministers. Sixteen years later, Katharine O'Shea Parnell published her memoir of her late husband, Charles Stewart Parnell: His Love Story and Political Life.[23] Its text was liberally sprinkled with Parnell's letters to her and also included a few excerpts from a diary she had kept. This work contained some information about political events which had not been known previously, but its principal interest lay in what it revealed about the love affair and the more private side of Parnell's personality. It is just about the only source, even now, for information about Parnell's relationship with Katharine. It also represented the last substantial addition of new information to Parnell's story. What has remained has been the reinterpretation of that story by succeeding generations..

In the remaining pages of this chapter, I survey the contributions made to the Parnell Myth by T. P. O'Connor, Barry O'Brien, Katharine Parnell and several Antiparnellite authors. Succeeding chapters offer analysis of the Parnell Myth taken as a whole. The purpose of the following section is to acquaint the reader with a few of the Myth's individual contributors and their works, and to demonstrate that the Myth was the largely unintentional product of many writers pursuing diverse aims and not the result of some conscious joint effort.

**T. P. O'Connor's Charles Stewart Parnell: A Memory**

T. P. O'Connor's biography of Parnell[24] appeared very shortly after his former leader's death. Parnell was buried on Sunday, October 11, 1891, and advance excerpts of the book appeared in the Dublin Evening Telegraph on Wednesday, the 14th. The Telegraph's sister publication, the influential Freeman's Journal, carried a summary of the book, with excerpts, the next morning. On Friday, the Freeman's Journal carried an advertisement announcing that the book was "Just Ready At all Booksellers and railway Bookstalls." It was available for two shillings, or, in a paper wrapper, for one shilling.[25] The political purpose of the book was to neutralize as far as possible the revulsion of feeling in Parnell's favor after his death. Three elements in the book reflected that purpose: its acknowledgment of Parnell's greatness, its sympathetic tone, and its firm insistence that opposition to his leadership was the only choice the Antiparnellites had had in December 1890. Those three elements continued to be present in all of O'Connor's subsequent writing about Parnell--I discuss this a little further on--and they made up the standard Antiparnellite line on Parnell, as expressed by the Party leaders, for many years.

Charles Stewart Parnell: A Memory provoked angry reactions from the Parnellites. United Ireland's review, entitled "T. P. O'Connor's Shilling Shocker," was bitter:

> '....This proud resentment of English domination --even of English condescension--is the root of the hold he exercised over so many Irish hearts.' Our dear, brave Chief! It was this feeling, says Mr. O'Connor, 'that laid him last Sunday in a premature grave.' 'With the assistance of myself and friends,' the pleasant author should have added...

The review went on to point out several inconsistencies in the book, concluding that both the political and the personal analysis were self-serving. Its final judgment was: "What hypocrites and knaves these people are!"[26]

O'Connor did not fare much better at the hands of the Unionist Dublin Evening Mail, which noted the evident strain of his trying to reconcile his past and present attitudes toward Parnell. The Evening Mail's reviewer could not help but be skeptical:

> The 'narrowness' and want of capacity now spoken of, have only been discovered of late. They may be facts, and may only have been brought out under the trying

> circumstances of the past few months, but had they been so marked, as we are now led to believe, surely some signs of them would have been noticed before.

Even more difficult for the reviewer to accept was O'Connor's assertion that Timothy Healy would have been Parnell's friend if Parnell had let him. He repeated O'Connor's story of Healy's comment on the effect Parnell's Kilmainham imprisonment had had on his personality and politics, but in a tone of incredulity:

> All the same, shortly after Mr. Parnell's release, the farseeing Mr Tim Healy, as he watched the chief on the terrace of the House of Commons, remarked, 'with an inexpressible sadness,' 'They have broken another great Irishman.' The 'They,' adds Mr O'Connor, 'were the English rulers.' Whatever the 'English rulers' may have commenced, it remained for Irishmen and 'patriots' to complete the 'breaking' which ended in the grave--after all, a happier fate than the lunatic asylum [a reference to Healy's alleged vow to drive Parnell to a grave or to an asylum].[27]

Actually, the angry reactions of the reviewers for United Ireland and the Dublin Evening Mail were a testimony to O'Connor's success in meeting his political aims. He managed to portray the Antiparnellite position as a sad necessity for those who had respected or even loved Parnell. The Dublin Evening Mail's reviewer was nevertheless right about O'Connor's inconsistencies. The speed at which he wrote it did have an effect on the book. He wrote it by appropriating large chunks of The Parnell Movement, which he had written five years earlier. Since his thesis in the second book was that Parnell's love affair with Katharine O'Shea (which had begun in 1880) and his Kilmainham imprisonment (in the winter of 1881-82) had significantly affected the quality of his performance as leader, he was forced to argue that Parnell had been virtually a broken man during the latter two-thirds of his career, including nearly all his time as leader. Naturally, this thesis, which he inserted into the text of the first book at various points, did not square with the enthusiastic portrayal of Parnell's leadership which he had written in 1886.

O'Connor's portrait of Parnell was, nevertheless, an interesting, even a compelling one. Two themes he used quite successfully were the influence of Parnell's ancestry and family traditions (a motif in the Parnell Myth) and the fascinating effect of Parnell's eyes. And, since his was the only complete biography of Parnell available for seven years, O'Connor exercised considerable influence on the early development of the Parnell Myth. Contemporary and succeeding writers repeated his stories and utilized some of the same motifs.

**Barry O'Brien's The Life of Charles Stewart Parnell 1846-1891**

The giant among the biographical studies of Parnell has always been Barry O'Brien's The Life of Charles Stewart Parnell.[28] This remarkable book was the product of a Parnellite author and journalist who was personally close to Parnell during his last campaign. One reason for O'Brien's success was that he fitted his book to the material he had, rather than the material to the book. He enjoyed access to many important people in the physical force camp as well as to men in the highest reaches of British and Irish politics. He sprinkled The Life of Charles Stewart Parnell with long extracts from interviews he conducted with them. One chapter, describing Parnell's secret meeting with the Tory Lord Lieutenant of Ireland, the Earl of Carnarvon, was written by Sir Charles Gavan Duffy, who had helped arrange it. This was only the longest of a number of first-hand accounts that O'Brien incorporated into the book. Its most remarkable chapter, an assessment of Parnell's character and career, consisted of Gladstone's written and oral responses to questions about Parnell that O'Brien had put to him in 1895 and 1897. These interviews and first-hand accounts enabled O'Brien to explore the backgrounds of many controversial events and to obtain assessments of Parnell from some of his most famous contemporaries.

The Life of Charles Stewart Parnell very accurately reflects the structure of the Parnell Myth. In it, O'Brien consistently portrays Parnell in that posture of independence and dignity which is the central symbol of the Myth, and he does this while emphasizing Parnell's Irish nationality. As I explain in Chapter 4, Parnell's independence, dignity and nationality are fused together in the Myth in Parnell's symbolic uncrowned kingship of the Irish nation. O'Brien employs this symbol effectively and, I think, deliberately. I would not claim that O'Brien articulated to himself the interrelationships of independence, dignity and nationality implicit in that kingship, but rather that he felt satisfaction in depicting his dead leader as a king, with that title's implications of sovereignty for Ireland and of princely qualities for Parnell.

The Life of Charles Stewart Parnell is a good example of the reason why I refer to a Parnell Myth rather than a Parnellite myth. O'Brien was a conviced Parnellite, but the book was not just another piece of Parnellite propaganda. It represented an honest attempt to present an accurate portrayal of the man, and, if O'Brien admired Parnell, he said so frankly and directly. More important, the focus of the book was on the totality of Parnell's career rather than on the arguments of the Split. True, it emphasized the question of independence, which Parnell had made the theme of his last campaign, but it did that because the question of independence represented the fundamental thrust of Irish nationalism and not because Parnell had appropriated it as the basis of his campaign to regain the leadership. In fact, O'Brien's emphasis, like that of the Parnell Myth generally, was centered on Parnell's relationship with the British, not on the disputes of the Split. His Life of Charles Stewart Parnell is the most important publication in the body of material comprising the Myth not just because of the new information it offers but because of the way it reflects the structure of the Parnell Myth, and especially because it makes such effective use of the Myth's principal symbols and central theme.

**Katharine O'Shea Parnell's Charles Stewart Parnell: His Love Story and Political Life**

The last significant accrual of new material to the Parnell Myth was Katharine Parnell's memoir of her husband. It is an odd book, the subject of immediate and lasting speculation. The speculation has concerned the extent to which the manuscript was edited by other hands. According to Katharine Parnell's preface, she had long intended to publish Parnell's love letters after her own death, but she decided to make them public sooner when she learned that William O'Brien had published a letter of Parnell's in the Cork Free Press and had added his own conclusion that Parnell had been "rather the victim than the destroyer of a happy home."[29] Katharine Parnell's son, Gerard O'Shea, "jealous for his father's honour," convinced her that O'Brien should not go unanswered, and she herself decided, she said, that she did not want Parnell's life to "seem in these softer days a lesser thing, beset with fears and indecisions that he did not know." She explained that

> Parnell never posed as 'rather the victim than the destroyer of a happy home,' as Mr. O'Brien suggested in the Cork Free Press of last year, and he maintained to the last year of his life that he suffered no 'dishonour and discredit' in making the woman he loved his own.[30]

What she said was true, but Parnell had never insisted that his bitter enemy, William O'Shea, had emerged from the affair without dishonor and discredit--rather the opposite, in fact. Katharine Parnell's implied thesis was that all three principals had behaved honorably. Actually, since she had borne two of Parnell's children during a period when she had pledged her fidelity to Parnell, that was impossible. Either O'Shea had colluded in the adultery or she had deceived both men. The book avoided addressing this problem by failing to mention either of the children. This fact gave rise to the suspicion--which has persisted to the present--that her son Gerard O'Shea had some hand in editing the manuscript, to preserve what remained of his dead father's reputation.

The question of tampering with the manuscript, interesting as it is in other respects, is of marginal significance for the Parnell Myth. Two things about Charles Stewart Parnell: His Love Story and Political Life are important: the love story provided an added dimension to Parnell's character and personality in the Myth, and the book as a whole reinforced the principal elements of the Myth.

Almost nothing had been known about Parnell's romance with Katharine O'Shea before the publication of her memoir. There had been some colorful--and inaccurate--recitation of squalid details in the divorce court testimony, including the famous, invented story of Parnell's escape from discovery in Mrs. O'Shea's bedroom by means of a fire escape. The only other description of the affair had come from Parnell himself, on the day he had been reelected chairman of the Irish Parliamentary Party. That day he had lifted, as he said, "a corner of the curtain," telling his colleagues that he had not broken up a happy home or betrayed a friendship, because neither had existed. This was all he could say "until the brief period of time will have elapsed [until the divorce decree would become permanent] when I can vindicate myself."[31] The Party, of course, split over Parnell's leadership shortly afterwards, and he never again made a public statement on the affair.

Charles Stewart Parnell: His Love Story and Political Life filled a void in the Myth by portraying a side of Parnell otherwise hidden. His love affair with Katharine was at once passionate and prosaic, tender and melodramatic. To many observers, it even represented the apogee of a kind of fidelity: whatever the moral and legal status of their liaison, Parnell and his "Queenie" never wavered in their love for each other. If their communications did not reach the level of high poetry--and they certainly did not--they were constant, warm, and intimate. Whenever the lovers were apart, Parnell wired Katharine "good night" every night.

The publication of Katharine Parnell's memoir in 1914 was widely noticed. It was serialized in the London Daily Sketch,[32] and reviews of it appeared in the Spectator, English Review, Nineteenth Century, New York Nation, Dial and Harper's Weekly.[33] It provided the occasion for a characteristically vitriolic pamphlet by Frank Hugh O'Donnell, The Lost Hat, directed at the reputations of Parnell, Katharine and William J. Walsh, the Roman Catholic Archbishop of Dublin.[34] As long as eleven years afterwards, St. John Ervine relied heavily on Katharine Parnell's revelations in putting together his "psychological biography" of Parnell.[35] The circle was completed the following year (1926) when, partly in reply to Ervine, William O'Brien published The Parnell of Real Life.[36] Still, even though O'Brien was able to offer personal accounts of many important political events, the most he or any other contemporary witness could offer about the ruling passion of the last ten years of Parnell's life was speculation and a judicious interpretation of the published letters and Katharine Parnell's personal testimony. This fact gave, and continues to give, Charles Stewart Parnell: His Love Story and Political Life great influence within the literature of the Parnell Myth. It is the only substantial primary source for the love story.

I said that, besides fleshing out the more personal side of Parnell's character, the book contributed to the development of the Parnell Myth by reinforcing its structure. It did this through its emphasis on Parnell's Irish nationality, his uncrowned kingship and his fiercely independent spirit. In her preface, for instance, Katharine Parnell even went so far as to make explicit the link she saw between Parnell's leadership and the independence and dignity of the Irish nation. She wrote that

> ...had he lived on dreams that Ireland might, long years ago, have come into her own, the honoured mother of her nobler sons, who, no longer sent forth to toil for other nations, should spend themselves in her service to earn for her a name that should no longer be a byword and a sneer among the Nations.[37]

Her bitter anger with Ireland was obvious, but so was her perception of the special importance which independence and dignity had for Ireland. It set the tone for her treatment of Parnell, Parnell's leadership and Ireland throughout the book.

**Three Antiparnellites: Justin McCarthy, T. P. O'Connor and Timothy Healy**

As leader of the Antiparnellites, Justin McCarthy was called upon several times to comment on Parnell's death for the British and Irish press. He gave three interviews during the evening and night of October 7, 1891 that appeared in the Irish newspapers the next day.[38] On the 9th, the Freeman's Journal also carried a special reminiscence of Parnell he had written.[39] Then, at the end of the month, his biographical sketch of his former leader appeared in the November Contemporary Review, with excerpts in the Freeman's Journal.[40] In these interviews and articles, McCarthy stressed Parnell's greatness, the tragedy of his fall, and the sad necessity the Antiparnellites had felt of opposing his continued leadership after Gladstone's letter and his manifesto.

In his subsequent writing, McCarthy stuck steadfastly to that political line. He repeated it, for instance, in A History of Our Own Times (1897), The Story of Gladstone's Life (1898) and Ireland and Her Story (1903).[41] In these books, while he expressed admiration for Parnell, his tone remained objective. His more personal books were different. In Reminiscences (1899) and An Irishman's Story (1905),[42] while he did not apologize for the political stand he had taken against Parnell, he described their personal friendship in very warm terms. McCarthy had known Parnell very early in Parnell's career, before McCarthy himself had won a seat in Parliament, and Parnell had been a frequent dinner guest in more personal books, describing Parnell's unaffected personal charm when he was in the privacy of the McCarthy family circle. McCarthy was clearly very proud to have been so personally close to so great a public man during that man's formative years.

The Split caused McCarthy much pain because of his affection for Parnell. One can glimpse it in Reminiscences and An Irishman's Story, but its true extent is best seen in Our Book of Memories (1912).[43] This book is a collection of the letters which McCarthy wrote to his collaborator and friend, Mrs. Campbell Praed, set in a narrative written partly by McCarthy (who died before the book was finished) and partly by Mrs. Praed. The letters in the book that date from 1890-91 show that McCarthy was gratified that his friendship with Parnell had persisted despite the Split and that he was concerned about Parnell's deteriorating health. Nevertheless, it became increasingly difficult for McCarthy to meet with Parnell--they were joint trustees for some Party funds--because of the evident effects the wearing political fight was having on Parnell. After one of these meetings, in mid-September 1891, McCarthy's report to Mrs. Praed included this cry of anguish:

> He was as friendly and familiar as if nothing whatever had occurred to divide us--and we smoked in intervals of work and drank whiskey and soda--and I thought it dismal and ghastly and hideous--and I hate to have to meet him.[44]

That was the last time McCarthy saw Parnell. The passage is one of the strongest outbursts of feeling in Our Book of Memories.

For the Parnell Myth, the important things about McCarthy's writing were that he held steadily to the Antiparnellite line and that he did this while professing friendship, not just respect or admiration, for Parnell. The descriptions of the early days of their friendship fleshed out Parnell's character and made his personality seem more attractive. (Very few of the other contributors to the Myth had known Parnell in his more relaxed, private moments.) McCarthy also firmly insisted on two crucial points about Parnell's politics: that his ultimate goal had been the independence of Ireland and that his methods had been non-violent. As a long-time resident of England, McCarthy was particularly annoyed by the English tendency to identify Parnell with the Fenians' dynamite campaign; he maintained over and over again in his writing that Parnell had had only scorn for the dynamiters and horror at their works. He portrayed Parnell as a strong, decisive leader with excellent judgment who had consistently exhibited the independence and dignity he had sought for Ireland.

T. P. O'Connor demonstrated a great deal of interest in Parnell in the years following Parnell's death. Charles Stewart Parnell: A Memory appeared only a few days after the funeral. In the ensuing years, O'Connor followed it with a number of newspaper and magazine articles. More important, however, was the very prominent place that Parnell occupied in O'Connor's Memoirs. The work practically ended with Parnell's death--

though it was finished thirty-eight years later, in 1929--and O'Connor offered this explanation:

> The most unforgettable years of my political life were so bound up with the remarkable career of this extraordinary man that I have little to add to the story...[45]

How little he had to add could be gauged from the book's index. Fifty-two lines of it were taken up with references to the author, while the references to Parnell filled eighty-eight, a remarkable testimony to the place Parnell occupied in O'Connor's public view of his own career.

What can be said about O'Connor's various portrayals of Parnell? They certainly depicted a great and powerful man: a sure decision-maker, a compelling leader and a formidable opponent. At the same time, they exhibited an odd emotional objectivity for the disclosures of one who had been so closely associated with Parnell. In "Orators Who Have Influenced Me" (1913) and "The Life Drama of the Parnells" (1921),[46] O'Connor betrayed no sympathy or affection for his subject, and his insights into Parnell's character seem to have come rather more from observation than from any disclosure Parnell had made to him. In the second article, O'Connor wrote that

> Parnell was one of the men who consumed their own smoke. He never had a moment of expansion, like other men; he never trusted anyone; he never unburdened himself to anybody.[47]

If this was not true of Parnell's relationships with all of his colleagues, it was true of his dealings with O'Connor. It influenced both the sympathy O'Connor displayed in his writing about Parnell and the depth of his understanding of the man. The result was a series of portrayals of Parnell that emphasized the air of mystery which surrounded him and that made of his personality an enigma.

O'Connor was careful, however, not to put too much political distance between himself and Parnell. In his Memoirs, he wrote

> I may say here that I was convinced, from my first days in the House of Commons, that the leadership of Parnell was the centre-stone in the arch of our fortunes; that I regarded every attempt to displace or overthrow him as a dagger aimed at the heart of Ireland; that I used every power and influence I possessed as a writer in newspapers to exalt him; that I was only too ready to regard with suspicion anybody whom I could think of as an enemy or a possible rival.[48]

The Split itself he did not care to discuss in his Memoirs. "Certainly," he wrote, "the time has passed when one should enter into the controversy as to whether the opponents or the defenders of Parnell took the wiser course for the future of Ireland."[49] But he wanted his readers to understand that he had taken the high road in 1890-91, writing that

> I hope that I may be forgiven for repeating that in expressing my dissent from the course of Parnell I did not allow myself to say anything personally insulting to him.[50]

In 1929, there was nothing for O'Connor to gain by insisting on the Antiparnellite line.

In Chapter 8, I discuss the influence that later events (for example, the Rising of 1916, the establishment of the Irish Free State) had on the popular perception of Parnell's place in history. Here, it is important to note how large Parnell loomed in O'Connor's memories of his fifty-year political career and how careful O'Connor was in his Memoirs, without recanting his Antiparnellite stand, to insist on his personal loyalty to and regard for Parnell. Memoirs of an Old Parliamentarian was, for this reason, a significant measure of Parnell's stature in the historical literature of his country.

Timothy Healy's Letters and Leaders of My Day[51] was published in 1928, the year before O'Connor's Memoirs. It consisted of letters Healy had written to his wife, father and brother, connected by a narrative. It was a very curious work: it was sometimes ruthlessly honest, quoting old letters of Healy's that showed the weak side of his character or illustrated instances of bad political judgment; at other times, it was plainly dishonest, as when Healy claimed that Parnell had not attended the House of Commons in 1890 until the day it was prorogued. (Actually, Parnell had spoken over a dozen times, including on the Estimates, the main subject of Healy's complaint.)[52] Healy's motives in writing the book must have been mixed in a complicated way. On the one hand, he clearly wanted to justify his career in the way that most writers of memoirs usually do. Since the most important political act of his career had been his decision to oppose Parnell in November 1890, he had to be critical of his former leader. This was especially true because of the highly personal line he had taken in attacking Parnell in Committee Room 15 and on the hustings. At the same time, he did not wish to appear mean-spirited or envious, as he felt Frank Hugh O'Donnell had done,[53] so he had to be careful to balance his criticism with credit where it was due. Healy's resolution of these difficulties was highly characteristic: rather than present a moderate, mildly-yet-firmly-critical portrait of the man, he focused first on good qualities, then on bad, describing all of them in the same blunt language, and he did not bother to integrate the qualities he depicted into a single, coherent portrait. He left the jumble as it was, each piece in high relief.

It would be far beyond the scope of this study to account for all of Healy's ambivalent feelings about Parnell--and we lack a good biography of this fascinating subject--but it is possible to sketch an outline of them. Healy admired Parnell's great qualities, his political ability and the power of his personality. At the same time, he seems to have been angered rather than disappointed by Parnell's flaws. At the outset of their relationship, Healy had practically worshipped Parnell, and he may have felt that Parnell's shortcomings were in some way a betrayal of his trust. Healy also appears to have envied the natural political advantages that Parnell had enjoyed. Healy had come from an obscure family in modest circumstances, while Parnell had inherited not only considerable wealth but also a famous name long associated with the nationalist cause. Parnell had been able to bear the expenses of his early election campaigns and to fight them as the great-grandson of Sir John Parnell. The ambitious Healy, on the other hand, had had no such advantages, and the very help which Parnell had given him must have rankled.

Healy has always been identified as Parnell's most virulent opponent. His language during the by-election campaigns of 1891 was vulgar and abusive. As soon, however, as he learned of Parnell's death, Healy tempered his language. In the weeks after Parnell's death, he spoke in a definitely conciliatory tone. He even admitted to an audience in Cavan that Parnell's tactics during the Split had helped the nationalist cause: by making Gladstone's Home Rule proposals an issue, he explained, Parnell had undoubtedly improved the terms of the expected bill.[54] Two weeks later, at Longford, he pleaded that the Antiparnellites had been reasonable with Parnell, that they had merely suggested that he retire until the impending general election.[55]

Two days later, however, lightning struck. While Healy had been temperate in his remarks about Parnell since his death, he had remained abusive as ever in his references to Katharine Parnell. When he referred to her as "that convicted British prostitute," the remark proved too much for Parnell's nephew, Alfred M'Dermott, a student at Trinity College Dublin. On the afternoon of November 3, 1891, he waited for Healy in Dublin's Four Courts, and, when Healy appeared, set upon him with a horsewhip. The incident was an immediate press sensation. M'Dermott granted interviews all around, while the obviously embarrassed Healy said nothing.[56] The editorial reactions were predictable. The Antiparnellite Freeman's Journal deplored the incident,[57] while the Unionist Dublin Evening Mail concluded that Healy had gotten what he had deserved.[58] This incident can only have reinforced the public's image of Healy as Parnell's most scurrilous opponent, an image that he still retains.

In a letter, reprinted in Letters and Leaders, that he wrote to his brother Maurice in 1888, Healy described himself as "wavering often as to this extraordinary man."[59] The phrase would have make a good epigraph for Letters and Leaders. The book was, as I have said, a jumble of positive and negative depictions of Parnell. I discuss this portrayal of Parnell in Chapter 5 (in connection with the central symbol of the Myth, Parnell's attitude exhibiting independence and dignity), but I should mention here Healy's one great contribution to the Myth's store of symbols. It was he--as he reminded the readers of Letters and Leaders--who first called Parnell "the uncrowned king of Ireland," in a speech that he gave in Montreal during Parnell's American tour in 1880. "This phrase," he explained, "was passed into currency by Preston [a reporter] through the New York Herald, although it had previously been applied to Daniel O'Connell."[60] Healy's description of the event did not indicate whether his hailing of Parnell as uncrowned King had carried the defiant implication of Ireland's essential sovereignty which the use of the phrase later acquired, but it did refer to two other elements associated with Parnell's symbolic kingship in the Myth: his great popular standing in Ireland and his position as successor to Daniel O'Connell.

One further point about Letters and Leaders is worth mentioning: the evidence it offered of Healy's wide reading in the literature about Parnell and his time. Healy demonstrated acquaintance with the writings of T. P. O'Connor, William O'Brien, Katharine Parnell, Michael Davitt, Lord Morley and Parnell's sister, Emily Dickenson, among others. T. P. O'Connor's Memoirs and William O'Brien's The Parnell of Real Life (1926) reflected the same extensive reading in this literature. This tendency of Healy, O'Connor, O'Brien and others to comment on other writers increased the cohesiveness and coherence of the Parnell Myth, reinforcing the patterns within it.

**William O'Brien**

William O'Brien was, in many ways, the most interesting contributor to the Parnell Myth. A close friend of Parnell's, he broke with him over Parnell's manifesto against Gladstone because he felt that Parnell had falsely represented Gladstone's position. But, rather than join the Antiparnellites immediately, he tried to mediate between the two Irish factions by negotiating Parnell's retirement. In the end, the negotiations failed, and, after six months in Galway Jail for a Plan of Campaign offense, he reluctantly joined John Dillon in denouncing Parnell. For years after Parnell's death, O'Brien remained very sensitive to criticism from both sides in the Split that his attempts at mediation had done more harm than good. This sensitivity was compounded by O'Brien's stormy relationships with the various nationalist factions in those years. He left Parliament in disgust in the mid 1890s and founded a movement patterned after the old Land League, called the United Irish League, which greatly facilitated the reunion of the old Party in 1900. He then was instrumental, through the Land Conference he initiated, in negotiating an amicable settlement of the land question. But he and Party leaders again quarrelled. He tried to put together a conference of nationalists and Unionists to settle the national question, the Party leaders objected, and they fell out for the second and last time.

These experiences encouraged O'Brien's romantic tendency to dwell on what might have happened had Parnell not fallen from power. As O'Brien saw it, every internecine Party quarrel, every political job accepted by a nationalist, every year that passed without Home Rule for Ireland, was a mark of how much Ireland missed Parnell. An early, and striking, indication of O'Brien's first disenchantment with his former colleagues--and a measure of his personal loss--the nostalgic article "London Revisited: Some Reminiscences," published in 1896.[61] O'Brien was only forty-three years old at the time, rather young to be publishing reminiscences. But the tone of the article indicated that he saw in the events of the previous six years the end, not just of the camaraderie of the Parnell years--his ostensible subject--but of their success too. "We are not the first nor the thirtieth generation of Irishmen," he commented sadly, "who have found the Irish cause a drama, in which you must not look for a too happy ending."[62] To William O'Brien, his generation's chapter of this story was coming to a close as early as 1896.

The nationalistic cause did find new life a few years later--in part due to O'Brien's United Irish League--but then came further disappointment: the slow death of Home Rule and then Partition and Civil War. As he watched these events take place, O'Brien wasted little sympathy on what he called "the dregs of Parnell's denationalised and sectarianised Party."[63] His sympathies were with the younger generation:

> Prate of the wild unreason of Easter Week insurrections!--to the new generation whose hot eyes peruse the story, the unending trickery, insincerity, incompetence, or downright treachery of English politicians of all parties in bedevilling a national claim....Those of us who have fretted thankless years out in search for peace with England will find any reproof of the impatience of our young countrymen with 'Parliamentarianism' perish on our lips.[64]

But his denunciation of the Irish Parliamentary Party's irrelevance did not extend to its late founder. "Parnell," he insisted, "remains an even more powerful factor of contemporary Irish history to-day [in 1926] than he was when a more or less remorseful nation saw his coffin pass a generation ago."[65] Had Parnell lived to win Home Rule, he maintained, Ireland's history down to 1926 would have been much happier: "that victory he would have been able to turn to account as no man who has come after him can hope to do."[66]

If those statements seemed Parnellite, they very nearly were. After reading Lord Morley's Recollections, O'Brien had more or less recanted his Antiparnellism:

> History will quite possibly pronounce Parnell to have been right and his opponents wrong in the struggle in Committee Room 15. Its cėnsures will not, it may be, spare the five delegates in America (of which O'Brien was one) for acting so far away and upon information which was inadequate then and has since proved to be absolutely false.
>
> ...The point was that there was no Parnell but one, and that, for good or ill, he held in his hands the thread of life or death for Ireland...[67]

For O'Brien in the 1920s, the crucial factor in the decision to oppose Parnell had been the intentions of the Liberal leadership. And, to him, the years had proven that "Parnell was not astray either in his anticipations as to the unreliability of his Liberal allies or as to the ineffectiveness of his divided successors."[68]

This conclusion represented a significant change of opinion for O'Brien, even since 1913. In the Cork Free Press article that had provided the occasion for the publication of Katharine Parnell's book, O'Brien had argued that Parnell--and Ireland--had been victims of the O'Sheas. His new argument was that misfortune had come to Ireland, not through private treachery or the Irish leader's weakness, but because, as usual, lesser men had failed to heed the leader's warnings about the English foe.

> For we now know that it was not Gladstone who made war on Parnell in his hour of stress, but Morley...The hapless Irish race were not only devoted to destruction for Parnell's private sin, but by the Englishmen they most trusted were kept in the dark as to Gladstone's real opinion on the point which meant all to Ireland, and were dragged through ten miserable years of civil strife under the utterly false delusion that they were asked to choose between sending Gladstone and Home Rule to their graves, or immolating an Irish leader greater than Gladstone, and worlds more truly respectable than Morley's electioneering caucus.[69]

The nearness of victory, the dashed hopes, and the helpless frustration were ancient themes, well known to his audience. What was important for the Parnell Myth, however, was his emphasis on Parnell's fundamental importance to the nationalist cause--and, on the question of nationality: the culprits O'Brien identified had, after all, turned out to be English.

This review has encompassed only a few of the most important contributors to the Parnell Myth, but it should have been extensive enough to demonstrate that their opinions and purposes varied widely. This diversity notwithstanding, the material comprising the Myth exhibits discernible characteristics which can be identified inductively. In the chapters which follow, I discuss those characteristics and their meaning.

## Notes to Chapter 2

[1]Description of funeral, National Press, (Dublin), 12 October 1891.

[2]"Sunday's Sad Parade: By One of Its Organizers," United Ireland (Dublin), 12 October 1891.

[3]"Glasnevin: James Stephens at Parnell's Grave: An Historic Incident," Freeman's Journal (Dublin), 26 October 1891.

[4]United Ireland (Dublin), 7 November 1891.

[5]"Parnell's Grave Visited by Royalty," Freeman's Journal (Dublin), 31 October 1891.

[6]William E. Gladstone, interview with R. Barry O'Brien, London, 28 January 1897, quoted in RBOB, 2:363-64.

[7]Katharine O'Shea Parnell, Charles Stewart Parnell: His Love Story and Political Life, 2 vols. (New York: George H. Doran Co., 1914), 2:42. Hereinafter referred to as KOSP.

[8]The version on the obelisk is taken from Parnell's speech in Cork, 21 January 1885. It is quoted in RBOB, 2:38.

[9]Sinn Féin's real target was Redmond and the Party. "Parnell," Sinn Féin (Dublin), 7 October 1911.

[10]William O'Brien, The Parnell of Real Life (London: T. Fisher Unwin, 1926), p. 33.

[11]Dublin Evening Mail, 10 October 1892.

[12]Irish Daily Independent (Dublin), 1 October 1892.

[13]Advertisement, Irish Daily Independent (Dublin), 4 and 5 October 1892. The same advertisement, with the last paragraph omitted, ran on 6 October 1892.

[14]"Ivy Day," Irish Daily Independent (Dublin), 6 October 1892.

[15]Irish Daily Independent (Dublin), 7 October 1892.

[16]Katharine Tynan, "The Green Ivy," Irish Daily Independent (Dublin), 7 October 1892.

[17]Daily Chronicle (London), 9 October 1893, quoted in Irish Daily Independent (Dublin), 9 October 1893.

[18]P. H. Meade, speech at a Parnell commemoration meeting in Cork, 4 October 1895, quoted in Irish Daily Independent (Dublin), 5 October 1895.

[19]Advertisements for both badges were carried in the Irish Weekly Independent (Dublin), 3 October 1896.

[20]"Ivy Day in Dublin," Irish Daily Independent (Dublin), 7 October 1896.

[21]Sung to "The Wearing of the Green" by "the secretary of the Irish National Club at the celebration of the anniversary of the Manchester Martyrs [23 November 1867] by the Speranza Club of New York." Quoted in Irish Weekly Independent (Dublin), 12 January 1895.

[22]R. Barry O'Brien, The Life of Charles Stewart Parnell 1846-1891, 2 vols. (London: Smith, Elder, & Co., 1898).

[23]Katharine O'Shea Parnell, Charles Stewart Parnell: His Love Story and Political Life, 2 vols. (New York: George H. Doran, 1914).

[24]T. P. O'Connor, Charles Stewart Parnell: A Memory (London: Ward, Lock, Bowden & Co., 1891). Hereinafter referred to as TPOC.

[25]Evening Telegraph (Dublin), 14 October 1891; "Mr. T. P. O'Connor's Life of Mr. Parnell: Interesting Reminiscences: The Leinster Hall Meeting," Freeman's Journal (Dublin), 15 October 1891; advertisement, Freeman's Journal (Dublin), 16 October 1891.

[26]"T. P. O'Connor's Shilling Shocker," review of TPOC, in United Ireland (Dublin), 14 November 1891.

[27]Review of TPOC, in Dublin Evening Mail, 21 October 1891.

[28]In addition to the first edition (1898), which I have already noted, there were two more editions in 1899 and a one-volume edition, with a preface by John E. Redmond, in Nelson's Shilling Library (London: Nelson & Sons, 1908). The Smith, Elder & Co. clothbound edition cost 21s in 1899.

[29]William O'Brien, "Two Pages of Secret History," Cork Free Press, 6 September 1913.

[30]KOSP, 1:viii-x.

[31]Charles Stewart Parnell, remarks at meeting of the Irish Parliamentary Party, London, 25 November 1890, quoted in Joan Haslip, Parnell: A Biography (New York: Frederick A. Stokes Co., 1937), pp. 379-80.

[32]Katharine O'Shea Parnell, "The Love Story of Charles Stewart Parnell," Daily Sketch (London), 5-30 May (except 10, 17, 24 May) 1914.

[33]Reviews of KOSP, in Spectator, 30 May 1914, pp. 912-14, and 6 June 1914, pp. 953-54; in English Review, June 1914, pp. 421-22; by Darrell Figgis, in Nineteenth Century and After, July 1914, pp. 217-27, reprinted in Living Age, 22 August 1914, pp. 495-503, reprinted, with revisions, in Darrell Figgis, Bye-ways of Study (Dublin: Talbot Press, 1918), pp. 1-24; in Nation (New York), 5 November 1914, pp. 551-552; by Laurence M. Larson, in Dial, 16 December 1914, pp. 498-500; by Neith Boyce, in Harper's Weekly, 20 February 1915, p. 187.

[34]Frank Hugh O'Donnell, The Lost Hat: The Clergy, the Collection, the Hidden Life [London: Murray & Co., 1914].

[35]St. John Ervine, Parnell (London: Ernest Benn, 1925).

[36]William O'Brien, The Parnell of Real Life (London: T. Fisher Unwin, 1926).

[37]KOSP, 1:ix.

[38]Justin McCarthy, interviews with Freeman's Journal London correspondent [J. M. Tuohy], Press Association, and Central News Agency, London, 7 October 1891, collected in "Special Interviews with Mr. Justin M'Carthy: The Position of the Irish Party: The Paris Funds," Freeman's Journal (Dublin), 8 October 1891.

[39]Justin McCarthy, "Mr. Justin M'Carthy's Reminiscences of Mr. Parnell," Freeman's Journal, (Dublin), 9 October 1891.

[40]Justin McCarthy, "Charles Stewart Parnell," Contemporary Review, November 1891, pp. 625-36, reprinted in Living Age, 12 December 1891, pp. 669-76, excerpted in Freeman's Journal (Dublin), 30 October 1891.

[41]Justin McCarthy, A History of Our Own Times, vol. 5: From 1889 to the Diamond Jubilee (London: Chatto & Windus, 1897); The Story of Gladstone's Life (London: Adam & Charles Black, 1898); Ireland and Her Story (New York: Funk & Wagnalls, 1903).

[42]Justin McCarthy, "Charles Stewart Parnell," Reminiscences 2 vols. (London: Chatto & Windus, 1899), 2:89-116; An Irishman's Story (New York: Macmillan Co., 1905).

[43]Mrs. Campbell [Rosa C.] Praed, ed., Our Book of Memories: Letters of Justin McCarthy to Mrs. Campbell Praed (London: Chatto & Windus, 1912).

[44]Ibid., p. 300.

[45]T. P. O'Connor, Memoirs of an Old Parliamentarian, 2 vols. (London: Ernest Benn, 1929), 2:322.

[46]T. P. O'Connor, "Orators Who Have Influenced Me," Harper's Weekly, 30 August 1913, pp. 21-22; "The Life Drama of the Parnells," Daily Telegraph (London), n.d., reprinted in Living Age, 26 March 1921, pp. 776-85, 2 April 1921, pp. 56-61.

[47]T. P. O'Connor, "The Life Drama of the Parnells," p. 782.

[48]T. P. O'Connor, Memoirs, 1:127.

[49]Ibid., 2:322.

[50]Ibid.

[51]Timothy M. Healy, Letters and Leaders of My Day, 2 vols. (London: Thornton Butterworth, [1928]).

[52]Timothy M. Healy, Letters and Leaders of My Day, 1:318; Great Britain, Parliament, Hansard's Parliamentary Debates (Commons), 3rd series, vol. 348 (1890), index, s.v. "Parnell, Mr. C. S."

[53]Healy was very critical of O'Donnell's portrait of Parnell. See Timothy M. Healy, Letters and Leaders of My Day, 1:279.

[54]Timothy M. Healy, speech at Cavan, 15 October 1891, quoted in Daily Express (Dublin), 16 October 1891.

[55]Timothy M. Healy, speech at Longford, 1 November 1891, quoted in Dublin Evening Mail, 2 November 1891.

[56]"Mr. T. M. Healy Assaulted at the Four Courts: Mr. Parnell's Nephew the Aggressor: Interview with Mr. M'Dermott: Mr. Healy Refuses to Say Anything: How the Evening Papers Descibe the Fracas," Freeman's Journal (Dublin), 4 November 1891.

[57]"The Assault on Mr. Healy," Freeman's Journal (Dublin), 4 November 1891.

[58]Leading article, Dublin Evening Mail, 4 November 1891.

[59]Timothy M. Healy, Letters and Leaders of My Day, 1:293.

[60]Ibid., 1:83.

[61]William O'Brien, "London Revisited: Some Reminiscences," Contemporary Review, June 1896, pp. 805-12.

[62]Ibid., p. 807.

[63]William O'Brien, The Parnell of Real Life, p. 207.

[64]Ibid., pp. 103-4.

[65]Ibid.

[66]The information O'Brien refers to led the delegates, in his opinion, to judge Gladstone's "nullity" letter to mean he would retire if Parnell did not and Parnell's replying manifesto, therefore, to be treacherous to Gladstone and the Liberals. William O'Brien, "A Missing Page of Irish History," review of The Life of Sir William Harcourt, by

A.G. Gardiner, in Catholic Bulletin and Book Review, October 1923, pp. 693-96.

[67]Ibid., p. 691.

[68]William O'Brien, The Parnell of Real Life, p. 147.

## CHAPTER 3

## THE PARNELL MYTH 1891-99: MOTIFS

The Parnell Myth has a simple structure. Its most important characteristics are a central theme, independence and dignity, and a central symbol, Parnell's defiant attitude projecting those qualities. Theme and symbol give the Myth unity, tying together the many books and articles which comprise it. Surrounding theme and symbol are a number of other core characteristics which are very closely related to them. They include the motif of nationality, which links Parnell to the people he represents; Parnell's symbolic uncrowned kingship of Ireland, which explicitly connects Parnell's leadership role to the independence and dignity of his people; and the motif of contempt/disdain/scorn, which not only presents the central theme in its most powerful form but also demonstrates that dignity is equally as important an element in theme and symbol as is independence. Finally, the metaphors for Parnell ascribe to him independence, dignity and complementary qualities, while the metaphorical roles assigned to him describe the various facets of the leader's relationship to his people.

In addition to these core characteristics, the Myth exhibits a number of others which, although they are compatible with theme and symbol and even provide them with modest support, make a more independent contribution to the shape of the Myth. These characteristics include four motifs, all of which echo themes from literature: ancestry, Providence/destiny/fate, treachery/betrayal and tragedy. They also include two other elements: a group of speculations on What Might Have Been and a sizable number of comparisons of Parnell with great figures from history, literature and the Bible.

This structure emerged from my analysis of the first index I compiled. It covered the material published between Parnell's death on October 6, 1891 and the last day of 1899. This was approximately the period of the Split in the Irish Parliamentary Party after Parnell's death, which ended in the spring of 1900. The body of material was of manageable size--about 250 pages of my notes--and could be compared with the twentieth century evidence to discover possible changes over time. I used a relatively large number of subject headings, 794, in order to maximize my chances of uncovering all the patterns in the evidence. The result was an index with 11,000 entries. (Table 1 lists the subject headings in one general category and shows how many entries appear under each.) The purpose of this approach was to discover the underlying structure in the mass

TABLE 1

THE NUMBERS OF ENTRIES UNDER EACH SUBJECT HEADING IN THE CATEGORY ISSUES OF THE SPLIT

Unworthy to lead (7)
Moral question (10)
English dictation (100)
Retirement (23)
Temporary withdrawal (23)
Parnell's ambition (37)
Efforts to remain leader (5)
Whether leader or sessional chairman (3)
Demeanor in Room 15 (3)
Parnell-I. P. P. relationship (20)
Room 15 (4)
Ingratitude/men made by Parnell (25)
First for Parnell, then against (25)
Desertion of Parnell (47)
Abandoned only when he went wrong (6)
Imperiled own achievements (41)
Parnell's principles (64)
Parnell indispensable (13)
Terrible attacks, vituperation (21)
Fidelity to New Departure (1)
Promises about Divorce Court results (8)
Parnell's manifesto (14)
Castlecomer lime (4)
Who knew of liaison (15)
Katharine O'Shea's influence (4)[a]
Paris funds (1)[a]
Leinster Hall Meeting (9)

I. P. P. Split (2)
Nonconformist conscience (4)
Maurice Healy's challenge (1)
Liberal alliance (5)
Parnell's strategy (3)
Irish opinion (1)
Effects of the Split (1)
Effects of Split on Parnell (3)
Parnell's pride (1)
Parnell's popularity (1)
Phoenix Park murders letter to Gladstone (4)[a]
Tory alliance with Parnell (6)
Liberal guarantees (7)
American money (2)
Parnell quoted (13)
The roles of
- The clergy (77)
- Timothy Healy (25)
- Gladstone/his letter (57)
- Michael Davitt (8)
- The Antiparnellites (27)
- The Irish (6)
- Parnell himself (8)
- The Liberals (3)
- The Parnellites (39)
- Flatterers (3)
- The American delegates (3)

[a]These are amplified by entries under headings elsewhere in the index.

of the published writing about Parnell--if there was any--rather than to impose one myself or to arrive at one impressionistically.

I discuss the core characteristics of the Myth in Chapter 4, contrast the nineteenth and twentieth century material in Chapter 5, and then discuss the differences between my findings and some traditional assumptions about the terms Parnell myth and myth in Chapter 6. I begin my analysis here with the more independent characteristics of the Myth, starting with the motif of ancestry.

Charles Stewart Parnell was descended from two distinguished lines of forebears. His mother was the daughter of the American hero of the War of 1812, Admiral Charles Stewart, nicknamed "Old Ironsides," and commander of the warship, U.S.S. Constitution, which bore the same sobriquet. On his father's side, Parnell was descended from the notable Irish family whose shining star had been Sir John Parnell, opponent of the Act of Union and Chancellor of the Irish Exchequer; but which had also included the poet Thomas Parnell; Lord Congleton, a member of British Whig cabinets in the 1830s; and his own grandfather, William Parnell, a pamphleteer who championed the rights of Irish tenant farmers and Roman Catholics. It was a distinguished pedigree for an Irish nationalist politician, and the authors of the Parnell Myth make good use of it. Mentions of the illustriousness of Parnell's ancestors or of the family names he bore, Stewart and Parnell, enhance Parnell's stature within the Myth. References to the qualities Parnell inherited from one or both sides of his family are used to account for many of the elements in his personality. Many of the writers use brief accounts of Parnell's ancestry to open their analyses of his career. This device not only gets the story going; it points it in a certain direction.

Eleven sources in the nineteenth century evidence mention the illustriousness of Parnell's heritage; sixteen use it to explain personality traits. Justin McCarthy is one of the former. In the volume of A History of Our Own Time entitled From 1880 to the Diamond Jubilee, he alludes to Sir John Parnell, Lord Congleton, Thomas Parnell and Admiral Stewart.[1] In his recollection of Parnell for the Contemporary Review, written just after Parnell's death, he describes the impression which the name Parnell had made upon him at the time of their first meeting in 1875:

> I knew nothing of him up to that time except his historic name. I knew that he belonged to the family of the Sir John Parnell who stood by Grattan's side in the long struggle against the passing of the fatal Act of Union. The mere name was naturally a recommendation to me.[2]

In ten of eleven sources that refer to Parnell's honored name, the author means it to be just as much a recommendation to his readers as it was to McCarthy in 1875. The exception is a book by Patrick Tynan, an old Invincible terrorist, who uses it as an index of Parnell's failure as a nationalist. Tynan complains that Parnell, "who bore an honoured name, told these British persecutors of Ireland [at a Liberal gathering in 1886] that Irishmen [dynamiters] were criminals."[3]

Throughout the evidence, Parnell is consistently portrayed as "A Chip of the Old Block,"[4] although the blocks named are many and various. The one singled out most often is Admiral Stewart, his maternal grandfather. T. P. O'Connor claims, for instance, that Parnell exhibited a personality much like Stewart's: dignified, engaging, bold, and kind, with a firm control over his passions and a tendency to icy calm in a crisis.[5] An American author, Ralph St. John, points out that both Admiral Stewart and Cromwell's soldiers--one of whom founded the Parnell line in Ireland--shared the sobriquet, "Ironsides." "Thus on both the paternal and the maternal side," he concludes, "there had come to this leader as an inheritance, qualities which had won this most expressive of all names for unyielding strength of character."[6] A second, anonymous, American writer explains that, while it was the blood of the Cromwellian Parnells that enabled Parnell to forge and discipline an effective party, the very "proper" Parnell blood was reinvigorated by union with the American Stewarts.[7] According to that same source, the Stewart influence was not entirely a salutary one. Parnell inherited from the old Admiral not only a "callous contempt of public opinion," but also a lamentable weakness for adultery, and "a more marked example of pertinacious heredity than the attitude of grandsire and grandson in [that] one particular of conduct has never been recorded."[8]

Parnell's mother also discusses his ancestry. In an interview with Barry O'Brien, she stresses the importance of family tradition. "Have not his ancestors been always opposed to England?" she asks. She answers this rhetorical question by reciting a long litany of names from both sides of the family.[9] This item illustrates the importance of the ancestry motif: in the Myth, as in life, Parnell's ancestry helped make him what he was. Eighteen of the twenty-one items of evidence mentioning Parnell's ancestry support the motif; three do not. Two of the three exceptions come from Patrick Tynan, who charges that Parnell betrayed his family's legacy of patriotism, and the third, less important from the standpoint of the central symbol, comes from an American writer puzzled why a man "descended from poets and judges seemed to hate books."[10] This is a clear pattern of support for the motif. By celebrating Parnell's famous name, listing his illustrious forebears or tracing his more noble qualities back to them, the items of evidence which comprise the motif enhance Parnell's stature within the Myth and contribute to the effectiveness of the Myth's central symbol, his independent, dignified <u>attitude</u>.

The motif of Providence/destiny/fate is both weaker and less important than the ancestry motif in the sources for the Parnell Myth published in the 1890s. Six items of evidence depict Providence as objectively real. In two of them, commentators sympathetic to Parnell describe him as a gift from God. One of them characterizes him as Heaven's messenger sent to deliver the Irish people from famine and bondage,[11] the other as Providence's gift to protect Ireland.[12] The remaining sources attribute Parnell's death to the action of Providence. Two explicitly say that Providence's purpose in bringing about his death was to save Ireland.[13] The other two are individual enough to merit direct quotation.

> There is something awful and mysterious in the reflection that his death has followed so closely the extinction of Balmaceda and Boulanger, whose careers and purposes corresponded so nearly to his....The purposes of Providence are great and in all these things it is not impossible to see a hand before the operation of which quails all the majesty of earth.[14]

> Leave him to God! that at least we can do.
> 'The mills of God that grind so slow', but small
> Have crushed him surely under their rough wheels;
> And now he stands before the tribunal...[15]

In the first quotation, the writer presents Parnell, by implication, as a threat to constitutional politics removed by Providence to preserve the peace. In the second, Providence's purpose is not quite so clear. It is retribution of some sort, for offenses that would presumably have been perfectly obvious to a Unionist audience.

Three more sources portray Providence as a function of human perceptions. One refers to "the opponents of the late Mr. Parnell who speak of his death as a providential deliverance,"[16] in a tone which suggests that that interpretation is likely a valid one. (I will discuss the remark at greater length in my treatment of the relationship between fate and the month of October, a little further on in this analysis.) The other two employ a more skeptical tone. One is a dramatized dialogue, a conversation in the Shades between Oliver Cromwell and Parnell. An urbanely skeptical Parnell tells Cromwell, "I can scarcely accept your theory of a special Providence in political matters."[17] He has to take this position, of course, not only to remain consistent with the popular perception of his theological opinions, but to justify his career. If Hannigan's Parnell admitted the existence of Providence, he would have to concede that Heaven had surely smiled on Cromwell and frowned on him--and Hannigan portrays both men as amiably competitive, each anxious to justify his historical importance. The other mention of Providence seeks to ridicule Gladstonian Liberalism, but it also implicitly casts doubt on the very idea of an intervening Providence when it refers to the opinions of

> ...Nonconformist papers regarding [Parnell's death] as a judgement from God on Mr. Parnell, for being impiously inquisitive as to Mr. Gladstone's intentions about Home Rule.[18]

Since these last two comments portray Providence as a function of human perception rather than of objective reality, they tend to undermine the motif.

In summary, then, Providence is depicted nine times in the nineteenth century sources for the Myth, six times as objectively real, three times as subjectively so. In the six references to an objectively real Providence, God acts out of concern for Ireland's welfare four times and in retribution for Parnell's actions twice. This Providence is readily recognizable from literature and mythology: God acting to preserve His chosen nation and to punish sin. At the same time, the depictions of Providence are very few (relative to the representation of other motifs within the Myth), and all but one of them dates from October 1891.

There are thirteen references to destiny or fate in the nineteenth century evidence, ten of them similar to the depictions of Providence. Most show destiny/fate in direct relationship to Ireland or to Parnell himself, but not from any consistent point of view. Sometimes destiny/fate smiles on Ireland and/or Parnell, sometimes it stands in the way of success. The difference between destiny/fate and Providence is that it can be a force for either good or ill, while Providence does only good. Providence guards the nation, rewards virtuous behavior, and punishes sin. Fate--as destiny--may be the force which guides the nation to the ultimate goal of the Promised Land or--as nemesis--it may be the cause of a series of catastrophes which prevents the nation from ever getting there.

Four of the references to destiny/fate portray its relationship to Ireland. Two of them depict it as friendly but as only subjectively real:

> To his own people he was the Man of Destiny...[19]
>
> It may have been that ... he had become convinced that fate had appointed him its special instrument to secure for his countrymen the fulfilment of their aspirations.[20]

The other two depict destiny/fate as real, but as hostile to Ireland:

> His remarkable career, with his extraordinary ability and his incredible weakness, adds another to the memorable illustrations of the singular fate which has baffled all great Irish Leadership.[21]
>
> Eire's ill fate cried--'For he dares the storm,
> No force afrights him nor disasters damn,

Slay now.' Beside her rose the susk-webbed form,

And 'whom thou seek'st I am.'

Said[22]

Of the five items that portray a direct relationship between destiny/fate and Parnell, two present it as friendly and three as unfriendly. The representations of a friendly destiny/fate are less explicit. An inexorable force is there, but between the lines: it is not depicted literally. In one of the passages, the writer describes " the one figure of the leader...moving persistently forward in pursuit of its predestined aim";[23] in the others, the author refers to Parnell's time of triumph after the Special Commission verdict in his favor as "the predominance of his lucky star."[24] The depictions of an unfriendly force are more literal:

> ...we must hold faction responsible. That he raised himself the Evil Fate that dragged him to his grave, that he planned his own ruin and immolated himself on the altar of his own vanity but adds to the bitterness and the pity of it.[25]
>
> The fierce bolt of fate dashed him dead from the crag.[26]

The most interesting of all the references to destiny/fate comes from Timothy Healy, who links it with the month of October. Healy tells this story of a political meeting he had with Parnell in October 1882, when Parnell seemed quite ill:

> 'Oh, no' said he; 'it is nothing.' After a pause he added, musingly 'Something happens to me always in October.' This remark fell from him as if he were announcing a decree of fate, and struck me intensely. October, in Mr. Parnell's horoscope, was a month of 'influence,' and he always regarded it with apprehension. [Here follows a list of significant events in Parnell's life which occurred in October]...
>
> ...Strangest of all, in view of his premonitions, is the fact that it was in the month of October that he died so unexpectedly in 1891. A belief that a particular month might be 'influential' would probably react with depressing effect on physical health at the critical period and thus weaken the resisting power at that time. Nevertheless, the stoutest disbeliever in unseen influence will deem the coincidence noteworthy.[27]

This linkage of fate to Parnell's well-known superstition[28] presents it as both subjectively and objectively real. Surprisingly, although Healy's article was widely reprinted,[29] no other author picked up his point and elaborated on it.

Fate is mentioned four more times in the evidence. Twice, it stands for the end result of things:

> It is the fate of every great patriot Irishman to die for his country. It has been

Parnell's lot.[30]

How pitiful the fate![31]

Once, Parnell's rigid sense of duty is characterized as "as unbending as fate,"[32] and once fate is blamed for putting Gladstone in a position which forced him to criticize the dead Parnell.[33] I have been exhaustive in cataloging the references to destiny/fate for two reasons: to illustrate my method of of sorting the evidence--I will present as much of it as possible in table form as this analysis proceeds--and to illustrate why a simple counting of words without reference to their meaning in context would be insufficient. The last three items of evidence, though they mention fate explicitly, are neutral with respect to the destiny/fate motif.

Providence/destiny/fate is a weak motif for two reasons. First, the number of items supporting it is relatively small compared to the numbers supporting the other motifs. Six items depict Providence as objectively real, one as only subjectively so, and two really debunk its existence. Eight items portray destiny/fate as having objective existence and two as existing in people's perceptions, while three are neutral. Not only is the pattern of support weak, but chronology is a factor. Five of the six positive references to Providence date from the emotional atmosphere of 1891 (the sixth from 1892) and the six strongest representations of fate from 1893 or earlier (three of them from 1891). Since they were not picked up and repeated by other writers later in the 1890s, the continuity of their appeal becomes a question. As a matter of fact, analysis of the twentieth century sources, which I discuss in Chapter 5, reveals that Providence did not continue as a motif in the Parnell Myth after 1900, but that destiny/fate actually grew stronger.

The meaning and importance of the Providence/destiny/fate motif is easily told. Essentially, the terms serve as a literary device, the representation in romantic language of two conflicting ideas. The positive one, usually represented as Providence or destiny, is the ultimate good of the nation (variously conceived, according to the writer's politics). The negative one, almost always fate, is adversity, the thwarting of the individual's or the nation's drive to achieve its purpose. The importance of this motif to the Parnell Myth is the quality of romance it brings to the story, along with the heightened importance given to its central character (whether he is guided or thwarted by the unseen forces). Every characteristic of the Myth which increases Parnell's importance enhances the effectiveness of the Myth's central symbol, Parnell's <u>attitude</u> of independence and dignity.

A third motif is treachery/betrayal. It is considerably stronger than Providence/ destiny/fate. Fifty-five items of evidence, from forty sources, support it, while only nine items, from nine sources, break the pattern. Like Providence/destiny/fate, it is colored by political interpretation: twenty-eight items portray the Antiparnellites as treacherous either to Parnell or to Ireland (five items deny this), while eighteen items from twelve sources claim Parnell betrayed Ireland or particular individuals (two items deny such a charge) and six items accuse him of treachery to Britain (one item maintaining the opposite). While, therefore, there is a definite pattern of support for the motif, there are significant interpretive differences among the items of evidence which support it.

Two angry outbursts from the Parnellite weekly, United Ireland, will illustrate the accusations of treachery/betrayal made against the Antiparnellites:

> Nine months ago the traitorous Seceders boasted that they would drive him into a lunatic asylum or into the grave. They have driven him into the grave.[34]

> ...the cruel baseness of the wretched creatures whose treachery last December was the beginning of the end of his great life.[35]

The charges made by the Antiparnellites are similar. The Irish Catholic refers, for instance, to "Mr. Parnell's gross outrage against the laws of morality and his later treason to Ireland."[36] The Unionist claims of Parnell's treachery to Britain, on the other hand, are less shrill. The Spectator's interpretation of Parnell's intention on his American tour is a good example:

> ...Parnell went to America in 1879 determined to capture the extremist movement in America, and bend it to his own purposes, paying, at the same time, the minimum price in the way of treason...[37]

The portrayals of treachery/betrayal which these examples represent differ in two essentials, their political orientations and the times at which they were written.

The great bulk of the references to treachery/betrayal grow out of the issues of the Split. Of these, twenty-eight come from twenty sources published in the emotionally-charged last three months of 1891. The remainder, sixteen items, come from fourteen sources scattered the remaining eight years of the nineteenth century.[38] The proximity of painful events--the divorce court revelation, Parnell's fall from power and his death--clearly influence the writers' choice of the loaded terms treason, treachery, and betrayal. This abusive language was music to the Unionist ears, of course. The London newspaper, England and Primrose Record, gleefully noted in October 1891 that

> 'Leprous traitors, infamous conspirators, perfidious murderers.' Such are the terms hurled at the Macarthyites, and, above all, at Mr. Healy.[39]

Five years later, the most emotional of the Parnellite organs had had a change of heart. It urged:

> Let us talk no more about 'betrayals,' 'treacheries,' 'murderers,' 'Whigs.' There is nothing of Parnell in that exaggerated vocabulary.[40]

"That exaggerated vocabulary" was always easier to employ in the heat of controversy. While the Split-related accusations of treachery/betrayal were concentrated in 1891, the complaints of Parnell's treachery/betrayal to Britain were scattered through the last six years of the nineties, reflecting Home Rule's continuing status as an emotional issue.[41]

The motif of treachery/betrayal helps shape the Parnell Myth. The items charging the Antiparnellites with betrayal contribute to Parnell's stature by accounting for his fall in this way--they imply that he could only have been overcome by treachery--and they implicitly affirm the legitimacy of his role as leader of the Irish people. The items accusing him of treachery to the Irish nation also affirm his leadership role, before his fall. They emphasize the extent to which the nation had entrusted its aspirations to him. This link between Parnell and Irish aspirations is vital to the operation of Parnell's attitude as the Myth's central symbol. So long as the Antiparnellite accusations concede Parnell's faithful performance of his duties as leader before the Split--and they do--they do not detract from the representation of his indepencence and dignity as leader. His betrayal of Ireland at the end is portrayed as a departure from his true role. Nor do the Unionist accusations of treachery take away from the central symbol. Rather, by equating Parnell's treason with his stirring up of Irish nationalist aspirations, they support it. The motif of treachery/betrayal, then, is compatible with the central theme and central symbol of the Parnell Myth, and many of the items supporting it come from sources published in 1891. This raises serious questions about its continuity in the Myth, and, in fact, my analysis of the twentieth century evidence in Chapter 5 shows that it became very weak indeed.

Tragedy is, on the other hand, a consistently strong motif throughout the Myth. In the nineteenth century material, twenty-three items from twenty sources present an unmistakable pattern of support. There are only three items which equivocate on the point, calling Parnell's story "almost tragic"[42] or "more or less tragic"[43] and none at all which assert that Parnell's story was not a tragedy. Here is a sampling of items supporting the motif:

> ...a tragedy dark enough for a Sophocles' chorus...[44]

> ...[Parnell's eyes] always had a strange glow in them that arrested your attention. It was this latent expression that suggested to so many people the impression that his end would be tragic. I once heard a poet declare that with such a face and air, Mr. Parnell was foredoomed to the scaffold. The reality has proved almost worse than such forecasts...[45]

> Poor fellow! I suppose he did [suffer]; dear, dear, what a tragedy! I cannot tell you how much I think about him, and what an interest I take in everything concerning him. A marvellous man, a terrible fall.[46]

The pattern of support among the items explicitly mentioning tragedy would be sufficient evidence to establish the existence of the tragedy motif, but there is more. Other items, such as these two examples, clearly imply that Parnell's story was a tragedy by encompassing language with tragic associations:

> Somewhere his strenuous soul unsoundly rang, When closely tested....[47]

> ...him who loved not wisely but too well...[48]

More important, the general outline of the story of Parnell's fall fits the pattern of a tragedy: first, the betrayal (or the moral offense and its effects, depending on one's political preferences); next, the fall itself; then, its effects; and, finally, the assessment that the story was a tragedy. To illustrate this pattern, I have assembled a dozen subject headings from my index to the nineteenth century evidence in Table 2.

The tragedy motif integrates very well with other elements of the Parnell Myth. The tragic event is the downfall of a great man. It is explained in various ways, but each explanation links the tragedy motif to a different element in the Myth, increasing the Myth's unity. Parnell is overcome by either his own flawed character (the Antiparnellite interpretation) or by superior unseen forces (Providence/destiny/fate motif). The presentation of Parnell's fall as high tragedy also reinforces the central theme of the Myth because of its air of dignity; it contributes to the central symbol by increasing Parnell's stature within the Myth and by describing his fall in dignified terms.

The motifs I have just outlined--ancestry, Providence/destiny/fate, treachery/betrayal and tragedy--help make the Parnell Myth what it is. They do this in part by contributing support to the central theme and central symbol--the sources of the Myth's unity and coherence--but they go beyond that. They add to the richness of the story because they themselves represent powerful themes from history and literature. The elements of the Myth I will discuss next add color to Parnell's story, while supporting the motifs I have just discussed and lending support to the central theme and central symbol.

One of those elements is the group of speculations on What Might Have Been. Some of these items are used to make points in controversy by indicating the consequences that would have necessarily followed a particular course of action. When, for instance, the Liberal writer J. L. Garvin asserts that, had the Home Rule Bill passed in 1886, Parnell

TABLE 2

SCHEMA FOR TRAGEDY IN THE FALL OF PARNELL

| Classification | Subject Heading | Number of Entries |
|---|---|---|
| moral offense | gravity | 36 |
| moral offense | punishment for | 4[a] |
| moral offense | effects of liaison | 5 |
| themes | treachery | 13 |
| themes | betrayal | 13 |
| fall | his own fault | 14 |
| themes | fate | 7 |
| fall | faults, sins that led to | 23[b] |
| fall | Katharine O'Shea's fault | 5 |
| fall | description | 5 |
| fall | effects | 6 |
| themes | tragedy | 19 |

Note: Tabulation reflects the number of items in which the information was explicitly stated, and not those in which it was merely implied.

[a]Sixteen other items refer to Parnell's spiritual punishment.

[b]This heading combines seven more specific headings from the index.

would have won consensus support for his new regime within six months, made himself autocrat of Ireland and become more imperialist than Cecil Rhodes,[49] he is countering the traditional Tory argument that Home Rule would be the first step to separation. Michael McCarthy, an Irish Tory, takes the opposite position, but by using the same type of speculation. If Parnell had won Home Rule, McCarthy argues, he would have demanded great concessions from Britain the first time Britain found herself in some international emergency.[50] There are six other items of this type in the nineteenth century evidence that are used to further political arguments, four on issues of the Split, one more on Home Rule, and one on the Irish Parliamentary Party.

Speculations about What Might Have Been also strengthen the tragedy motif. In an interview with Barry O'Brien in 1897, Gladstone twice used them to substantiate his point that Parnell's fall had been a terrible tragedy for Ireland:

> I do believe that if these divorce proceedings had not taken place there would be a Parliament in Ireland now. Oh, it was a terrible tragedy.[51]

These remarks support the tragedy motif in a special way, because the depiction of tragedy rests on more than mere assertion. They make so compelling an argument for tragedy, in fact, that the second remark is quoted in three different reviews of O'Brien's book.[52]

The other speculations about What Might Have Been increase our estimate of Parnell's greatness. An American critic of Dublin's Royal University, established in 1895, maintains vigorously that Parnell would have had the wisdom and power to prevent its foundation.[53] A Spectator epitaph on Parnell's career concludes that ambition could not have been Parnell's "master-impulse," because Parnell ignored his very good chances for success in the wider field of British Empire in order to work for Ireland.[54] Finally, an American writer employs the very refusal to speculate to make his point about Parnell's greatness.

> It seems temerity, impudence, almost, to ask what he would have done had he not fallen. Surely in a life of forty-five years, in a Parliamentary career of fifteen, this man had done enough.[55]

By emphasizing Parnell's greatness, these items increase his stature in the Myth and thereby strengthen the central symbol. Taken together, the speculations about What Might Have Been add color to the Myth by injecting an imaginative quality into the arguments and historical evaluations which partly comprise it.

Another group of items adds yet more color and performs a number of other functions as well. This is the collection of comparisons--or contrasts--of Parnell with historical, Biblical and fictional characters. Table 3 contains a summary of these comparisons. One

TABLE 3

PERSONS COMPARED WITH PARNELL 1891-99, WITH THE NUMBER OF COMPARISONS MADE

Characters from Irish History

Brian Boru (1)
Isaac Butt (5)
Thomas Davis (4)
Robert Emmet (2)
Lord Edward Fitzgerald (2)
Henry Grattan (12)
Terence McManus (1)
Dermot McMorrough (1)
Thomas Meagher (1)
John Mitchel (1)
William Smith O'Brien (1)
Daniel O'Connell (25)
Owen Roe O'Neill (4)
William Shaw (1)
James Stephens (1)
Jonathan Swift (1)
Wolfe Tone (6)

Other Historical Characters

Alfred the Great (1)
Marc Antony (1)
Athanasius (1)
Augustus (1)
Balmaceda (3)
Bismark (6)
Joseph Bonaparte (1)
Napoleon Bonaparte (22)
Boulanger (7)
Admiral Byng (1)
Julius Caesar (9)
Cassius (1)
Catherine of Aragon (1)
Cavour (3)
Charles I (2)
Charles II (1)
Bonnie Prince Charlie (1)
Constantine (1)
Oliver Cromwell (2)
Disraeli (2)
Gambetta (2)
Gladstone (4)
Grant (1)
Hannibal (2)
Hartington (1)
Kossuth (1)
Mary, Queen of Scots (1)
Mokanna (1)
Napoleon III (1)
Palmerston (1)
Peter the Great (1)
Pisistratus (1)
Pius IX (1)
The Princes in the Tower (1)
Cecil Rhodes (1)
Rienzi (1)
Stambuloff (1)
Strafford (1)
Washington (3)
William III (1)

Biblical Characters

David (2)
Jesus (14)
Jonas (1)
Moses (14)
Samson (2)
Saul (2)

Characters from Literature

Achilles (1)
Actaeon (1)
Ancient Mariner (1)
Banquo's Ghost (2)
Coriolanus (1)
Marmion (1)
Othello (1)
Sisyphus (1)
The woman who threw herself and children in the Sultan's path (1)

of the functions they perform is to illustrate or strengthen arguments in controversy. The items comparing Parnell to General Georges Boulanger are a good example. The names are linked, according to the various writers, because Boulanger's fall was his own fault,[56] because it was the result of a moral lapse,[57] because his reputation was "ruined through feminine fascinations,"[58] and because it was "not impossible" to see the hand of Providence in his fall.[59] In all, Parnell is compared to twenty-nine different individuals (a total of fifty-nine times, in forty-seven items of evidence) for purposes of argument: twenty-one historical persons, four Biblical characters and four fictional characters.

The comparisons also contribute support to the motifs of tragedy and treachery/ betrayal. Two of them explicitly say that Parnell's fall was a tragedy. One links Parnell and Leon Gambetta, lamenting the "two foremost statesmen of France and Ireland dying in the flower of their age and under more or less tragic conditions."[60] The other declares that "his fate was as tragic as that of Antony or Mary [Queen of Scots]."[61] Seven other items support the treachery/betrayal motif. In four of them, Parnell is compared to Julius Caesar and his opponents to Brutus (William O'Brien three times[62] and Gladstone once[63]). In the other three, he is compared to Jesus Christ and they--William O'Brien,[64] the political team of Dillon and O'Brien[65] and Timothy Healy[66]--are likened to Judas Iscariot.

There are a number of other comparisons of Parnell with Christ and Caesar, but they are not related to any motif. Instead, their principal effect is to increase Parnell's stature within the Myth while heightening the drama inherent in the story. The most extensive comparison is offered by Parnell's mother, who tells an interviewer that "he died as Christ died, hounded to death by those who should have stood by him." He forgave the Irish people, she explains, in his last words when he said, "Give my love to my colleagues and to the Irish people,"--just as Christ had forgiven those who had killed Him. "He was crucified," she insists again. The coalition which defeated him "was like Pontius Pilate and Herod becoming friends."[67] In striking contrast to the emotionalism of Mrs. Parnell's interview, Justin McCarthy offers a comparison of Parnell not in controversy but in simple wonder at Parnell's great career:

> He could no more have intended at the beginning to do all that he did than Julius Caesar could have started in life with the determination to become the greatest man in the world.[68]

The Myth's authors also use comparisons for purposes of historical evaluation or explanation. One writer, for instance, compares Parnell to President Ulysses S. Grant for his mixture of poor oratory and resolute leadership and to "certain leaders of Tammany Hall" for the narrow horizons of his imagination.[69] A second offeres this capsule review of Parnell's government of party and nation: "Like Strafford, he was thorough; like Pius IX., he knew the power of a brief non possumus."[70] Some of these comparisons are colorful and striking. A few are merely workmanlike. The Spectator writes of Parnell that "in all but principle, the man he is most like in history is William III, who, however, cared more for individuals."[71]. The primary function of these evaluative comparisons, which number eighteen, is to enhance Parnell's stature. They do this incidentally, because of the eminence of the men with whom Parnell is compared.

There is, however, another, much larger group of comparisons that deliberately estimate Parnell's stature in comparison to other great men. John Redmond, for instance, leads into a speech on Irish leaders this way:

> ...we see, to my thinking, four men standing out from amidst them all; four distinguished by their actual achievements from all the rest; four who, by those achievements, have left ineffaceable traces on the history of the nation; four whose achievements have been recognized abroad as fully as at home. I refer to Swift, Grattan, O'Connell, and Parnell.[72]

Another writer, a poet, makes roughly the same estimate of Parnell's stature but widens the field of comparison:

> Parnell shall rank in history not least
> In trio Grattan and O'Connell form:
> With Kossuth, Garibaldi, Washington --
> With men who nations found and peoples weld
> Shall he be named....[73]

Not all the comparisons are entirely favorable to Parnell. One estimation of his career concludes: "far less noble than Grattan, far less attractive than O'Connell, far less brilliant than either of them, [Parnell is] yet entitled to be remembered as one of the most remarkable figures of our time."[74] These items that use comparisons with history's great men to measure Parnell's stature perform an especially important function with respect to the central symbol of the Parnell Myth: by establishing Parnell's membership of what might be called the heroic pantheon, they help establish his worthiness to represent the Irish nation's aspirations. In all, there are seventy-three such items in the evidence, and Parnell is compared to thirty-six different individuals in them.

These, then, are the functions performed by the items comparing Parnell with historical, Biblical and fictional characters: some support controversial arguments, a few reinforce motifs in the Myth, some illustrate historical explanations or evaluations, many more establish Parnell's membership of the heroic pantheon, and virtually all of them add color to his story.

In this chapter, I have described four motifs--ancestry, Providence/destiny/fate, treachery/betrayal and tragedy--and two other characteristics of the Parnell Myth, speculations about What Might Have Been and comparisons of Parnell with other great men. In Chapter 4, I will discuss the central theme and central symbol of the Myth and several other characteristics directly related to them, and I will explain how they create the Myth's unity, coherence and emotive power. Before proceeding to that discussion, however, I should stress three points about the characteristics I have just described.

First, these characteristics are important on their own merits, outside their relationships to the central theme and central symbol. The motifs evoke timeless themes from literature. All of the characteristics add color, enlivening Parnell's story. The speculations about What Might Have Been add a fanciful element. They and the historical comparisons help define Parnell's place in history. All of the characteristics except the ancestry motif serve to buttress one side or another in the controversy about the meaning of Parnell's career, and the ancestry motif helps certify Parnell's credentials as a nationalist.

Second, these characteristics do strengthen the central theme and central symbol. They do this especially by increasing Parnell's stature within the story. The motifs of Providence/destiny/fate, treachery/betrayal and tragedy solve one of the thorniest problems for the symbol by providing a dignified interpretation of Parnell's fall from power (or, in the case of the Antiparnellite sources, an interpretation of Parnell's fall that emphasizes his central leadership role before his fatal error). This allows the symbol to convey an unambiguous message about independence and dignity. The comparisons that include Parnell in the heroic pantheon not only add to his stature within the story but, by linking him, an Irishman, with the world's great men, confer honor on the Irish nation as a whole. This process parallels the operation of the central symbol and reinforces it.

Third, these characteristics fit together well, reinforcing the Myth's unity and coherence. The tragedy motif, in fact, incorporates several items of evidence that also support either Providence/destiny/fate or treachery/betrayal. The speculations about What Might Have Been underline the scope of the tragedy which Parnell's fall represents. And the comparisons of Parnell with Biblical, fictional and historical figures often evoke or underline the motifs of treachery/betrayal, tragedy or Providence/destiny/fate.

The characteristics described in this chapter, then, do much to shape the Parnell Myth. The characteristics I will discuss next do more: they give it unity, coherence and emotive power.

## Notes to Chapter 3

[1]Justin McCarthy, A History of Our Own Times, 5:75.

[2]Justin McCarthy, "Charles Stewart Parnell," p. 669.

[3]Patrick J. P. Tynan, The Irish National Invincibles and Their Times (London: Chatham & Co., 1894), p. 402.

[4][Albert Shaw], "Three Fallen Leaders: I. Parnell--'The Uncrowned King of Ireland,' " American Review of Reviews, November 1891, p. 417.

[5]TPOC, pp. 15-16.

[6]Ralph D. St. John, "Charles Stewart Parnell," Chautauquan, December 1891, p. 322.

[7]"The 'King' is Dead," Harper's Weekly, 17 October 1891, p. 795.

[8]Ibid.

[9]Delia T. S. Parnell, interview with R. Barry O'Brien, RBOB, 1:29, quoted in [W. T. Stead], "The Book of the Month: Parnell the Avenger," review of RBOB, in Review of Reviews, December 1898, p. 599.

[10]Charles de Kay, "An Intellectual Phenomenon," review of RBOB, in Critic, August 1899, p. 730.

[11]Leading article, Irish Daily Independent (Dublin), 18 December 1891.

[12]"No!" United Ireland (Dublin), 17 October 1891.

[13]Mac and O', The Parnell Leadership and Home Rule: From an Historical, Ethical and Ethnological Point of View (Dublin: Gill & Son, 1892), p. 24; Monde (Paris), n.d., quoted in "Catholic Opinion on Mr. Parnell," Irish Catholic and Nation (Dublin), 17 October 1891. The first was Antiparnellite, the second Roman Catholic.

[14]Evening Press (Dublin), 7 October 1891, quoted in Dublin Evening Mail, 7 October 1891. The first was Antiparnellite, the second Unionist.

[15]Primrose, "Charles Stewart Parnell," Dublin Evening Mail, 8 October 1891. The writer was a Unionist.

[16]Daily Express (Dublin), 10 October 1891.

[17]D. F. Hannigan, "Parnell and Cromwell: A Dialogue between Two Ghosts," Westminster Review, September 1899, p. 248.

[18]Dublin Evening Mail, 17 October 1891.

[19]Lionel Johnson, "The Man Who Would Be King," review of RBOB, in Academy, 19 November 1898, p. 293.

[20][J. M. Tuohy], reminiscences of Charles Stewart Parnell, Freeman's Journal (Dublin), 8 October 1891, reprinted in Dublin Evening Mail, 8 October 1891, in Evening Telegraph (Dublin), 8, 9 October 1891, in Weekly Freeman (Dublin), 17 October 1891.

[21]"Parnell," Harper's Weekly, 17 October 1891, p. 791.

[22]W. I. P., "Ireland's Leader," United Ireland (Dublin), 31 October 1891.

[23]Leonard Courtney, "Parnell and Ireland," review of RBOB, in Nineteenth Century, June 1899, p. 880.

[24][J. H. Millar], "The Rebel King," review of RBOB, in Blackwood's Magazine, January 1899, p. 147.

[25]"1891," Weekly Freeman (Dublin), 9 January 1892.

[26]"A Lament," United Ireland, (Dublin), 7 October 1893. United Ireland published this poem noting that it was taken from [Alfred] Percival Graves's Irish Songs and Ballads (Manchester: A. Ireland & Co., 1880), but neglecting to mention the date of publication. Readers may have been misled by United Ireland's suggestion that the poem "will seem to many to have been inspired by the death of the Irish leader."

[27]Timothy M. Healy, "A Great Man's Fancies," Westminster Gazette, 3 November 1893.

[28]It was foreshadowed only eight days after Parnell's death by a columnist (Healy again?) in the National Press: "Strange that one of Mr. Parnell's many superstitions was that 'something always happens to me in October.' " "Day by Day," National Press (Dublin), 14 October 1891.

[29]In Daily Express (Dublin), 3 November 1893; Evening Telegraph (Dublin), 3 November 1893; Dublin Evening Mail, 3 November 1893; Weekly Freeman (Dublin), 11 November 1893; RBOB, 1:367-68.

[30]Timothy Harrington, quoted in Weekly Freeman (Dublin), 10 October 1891.

[31]T. H. Farnham, "Parnell," New England Magazine, December 1891, p. 469.

[32]T. P. O'Connor uses a description of Admiral Charles Stewart as a device for indirectly describing Parnell. TPOC, p. 16.

[33]"Topics of the Day: Banquo's Ghost," Spectator, 15 April 1893, pp. 473-74.

[34]"The Week's Work," United Ireland (Dublin), 10 October 1891.

[35]"Mr. Parnell As I Knew Him: (By a Physical Force Man)," United Ireland (Dublin), 10 October 1891.

[36]"The Duty of a Catholic Journalist: A Word to Our Assailants," Irish Catholic and Nation, (Dublin), 24 October 1891.

[37]"Books: Mr. Parnell," review of Dictionary of National Biography, s.v. "Parnell, Charles Stewart," in Spectator, 6 July 1895, p. 20.

[38]Here is a summary of sources: 20 in 1891, 3 in 1892, 1 in 1893, 1 in 1894, 3 in 1895, 0 in 1896, 2 in 1897, 3 in 1898, 1 in 1899.

[39]"Irish Notes," England and Primrose Record (London), 17 October 1891.

[40]"Our Fealty to the Dead: (By Our Special Correspondent in England)," United Ireland (Dublin), 10 October 1896.

[41]One source was published in 1894, 2 in 1895, 1 in 1898 and 1 in 1899.

[42]"Charles Stewart Parnell," review of RBOB, in Westminster Review, January 1899, p. 1; [Arthur R. Elliot], "Parnell and His Work," review of RBOB, in Edinburgh Review, April 1899, p. 569.

[43]John O'Leary, Recollections of Fenians and Fenianism, 2 vols. (London: Downey & Co., 1896; reprint ed., Shannon: Irish University Press, 1969), 1:170.

[44]William O'Brien, "Was Mr. Parnell Badly Treated?" Contemporary Review, November 1896, p. 680.

[45]TPOC, p. 214.

[46]William E. Gladstone, interview with R. Barry O'Brien, London, 28 January 1897, quoted in RBOB, 2:367.

[47]"A Fallen Leader," Punch, 17 October 1891, p. 191, quoted in Dublin Evening Mail, 19 October 1891.

[48]T. H. Farnham, "Parnell," p. 469.

[49]J. Louis Garvin, "Parnell and His Power," review of RBOB, in Fortnightly Review, 1 December 1898, pp. 882-83, quoted in "Parnell As an Interracial Type," American Review of Reviews, January 1899, p. 94.

[50]Michael J. F. McCarthy, Mr. Balfour's Rule in Ireland (Dublin: Hodges, Figgis & Co., 1891), p. 69.

[51]RBOB, 2:357-58, 366.

[52]"Charles Stewart Parnell," Westminster Review, January 1899, p. 11; [W. T. Stead], "The Book of the Month: Parnell the Avenger," p. 604; E. G. J., "Parnell, Irish Patriot and Nationalist," review of RBOB, in Dial, 1 February 1899, p. 75.

[53]Quoted in J. B. K., "American Opinions on Mr. Parnell," United Ireland (Dublin), 12 October 1895.

[54]"Topics of the Day: The Death of Mr. Parnell," Spectator, 10 October 1891, p. 484.

[55]"The 'King' is Dead," Harper's Weekly, 17 October 1891, p. 795.

[56]National Zeitung (Vienna), n.d., quoted in "Continental Opinion on Mr. Parnell," Irish Catholic and Nation (Dublin), 17 October 1891.

[57]As was Leon Gambetta's. Gazette de France (Paris), n.d., quoted in "Continental Opinion on Mr. Parnell," Irish Catholic and Nation (Dublin), 17 October 1891.

[58]As were those of Napoleon I and Napoleon III. "Notes of the Week," Irish Ecclesiastical Gazette (Dublin), 9 October 1891.

[59]Or Jose Manuel Balmaceda's. "Dead!" Evening Press (Dublin), 7 October 1891, quoted in Dublin Evening Mail, 7 October 1891.

[60]John O'Leary, Recollections, 1:170.

[61]J. Louis Garvin, "Parnell and His Power," p. 94.

[62]"Dead Caesar's Brutus," Dublin Evening Mail, 21 October 1891; "The Dead Chief," United Ireland (Dublin), 10 October 1891; leading article, United Ireland (Dublin) 24 October 1891.

[63]Robert Buchanan, untitled poem, Echo (London), n.d., reprinted, under the epigraph "We come to bury Caesar, not to praise him," in "Englishmen Reproach Irish Ingratitude," United Ireland (Dublin), 17 October 1891.

[64]Ibid.

[65]The Dublin Evening Mail's correspondent draws a slightly different inference from Robert Buchanan's lines: that they refer to both Dillon and O'Brien. Ibid., quoted in "Dead Caesar's Brutus," Dublin Evening Mail, 21 October 1891.

[66]John Clancy, City of Dublin Sub-sheriff, speech at the National Club meeting, Dublin, 7 October 1891, quoted in "Meeting at the National Club," National Press (Dublin), 8 October 1891.

[67]Delia T. S. Parnell, interview, Daily News (London), n.d., reprinted in National Press (Dublin), 16 October 1891, and in Dublin Evening Mail, 16 October 1891.

[68]Justin McCarthy, "Charles Stewart Parnell," p. 632.

[69]Charles de Kay, "An Intellectual Phenomenon," p. 731.

[70]Lionel Johnson, "The Man Who Would Be King," p. 294.

[71]"News of the Week," Spectator, 10 October 1891, p. 481.

[72]John E. Redmond, "Irish Popular Leaders from Swift to Parnell," speech delivered in Ireland, 1898, Dublin, National Library of Ireland, John E. Redmond MSS, 15274.

[73]John Stuart, untitled poem, quoted in Jeremiah C. Curtain, Thomas C. Luby, and Robert F. Walsh, The Story of Ireland's Struggle for Self-government: With the Lives and Times of Her Great Leaders (New York: Gay Bros. & Co., 1893), p. 742.

[74]James Bryce [O.D.], "Charles Stewart Parnell," Nation (New York), 29 October 1891, p. 333, revised and reprinted in James Bryce, Studies in Contemporary Biography (London: Macmillan Co., 1903), pp. 248-49.

## CHAPTER 4

## THE PARNELL MYTH 1891-99
## CENTRAL THEME AND CENTRAL SYMBOL

The central theme and central symbol of the Parnell Myth are not just central, they are also pervasive. Many, many items of evidence support them, including items which support other characteristics of the Myth as well. For that reason, I will approach my analysis of them by discussing a number of those other characteristics that either reinforce them or serve to link the central symbol, Parnell's attitude, to the Irish people, the Myth's primary audience.

The metaphors that the Myth's authors use to describe Parnell evoke independence, dignity and complementary qualities. The metaphorical roles assigned to him also evoke those qualities while establishing Parnell as the nation's leader. The nationality motif reinforces the bond between leader and people. Parnell's symbolic kingship establishes the independence and dignity of both people and leader, ties the independence and dignity of the people to their leader and of the leader to his role, and reaffirms nationality as the element which binds all together. The motif of contempt/disdain/scorn depicts these relationships in high relief: in the confrontations involving contempt/disdain/scorn, independence and dignity are crucially at stake, nationality is the element that divides the antagonists, and Parnell emerges the victorious leader of his people.

Metaphors[1] play a colorful and important part in the telling of Parnell's story. The Myth's authors use them to represent qualities they see in Parnell, qualities that often comprise or complement Parnell's symbolic attitude. The most common metaphors are listed in Table 4. Within the table, the metaphors which represent similar or complementary images are grouped together.

So far as the central symbol of the Myth is concerned, the most important metaphors are the animal metaphors. Conor Cruise O'Brien once referred to "the zoology of Parnellite invective."[2] He could as well have noted the zoology of Parnellite praise. While the Parnellites accused their opponents of being "jackals," "vipers," "vultures," and "wolves," they were quick to depict their leader as an animal, too. The difference was that the animals with which they identified him, big jungle cats and birds of prey, are commonly thought of as far more noble beasts.

Not only the Parnellites, but many of the Myth's other authors have used animal

## TABLE 4

## PRINCIPAL METAPHORS FOR PARNELL 1891-99

| | |
|---|---|
| Fire (7) | |
| Ice (7) | |
| Volcano (2) | Star (1) |
| Iron (3) | Backbone (1) |
| Granite (2) | Right Arm (1) |
| Marble (1) | |
| Statue (1) | Lion (10) |
| Castle (1) | Eagle (4) |
| Tower (1) | Hawk (1) |
| | Tiger (1) |
| Sword (1) | Falcon (1) |
| Axe (1) | |
| Cannonball (1) | Stag (1) |
| Spring Lock (1) | Wild Beast (1) |
| Vice (1) | Hunted Hind (1) |
| Earthquake (1) | Sphinx (3) |
| Eclipse (1) | |
| Meteor (1) | |
| Sunburst (1) | |

images to represent aspects of Parnell's character, and, for the most part, they have used animals that suggest strength, fierceness and natural dignity. These images can be very effective. One source, an American priest complaining during the Split about those critics who presumed to judge Parnell on moral grounds, says that:

> They could as little comprehend the character and greatness of a man like Parnell as a gnat could the size of a lion it may succeed in stinging.[3]

This is one of ten items in the evidence depicting Parnell as a lion or as being lion-hearted. He is also likened to an eagle, tiger, falcon and--by himself--to a hawk.[4] All of the animals are strong, fierce, and even regal. By way of comparison, only two items of evidence depict Parnell as a lesser animal, one saying that "he perished, solitary, unpitied, and betrayed, like a wild beast in his den,"[5] and the other describing him as looking during the Split "like a hunted hind; his hair was dishevelled, his beard unkept, his eyes were wild and restless."[6] There is one final image, that of a great stag set upon by a pack of hounds.[7] This image, while it does not evoke fierceness, represents strength and natural dignity.

Most of the non-animal metaphors employed by the Myth's authors refer to Parnell's strength of character. He is, for instance, "the backbone of Home Rule"[8] in one and "Ireland's strong right arm"[9] in another. He is described as made of iron three times and of granite twice. There is also this description of Parnell's reaction to the very emotional welcome he received at Avondale when he returned home from his imprisonment in Kilmainham:

> Parnell was absolutely unmoved. I thought he was the most callous fellow I had ever met....He was like a statue.[10]

The same silent strength is evoked, although in a much more positive way, by Katharine Tynan's avowal that "you were our Tower, our Castle."[11]

Parnell's strength of character comprehended a number of allied qualities, and these, too, are represented metaphorically. One source describes "the unscrupulous and ruthless spirit with which he, in his political life, had gone like a cannon ball direct to his mark."[12] A second characterizes Parnell's mental processes this way:

> Parnell's mind seems to have acted like a spring-lock on some adamantine safe. It shut down with a snap, and then nothing could move the doors but the absolute destruction of the safe itself.[13]

A third describes Parnell's stoical behavior during his imprisonment in Kilmainham Jail:

> To the majority of his companions in durance he was the sphinx that they had known before, unaltered and unmoved in that novel environment, and neither more nor less conciliatory than it was at all times and in all places his wont to be.[14]

These metaphors evoke Parnell's strength of character by representing him as direct, ruthless, stubborn and aloof.

In a few instances, writers make use of natural phenomena as metaphors. One, a poet, addresses this petition to the dead Parnell:

> Illume our dark and penitential night,
> O King, our Saint, our Star![15]

Other authors refer to him as a meteor,[16] and a sunburst.[17] T. P. O'Connor offers the final two images of this type:

> No, there is no doubt about Parnell's greatness. He was a portent, a great and tragic exception to Nature's ordinary laws, like an eclipse or an earthquake.[18]

It is noteworthy that four of the five natural phenomena used as metaphors are "great and tragic exceptions" to the law of nature rather than equally great but more commonplace phenomena such as a mountain or towering tree. Even the star--though, of course, it is a frequently observed phenomenon--seems remote, inaccessible, beyond our understanding. These images are utilized more to express each writer's attitude toward Parnell than to represent some quality perceived in him. The images convey the feeling that Parnell was an exceptional being, remote and inscrutable.

The last group of images, the fire-and-ice-related metaphors, describe dual elements of Parnell's personality, his deeply passionate feelings and his usually rigid self-control. Katharine Tynan characterized one of Parnell's speeches as "full of indomitable spirit and fire,"[19] and Barry O'Brien describes his speaking, on another occasion, "in clear and icy accents."[20] Remarkably, writers often link together the qualities represented by these two quite opposite images, and sometimes they even combine the images themselves. One example is this explanation of the fascination that Parnell held for the English press:

> ...it is the man himself that conquered them, the Titan as he flamed out in the last struggle, like an unsuspected volcano breaking in red devastation through its accumulated ice.[21]

An even more striking example is a combination of metaphors first utilized by the Anglo-Irish writer Stanish O'Grady and later borrowed by Lionel Johnson, a poet whose own store of colorful language was far from meager. It is the image of "the ice-clear, ice-cold intellect working as if in the midst of fire."[22] The coupling of the metaphorical images of fire and ice enabled the writers to express a perception difficult to articulate: the coexistence in Parnell of both extraordinarily passionate feelings and a rigid self-control. It is for this reason that not only the fire and ice metaphors, but also the combination of them, were seized upon and utilized by writers throughout the Myth's history.

Metaphorical images play an important part in the Parnell Myth. They add color to the narrative. By depicting what was extraordinary about Parnell, they heighten his stature within the story. The metaphors which represent his strength of character complement the central symbol, and those which attribute to him strength, fierceness and natural dignity directly reinforce it.

The metaphorical roles assigned to Parnell fulfill similar functions. Most of them are leadership roles, represented in Table 5. Not included in the table are the more

TABLE 5

THE ROLES FOR PARNELL IN THE MYTH DIVIDED FUNCTIONALLY, WITH THE NUMBER OF TIMES EACH APPEARS

| Direction | Representation |
|---|---|
| Pioneer (1) | Champion (4) |
| Guerilla Leader (1) | Tribune (1) |
| Helmsman (4) | Knight (3) |
| Captain (2) | Avenger (1) |
| General (2) | Vindicator (1) |
| Pilot (1) | |

fundamental roles of chief and King, which I will discuss a little later in this analysis, and seven others which appear in three sources. Two of those sources characterize Parnell as a "Saint"[23] and an "evil genius."[24] The third has him all manner of men at once, as the author employs different images to express his perception of the various facets of Parnell's character:

> ...that sad, strange, shadowy figure, prophet, desperado, ruler, madman, martyr all in one--...[25]

In the first source just quoted, the word choice signifies the author's regard for Parnell; in the second, the writer's distrust of his politics; and, in the third, the author's attempt to capture in words a personality he does not understand by describing the roles he believes it to be capable of playing.

The metaphorical roles for Parnell listed in Table 5 are ways to describe the two functions Parnell performs for the Irish people as their leader, direction and representation. As captain[26] and general,[27] he directs their forces; as pilot[28] and helmsman,[29] he guides their ship of state; and, as pioneer,[30] he blazes the trail they will follow. As, on the other hand, the people's champion,[31] tribune,[32] knight,[33] avenger,[34] and vindicator,[35] he represents them in confrontations with their adversaries. The difference is really in the role which, by implication, the people play. When Parnell's function is direction, they participate actively--though they follow his lead--while, when his function is representation, they are more passive, and he carries confrontation......... burden of the confrontation. In both cases, Parnell's leadership role enhances his stature and explicitly links him to the people whom he leads.

Parnell's metaphorical role as chief performs the same function, but on a grander scale. Fifty-two times in forty-one sources, he is called "chief" or "the Chief." This term was often used in reference to Parnell during his lifetime. It signified his leadership of party and nation--it was used with deliberate ambiguity--and was meant to evoke the romantic image of the clan chief from Ireland's Gaelic past. (In Chapter 8, I discuss how Eamon de Valera wrote this image into the 1937 Constitution by bestowing the title Taoiseach on the Irish premier.) Use of the title Chief not only signified nationalist, and, later, Parnellite, loyalty to Parnell, it also established that nationality (depicted as tribal loyalty) was the bond between Parnell and his people. He was the Irish chief: it was Irishmen, as Irishmen, whom he led and whom he represented. The metaphorical role of chief carried the same meaning in the Parnell Myth.

Parnell was, of course, not only known as "the Chief," but as "the uncrowned King of Ireland." He was first called by that title in Montreal in 1880,[36] and, ever after, the uncrowned King he remained. He was, for example:

> ...never less than the uncrowned King of Ireland...[37]
>
> ...king--though crownless...[38]
>
> ...our dead Monarch...[39]
>
> My Chief, my king!--...[40]

This metaphoric kingship is a potent symbol in the Parnell Myth.

Three statements about Parnell are implicit in his kingship: he is successor to the ancient High Kings; he is a symbol of Ireland's sovereignty; and he is regal. Parnell is actually called Ard Rí (High King) three times in two sources.[41] There are, as well, three other allusions to his status as successor to Ireland's ancient kings. All three allusions are made by Irishmen--the authors calling him Ard Rí are also Irish--and in highly romantic language. One writer asks, for instance, that the Irish people "bury him standing, as kings of old."[42] A second calls back the High Kings' retainers from the grave:

> May all the wraiths of all the minstrels old,

Of Ireland's kings who sat in Tara's bowers,
And hurled a bold defiance from its towers,
Resume their harps, and with their fingers cold
Twang the loud strings in ghostly minstrelsy
Which is the only fitting dirge for thee.[43]

And the third acknowledges Parnell explicitly as

..as kingly
A king as ever dear Erin knew;...[44]

It is significant that these writers not only call Parnell King but place him in the line of High Kings: they elevate their claims for Parnell's kingship to include the highest stature and legitimacy, the greatest romance, and the closest ties of nationality possible.

The second inference to be drawn from Parnell's kingship is its implicit proclamation of Irish sovereignty. In their uncrowned King, the Irish people had not just a leader but a widely acknowledged symbol of their longed-for independence. Earlier in the nineteenth century, when Belgium and Italy had emerged as states, they had acquired kings as symbols of their sovereign status. When Irishmen proclaimed Parnell to be their King, they were asserting their own independence, and when outsiders called Parnell "the uncrowned King of Ireland," they were acknowledging the fact of the Irish claim even if they did not mean to signal their acceptance of it.

This interpretation of the implicit claim to sovereignty contained in Parnell's uncrowned kingship is based on the meaning of the institution itself rather than on explicit statements in the evidence. In fact, there is only one item in it which unmistakably makes the connection, the story that Barry O'Brien tells of the banners which greeted the Prince of Wales on his visit to Ireland in 1885. They proclaimed that "We will have no Prince but Charlie,"[45] clearly an assertion of defiance, of pride, and of independence.

Kings were, and are, by their very nature mutually exclusive. To acknowledge Parnell as one's king, crowned or uncrowned, was to renounce all others. Kings stand for independence; they embody the sovereignty of nations. To say that Ireland had a king was to say that she was virtually or rightfully sovereign. The American commentators who called Parnell "the uncrowned King" may not have been so aware of, or interested in, these connotations, but British and Irish writers can hardly have missed their significance. That very significance is, I think, behind one British writer's label, "The Rebel King,"[46] and it explains why another insists that Parnell "posed" as King of Ireland.[47] It is also, no doubt, one of Barry O'Brien's reasons for weaving the theme of royalty into the fabric of his biography.

O'Brien has, however, a second point to make. It is the same as my third inference from Parnell's kingship, that he is regal. In his review of O'Brien's Life of Parnell, "The Man Who Would Be King," Lionel Johnson comments upon O'Brien's frequent references to Parnell in regal terms. The word he notices is instructive. I have been discussing the implications of the noun king; Johnson chooses rather the adjective kingly.[48] These are the references to Parnell in royal terms which I have found in O'Brien's Life of Parnell:

> ...that position of eminence well described by the title which the people gave him--'the uncrowned King of Ireland.'
>
> ...; and it was a fine sight to see the 69th salute as we sailed off [from New York in 1880], and Parnell wave his hand in response, looking like a king.
>
> Every head was uncovered as he stepped out of the carriage, with the air of an emperor,...
>
> What a king he looked,...
>
> 'We will have no Prince but Charlie.'
>
> Parnell's visits to the provinces in Ireland were generally like the progress of a sovereign enthroned in the hearts of the nation....The crowd scanned him and his companions closely [in Galway, in 1886, for the by-election], but not an angry or a disrespectful word was addressed to the 'uncrowned king.' ... looking more regal than ever, ...
>
> This question [whether any member of the House of Commons did not consider the Pigott letters forgeries], asked with an air of dignity, hauteur, and kingliness, produced a deep impression upon the House.
>
> Parnell's reply [to Timothy Healy and Thomas Sexton in Committee Room 15] was full of the imperial dignity and strength which characterised almost all his utterances.
>
> ...that kingly air which was his chief characteristic.[49]

Only five of the nine selections are original O'Brien; one is from the banner described above, and the other three are descriptions of events which he obtained from witnesses. There does not seem to be any question, however, that he employs them quite deliberately.

The selections demonstrate the accuracy of Johnson's perception. The emphasis in them is unmistakably on Parnell's kingliness. "Kingly" is used by O'Brien to tell us that Parnell conducted himself with a dignity that was clearly perceived and was accorded respect. Nor is O'Brien the only writer to portray Parnell in this way. Sixteen times, in twelve sources, Parnell is called "kingly," "regal," "imperial," or is said to have exhibited "majesty." Parnell's regality quite clearly stands, not only for independence, but for dignity as well. He was, to repeat, "as kingly/A king as ever dear Erin knew."[50] That is why an English poet can properly include the title of uncrowned King in the middle of an assessment of Parnell's character:

> Posterity shall say: Then lived a man
> Of one unchangeable and stern resolve
> The Uncrowned King, calm silent and restrained,
> Passionless yet passionate, slow but sure.[51]

The title evokes an image conveying his dignity.

It is in Parnell's symbolic role as King, then, that three statements about him are represented: he is Irish, he leads Irishmen and represents them, and, as Ard Rí, he is heir to the ancient High Kings. He stands for independence: he is the uncrowned embodiment of the sovereignty that his nation asserts and seeks to have recognized. He has dignity: his actions have an air of majesty about them, and he is treated with respect. Since he is Irish, that dignity, as well as independence, are reflected onto his people who can identify, and be identified, with him.

Nationality is the link between Parnell and his people. It is also, quite obviously, a significant motif in the Parnell Myth. I have deferred directly discussing it until this point in the analysis, however, because the evidence for it is potentially confusing, and the analysis of Parnell's metaphorical roles, especially chief and King, makes a crucial distinction much easier to draw. The potential confusion stems from the bewildering variety of the characterizations of Parnell's nationality. Most items of evidence declare either that he was Irish (11) or English (10) or that he was not Irish (9), but a few others characterize him more specifically as Anglo-Irish (2), Irish-American (1), Anglo-American (2) or Anglo-American Irish (1). The key to understanding the diversity of these statements is the realization that they are concerned with Parnell's origins. They represent attempts to account for his personality characteristics. The most articulate of them is this analysis by James Bryce:

> It has often been observed that he was not Irish, and that he led the Irish people with success just because he did not share their characteristic weaknesses. But it is equally true he was not English. One always felt the difference between his temperament and that of the normal Englishman....the Anglo-Irish Protestants, a strong race who have produced a number of remarkable men disproportionate in their ratio to the whole population of the United Kingdom, are a group by themselves, in whom some of the fire and impulsiveness of the Celt has been

> blended with some of the firmness and tenacity of the Englishman. Mr. Parnell, however, though he might be reckoned to the Anglo-Irish type, was not a normal specimen of it. He was a man whom you could not refer to any category, peculiar both in his intellect and in his character generally.[52]

While this and similar efforts to explain elements in Parnell's character by linking them to particular nationalities are interesting, they are quite independent of the nationality motif, which is concerned with the phenomenon of national identification.

One might expect the two elements of national characteristics and national identification to be closely related, but that is not the case in the Parnell Myth. Queen Victoria provides a good illustration of the distinction. As Queen of the United Kingdom--to say nothing of her other titles--she was sovereign of four nations (English, Welsh, Scottish, Irish). No one would have claimed that she represented all four nationality types, but she stood for a state which included all four nations. An insult to her was an insult to them--indeed, to the British Empire--and praise of her reflected on the people of all four nations. Parnell's position as chief or uncrowned King of the Irish nation was analagous. Insult or courtesy to him as leader was insult or courtesy to the nation he led. The evidence bears out this distinction. The authors represented in Table 6 repeat Parnell's assertion that he was despised because of his Irish nationality, even though several of them ascribe his personality characteristics to English or American blood. In other words, no matter how they describe his heritage, they recognize that, when it came to a conflict based on nationality, Parnell counted himself an Irishman, and so did everyone else.

This identification of Parnell with Irish nationality is what gives the central symbol of the Parnell Myth much of its power. His <u>attitude</u> projects independence and dignity, and his fellow Irishmen identify those qualities with themselves because of the bond which nationality forms between them. This point is important, because nationality, in the sense of national identification that I am using here, is different from not only the racial heritage to which nineteenth century commentators assigned so many personality characteristics but also the exclusivist combination of blood, language and religion upon which many Gaelic nationalists later insisted.

This bond of nationality between Parnell and his people can be clearly seen in the motif of the Parnell Myth most heavily laden with meaning, contempt/disdain/scorn. The items of evidence containing those three words link together Parnell's <u>attitude</u>, the values of independence and dignity, and the question of nationality, explicitly and unmistakably. It was my reflection, early in my analysis, on the striking similarity of these passages that led me to recognize the operation of the Myth's central symbol and

TABLE 6

REPORTS OF PARNELL'S PERCEPTION THAT HE WAS DESPISED BECAUSE HE WAS IRISH, TOGETHER WITH OTHER REFLECTIONS ON HIS NATIONALITY BY THE SAME AUTHORS

---

...as little of the Celt in him as Swift.

'These English despise us,' so the unhappy creature told his brother John, 'because we are Irish'; and he seems to have kept harping on that string.[a]

---

...a man in temperament as in blood English and not Celtic--...

'These English,' he used to say to John, 'despise us because we are Irish; but we must stand up to them,...

In the United States, as in England, Parnell was ever haunted with the feeling that he was despised because he was an Irishman,...[b]

---

...Parnell was a very singular variety of patriot, perhaps so singular a variety that only Ireland could produce him;...[for Ireland is] a country where the population produces the greatest extremes of character...

Parnell was handicapped not only by his lack of learning and the clamminess of his manner, but by the fact he was partly American. In his day it was not a passport to favor in Great Britain to be to any degree an American.

It seems to me that as an American as well as an Irishman,..., Parnell was forced out of his indifference and selfishness by the contemptible manner and the unwarrantable speech in which many Britons used to show and hold with respect to all things Irish ...the galling produced by the measureless impertinence and dull malevolence hurled by Britons against Ireland and the Irish.[c]

---

...an Anglo-American Fenian.

'These English,' he would say to his brother John, 'despise us because we are Irish, but we must stand up to them. That's the way to beat the Englishman--stand up to him.'[d]

---

...spurred primarily by a mere fanatical hatred of England, partly inherited from his mother and partly grounded in his foolish early notion that people 'despised him because he was an Irishman,'...[e]

---

'The idea that the Irish were despised was always in Charles's mind,' wrote a sister.[f]

---

...this man who was so English in temperament and in method.

'These English,' he would say to his brother John, 'despise us because we are Irish; but we must stand up to them. That's the way to treat the Englishman--stand up to him.[g]

---

'The idea that the Irish were despised was always in Charlie's mind.'[h]

to understand its historical significance.

The motif consists of twenty-seven passages, from twenty-two sources, which contain the words contempt, disdain and scorn. The remarkable thing about them is their consistency. In twenty-three of them, the attitude which the words describe is Parnell's alone, while he shares it with his opponents in four, and in only one is it displayed towards him without being returned. In other words, as portrayed in the Myth by both allies and opponents, Parnell is simply too formidable a man to be the object of his adversaries' unanswered contempt. When they do show scorn for him, he returns it in a way which leaves little doubt as to who holds the higher ground.

The single item that depicts Parnell as the object of unanswered contempt comes from a Parnellite, who charges the Antiparnellites with having "scorned, betrayed, dishonoured" him.[53] In the four items that portray an exchange of scorn, Parnell hardly comes off the loser. Here are two of them:

> He gave them back scorn for their poor scorn
> That pierced them through![54]

> Parnell resented scorn. He repaid it in kind. In that kind of coin he was never a debtor.[55]

Both of these statements characterize Parnell's confrontational relationship with the British. In all, fourteen items (from thirteen sources) depict Parnell's contempt/disdain/scorn for the British, eleven (from eight sources) his contempt for his fellow Irishmen, either colleagues or opponents, and one his contempt for public opinion generally, besides the single item that describes the Antiparnellites' scorn for him. The items involving the British are most important because they affect the questions of independence and dignity expressly in terms of nationality, but the items involving Irishmen have significance, too, because they reinforce the reader's perception that Parnell was a man for whom one could have hatred but not contempt.

The passages reflecting the contempt/disdain/scorn motif that depict Parnell's contempt for his British adversaries lead directly, as I have said, to a consideration of Parnell's symbolic attitude in national terms. I have quoted two of the passages describing an exchange of scorn. Another occurs in T. P. O'Connor's biography of Parnell. O'Connor describes what the campaign of Parliamentary obstruction meant to the Irish people in these terms:

> ...what the Irish saw in Parnell was a man who was proud, scornful of English indignation....The strong nation was humbled by the weak, in the person of Parnell; the proud conqueror baffled; the scorn of the dominant race met with a scorn prouder, more daring and more deep.

Significantly, he goes on, beginning with the very next sentence, to explain Parnell's contribution to Ireland in terms of nationality:

> This entire change in the attitude of the two nations must always remain as the imperishable work of Parnell. It was a spirit in some respects evil, and at first decidedly malignant; but it was the spirit of self-confidence, pride and hope which Parnell thus inspired, that rendered possible the mighty movement and the splendid unity which have won for Ireland the vast gains of the last fifteen years. Parnell endeared himself--will ever endear himself--to the hearts of Irishmen as the first man who, for two generations, approached the proud and, as England then was, cruel and contemptuous conqueror, and compelled him to stand and listen--and obey.[56]

This is quite a remarkable statement, coming, as it does, from an Antiparnellite and a supporter of the Liberal alliance, because it directly links Parnell's haughty and scornful demeanor towards the British with a growing Irish "spirit of self-confidence, pride and hope."

The fourth passage which depicts an exchange of scorn makes the same point as O'Connor does, but in more emotional language that employs the kingship symbol and that explicitly connects Parnell's independence and dignity with those of his people. It comes from the leading article of the first issue of United Ireland following his death:

> ...he made every individual Irishman feel that he was a citizen of an Irish nation that had rights, and could claim and win them despite all opposition. He made Ireland and Irishmen respected by those whose only sentiment in our regard was contemptuous dislike. Who that ever saw him in the House of Commons proudly confronting the representatives of Great Britain, the rulers of the British Empire, meeting their scorn with a kinglier scorn, their hatred with a loftier hate, calm and implacable whilst the storm seethed around him--who that saw him so, as he often was to be seen, did not feel a thrill of joy at finding that this country could boast of having for a champion such a ruler of men?[57]

The contempt and defiance in Parnell's attitude were never more clearly displayed than in his reply to former Chief Secretary William Forster's indictment of him before the House of Commons in Feburary 1883. Forster accused Parnell of encouraging crime in Ireland. In the words of the Myth's authors, Parnell replied in "a few scornful words,"[58] "in chilling and scornful accents,"[59] "full of scorn and defiance, hurling back the charge on Forster and the Ministry as the really responsible parties,"[60] and told the House he did not care what it thought because he owed his explanations to the Irish people alone.[61] That incident was merely the most famous of a long series of confrontations between Parnell and the House of Commons, faithfully chronicled in the Parnell Myth, that both encouraged and exemplified Ireland's growing independence of mind and self-respect as a nation.

In one item of evidence, an Irish nationalist living in Britain explains what Parnell's House of Commons demeanor meant to Irish nationalists. The image he describes is virtually identical with Parnell's symbolic attitude:

> We imagined him standing there with folded arms like a marble man while the House raved and roared through all its benches and longed with a brute fury to be able to tear him from limb to limb. His cold scorn eating into them like an acid; his irresistible resolution; his miraculous wariness--what a fierce, an insolent pride we had in him and all this. In him there was not only success, there was National self-respect embodied.[62]

Notice that it is the British members who are carried away with impotent fury and the Irishman who remains unmoved, that the observer's response is to take pride in the spectacle, that the inclusive term is "National," and that what Parnell represents is "not only success," but "self-respect," a sense of the writer's own dignity as an Irishman founded on the independence of spirit exhibited by the nation's leader.

The writer says that Parnell himself embodied "National self-respect," but it should be clear, even from this passage, why it is Parnell's attitude which is the central symbol of the Parnell Myth and not Parnell himself. The writer is a Parnellite, so the distinction is an unnecessary one for him. To him, Parnell was his attitude; he himself stood for independence, and that is why the writer reveres him. For authors of other political persuasions--and nationalities--the distinction is crucial. Many of them do not trust Parnell's politics, but they do acknowledge the meaning of his public attitude. That is one reason why the Parnell Myth is so important in national terms: its characteristics, especially the central theme and central symbol, exist across the political spectrum of its authors.

As I have said, the passages comprising the motif of contempt/disdain/scorn led me to the discovery of the central theme and central symbol. The motif itself came directly from the index: contempt/disdain/scorn was a subject heading. I did not, however, have any headings for independence, dignity, or Parnell's attitude. To test my hypothesis, therefore, I turned to a group of subject headings dealing with Parnell's public relationships with other politicians. My question was whether the Myth's authors depicted Parnell's attitude consistently when portraying those relationships. Examination of the items under a number of subject headings confirmed that they did--and that the portrayal of certain of Parnell's character traits also supported the central symbol.

The items of evidence that most dramatically depict Parnell's symbolic attitude are those which describe his relationship with the House of Commons. I have quoted a few of them in discussing the motif of contempt/disdain/scorn, but there are many others. Among them is this brief analysis from the pen of J. L. Garvin:

> It was realised that here was a man whom even the whole House of Commons could not break, but who might break the whole House of Commons. That was the secret of his power.[63]

Another comes from Gladstone himself, in the interview with Barry O'Brien that closes O'Brien's Life of Parnell:

> He succeeded in surrounding himself with very clever men, with men exactly suited for his purpose...The absolute obedience, the strict discipline, the military discipline, in which he held them was unlike anything I have ever seen. They were always there, they were always ready, they were always united, they never shirked the combat, and Parnell was supreme all the time.[64]

In the same interview, Gladstone reinforces our perception of Parnell's attitude with an anecdote, the story of his first personal encounter with Parnell. Parnell, relates Gladstone, had been making rather violent speeches in Ireland in 1881, and Chief Secretary Forster had had some of them printed. When, one day, Gladstone read extracts from some of them to the House, one of them made an especially strong impact. Parnell appeared to be the only one in the House who remained unmoved. "He listed attentively, courteously, but showed no feeling, no excitement, no concern." Gladstone left the House some time after his speech, and Parnell followed him and asked to see his report of the speeches.

> Fastening at once on the most violent declaration, he said, very quietly: 'That's wrong: I never used those words. The report is quite wrong. I am much obliged to you for letting me see it.' And, sir (with vehemence), he was right....But Parnell went away quite unconcerned. He did not ask me to look into the matter. He was apparently wholly indifferent....That was my first interview with him and it made a deep impression on me. The immobility of the man, the laconic way of dealing with the subject, his utter indifference to the opinion of the House--the whole thing was so extraordinary and so unlike what one was accustomed to in such circumstances.[65]

None of the three passages I have just quoted describes Parnell's attitude of independence and dignity in the explicit way that the items comprising the motif of contempt/disdain/scorn do. They do, however, reinforce the symbol. In the first quotation, Parnell is strong, formidable. In the second, the Irish Parliamentary Party forms a powerful team, and Parnell remains "supreme," always in control. In the third, he is indifferent to the reaction of the House and firmly in control of his emotions. All three passages, in other words, present Parnell in a way that implies great independence of spirit, and the third also evokes an image of personal dignity.

Another anecdote, related by Justin McCarthy, has a similar effect. McCarthy describes the Irish reaction to Sir Henry Brand's retirement as Speaker of the House Commons in 1884. Both the Prime Minister and the Leader of the Opposition were generous in their praise and enthusiastic in their support of the customary vote of thanks.

> Mr. Parnell, speaking for the Irish Nationalist party explained that his colleagues and he could not actually support the vote of thanks, because they had publicly stated and fully believed that the action the Speaker had taken in the coup d'etat we have mentioned [ending the forty-one hour sitting of the House on 2 February 1881] was utterly unconstitutional, but that still they had no intention whatever of pressing their objection so far as to take a division.[66]

Parnell's action showed both firmness and restraint. An independent party could not thank even this popular and respected Speaker for a career of service that had included unconstitutional actions directed against the interests of the nation it represented, but it did not need to embarrass itself or him with a display of bitter vindictiveness. In this instance, the very way in which Parnell is presented as exercising his independence of the House bespeaks his dignity.

I have already quoted several descriptions of Parnell's scornful defiance of the opinion of the House in his reply to Forster's charges in 1883. Lionel Johnson goes beyond description to interpret the meaning of Parnell's famous speech. He explains that the basis of Parnell's reply was his

> ...essential conviction that England, being 'the enemy,' should be treated as such; that to the House of Commons, in which he sat as, in the Attic phrase, 'a resident alien,' explanations, self-defences, regrets, apologies, could never be due from an Irishman...[67]

That sums up Parnell's attitude in the House of Commons as the authors of the Parnell Myth depict it: defiantly projecting independence and dignity. In the index, I recorded explicit characterizations of Parnell's relationship with the House along with a few representative anecdotes. Of these, twenty-six items from twenty sources reinforce the symbol; there are no items which contradict it.

The items describing Parnell's relationships with British politicians present a similar pattern. In them, Parnell is strong, he is oriented to Ireland's interests exclusively, and he insists on being treated with respect. Justin McCarthy relates, for instance, that once, when Sir Stafford Northcotte was Leader of the House of Commons, he "objected...to Mr. Parnell's tone, as that of one who thought he ought to be dealt with by the Ministry on the conditions of equal powers."[68] Indeed, Sir Charles Dilke once explained to Barry O'Brien that

> He acted like a foreigner. We could not get at him as at any other man in English public life. He was not one of us in any sense. Dealing with him was like dealing with a foreign power.[69]

An English writer, recognizing the same quality, quotes Parnell's response to a question about the Liberal alliance:

> I think of Mr. Gladstone and the English people what I have always thought of them. They will do what we can make them do.[70]

John Redmond reports that the English people first hated Parnell, later respected and honored him, "at all times feared him."[71] Both the Irish Daily Independent and Barry O'Brien quote Chief Secretary Forster's famous reaction to Parnell's release from Kilmainham in 1882:

> I think we may remember what a Tudor king said to a great Irishman in former times: 'If all Ireland cannot govern the Earl of Kildare, then let the Earl of Kildare govern all Ireland.'...In like manner, if all England cannot govern the hon. member for Cork, then let us acknowledge that he is the greatest power in all Ireland to-day.[72]

The effect of these and similar passages is to evoke the image of Parnell's defiant attitude and to reinforce its meaning. In all, there are twenty-seven items under "Parnell and the English" (exclusive of items that overlap contempt/disdain/scorn) that portray Parnell in a posture projecting independence and dignity, while two items break the pattern and sixteen are neutral.

An alternate way of looking at Parnell's attitude is to analyze descriptions of his public manner. The entries under the subject headings "silent," taciturn," and "uncommunicative," are, for instance, nearly all relevant to the question of Parnell's attitude. They consistently portray him as exhibiting independence and dignity. Most are suitable for presentation in table form, but three of them are both important and too long for that type of presentation.

One of them, an analysis of Parnell's manner by J. L. Garvin, uses Parnell's silence as a vehicle for explaining his style of leadership:

> The lock-mouthed master of loose-lipped men, Mr. Parnell, amid the more volatile talents and passionate levities of his followers, had the absolute fixity of purpose with which feeling had never any more to do than emotion with the laws of

> gravity. He was equally beyond the contagion of enthusiasm and the provocation of hate. He was unexcitable. There never was a more remarkable exponent of the power of silence. His immobility and his silence were deeply related. As he neither was touched by devotion nor irritated by dislike, and as the exercise of words was in itself distasteful, he had no impulse to respond to supporters or to waste reply upon opposition which he intended to crush and did not care to answer. Mr. Parnell was exempt from the passion for replies.[73]

Silence, to Garvin's mind, gave Parnell power. It also gave him, as one can see, a way to assert his independence, even of his followers, and to safeguard his dignity.

The second item comes from an interview that an unnamed Fenian once granted to Barry O'Brien. Here is O'Brien's account of it:

> 'What was it about Parnell that struck you most?'
>
> X. 'His silence. It was extraordinary. One was not accustomed to it. All Irish agitators talked. He didn't. He listened with wonderful patience. His reserve was a revelation. We used to say: "If ever there was a man for a secret society, this is the man--he can hold his tongue!" But I could never discover that Parnell had the least notion at any time of joining us.'[74]

This brief discussion conveys not only Parnell's independence and dignity but the respect that they engendered in the observer.

The third and last item I have excluded from the table is rather curious. It comes from a phrenological study of Parnell. It is an analysis of his character, couched in the dispassionate language of science, based on the shape of his head. It reads:

> If the accompanying portrait is a good likeness of Mr. Parnell, then the popular conception as to one faculty, secretiveness, is undoubtedly correct. The head is most prominent where that organ is located. He has great power to conceal thoughts and plans, and will be strongly inclined to throw a veil over countenance, expression and conduct, and, though the moral faculties are well developed, he will employ many strategems calculated to cover up the real motives.[75]

This item, though odd and not particularly flattering to Parnell, still portrays him as independent-minded.

Turning to Table 7 for the remainder of the items describing Parnell as silent, one can see a general pattern of support for the Myth's central symbol. Fifteen items under "silent" reinforce portrayal of Parnell's independence and dignity (one item, the fifth, is neutral), while five items under "taciturn" also support it (the second item breaks the pattern and the fifth is neutral), as do all three items under "uncommunicative." All three of these subject headings are words that describe Parnell's manner, but, obviously,

## TABLE 7

## THE ITEMS UNDER "SILENT," "TACITURN" AND "UNCOMMUNICATIVE" NOT MENTIONED IN THE TEXT

silent

'The Only Irishman Who Can Keep a Secret'[a]

He had the art of saying what he wanted to say, and he had above all the art of keeping silent when silence was golden.[b]

...repaid/With silent scorn, the hate of open foes...[c]

He had force, virility, silence...[d]

[One of the press' mistaken notions about Parnell was] that he was silent because he had no ideas.[e]

He was still [during the years of the Liberal Alliance] the same silent, solitary, self-contained, mysterious figure...[f]

Silent, an observer, and ignorant enough to keep the instinct for essentials unobscured, Mr. Parnell was a wonderful and remorseless judge of men.[g]

...the undemonstrative, reserved, determined man, who always kept his own counsel, who hated rhetoric and speechmaking, but who always knew what to do in a crisis...[h]

He was 'the strong still man' in not 'a blatant' but a most loquacious land; and his countrymen looked for more fruit from his silences than from the eloquence of others.[i]

The Uncrowned King, calm, silent and restrained,
Passionless yet passionate, slow but sure.[k]

Here was, if you will, a strong, still man, a man to be feared by his foes, a man to be trusted and followed to the death by his friends.[l]

...the proud, silent, isolated attitude of the new dictator...[m]

He who had defied in stately silence the malice of alien foes...[n]

In the midst of a loquacious and nervously restless generation, Mr. Parnell achieved his unique success chiefly by the possession of a unique capacity for holding his tongue.[o]

Here was a man of profound ambition, silent, impassive, and undaunted.[p]

There is, it must be admitted, a sombre grandeur about the figure of Parnell the Avenger as he is depicted in Mr. O'Brien's pages. He paints him as the silent embodiment of brooding resentment, animated from his boyhood by a fierce animosity against the English, and cultivating all through his life an unrelenting thirst for vengeance.[q]

TABLE 7--Continued

---

Mr. Parnell never spoke a word more than he needed to about anything. No man was ever better at holding his tongue.[r]

taciturn

He was then [1886] a tall, stately-looking young man of reserved manners, who spoke little, but the little was always to the purpose.[s]

At moments [in the summer of 1891] he would have fits of depression and melancholy. He did not wish to be alone. He would often--a most unusual thing for him--talk for talking's sake.[t]

Of a reticent, cold nature, with an utter lack of all oratorical powers, this taciturn man seemed [in 1875] little likely ever to make an impression in that brilliant conclave of parliamentarians.[u]

...the anitithesis of the Celt in his taciturnity and imperturbability, his want of humor and geniality...[v]

Parnell answered as usual in a few words.[w]

The immobility of the man, the laconic way of dealing with the subject, his utter indifference to the opinion of the House--the whole thing was so extraordinary and so unlike what one was accustomed to in such circumstances.[x]

It's a curious thing that the two most laconic men I ever met were Irishmen, Parnell and Archdeacon Stopford.[y]

uncommunicative

He was cold, reserved, uncommunicative.[z]

He is very tall, grave and quiet; rather amusing, in a serious, dry way, and--though he gives one the impression of being very reserved and perfectly impassive--perfectly willing to talk over everybody and everything.[aa]

...and so self-contained was the man, so little given to personal anecdote or reminiscence, that those who sit down to the attempt of bringing before their own minds' eyes and the minds' eyes of others some simulacrum of what the man himself was off the hustings and outside the Commons are confronted at once with the paucity of materials for the making of a likeness.[bb]

they also imply characterizations of the way he conducted his public relationships. Since, quite often, the writer's conscious aim in his description seems to have had nothing to do with depicting Parnell's independence or his dignity, these qualities emerge all the more effectively from the passages in which they are inadvertently portrayed. Thus we find Parnell's attitude depicted by authors who would not have recognized the term, and the central symbol of the Myth created by writers who did not agree at all in their assessments of Parnell's character or his politics.

The evidence from 1891-99 shows a general pattern of reinforcement of the Myth's central symbol. While the subject headings "contempt/disdain/scorn," "Parnell and the House of Commons," and "Parnell and the English" are the most important--because they are the most likely categories for entries which would break the pattern--examination of the entries under other headings leads to the same conclusion. The subject headings "inscrutable" and "puzzling" are interesting because, while they describe Parnell's manner (as "silent" does), they say more about the observer than they do about Parnell. This makes them useful in illuminating the pattern of Parnell's public relationships. All thirteen items under "inscrutable" reinforce the symbol, while three items from "puzzling" also do so (one more is neutral and one breaks the pattern). The entries under another heading which describes Parnell's public manner, "militant," number fifteen; all of them reinforce the portrayal of Parnell's attitude.

One final heading, "Parnell's contribution," is worth describing at a little greater length because of the specific content of a few of the items recorded under it. Included are forty-three items that reinforce the central symbol, forty-seven items that are neutral and one that breaks the pattern. That item is an assessment of Parnell's movement which includes the charge that it induced in Irish farmers "idleness, constantly deteriorating husbandry, political gossipping, and undue expectations from Parliament,"[76] the very opposite of independence and dignity. Many of the items reinforcing the symbol are, however, equally clear in their meaning, as two examples will illustrate. The first is a bit of dialogue from a newspaper account of a reception held for Parnell during his American tour. It begins with a remark from an old Irishman.

> 'The Irish are respectable to-day I guess,'... 'Why?' says a bystander. 'Because,' he replied, 'they are showing they can unite, and are willing to fight, and have got a leader who is willing to fight too.'[77]

The other comes from the pen of John Redmond, who sums up Parnell's career this way:

> All that was the work of one masterly, cool and far-seeing brain, of one dauntless and unpurchasable heart. Parnell taught Irishmen to unite. Parnell taught Irishmen self-respect and self-reliance.[78]

I began this analysis by calling independence and dignity the central theme of the Parnell Myth and by calling Parnell's attitude its central symbol. In reviewing the evidence, I have focused my remarks on the symbol, because existence of the theme, which consists of the values represented by the symbol, can be inferred from the existence of the symbol. The evidence exhibits a general pattern of support for the central symbol.[79] Significantly, the pattern is very strong among the items describing Parnell's relationships with the British, in and out of the House of Commons, where negative evidence would have been more likely to show up.

The central symbol of the Myth really is central. It ties the various anecdotes and characterizations of Parnell together; this gives the Myth unity. It also focuses the meaning of the story--the Myth's constituent parts fit together in terms of it; this gives the Myth coherence. The motifs of Providence/destiny/fate and treachery/betrayal support the symbol by offering explanations for Parnell's fall consistent with his independence and dignity. The ancestry motif enhances Parnell's stature. The metaphors for Parnell's personal qualities, which represent strength, tenacity, fierceness and natural dignity, and the metaphorical roles assigned to him--leadership roles involving direction and representation--reinforce his attitude and link him to his people. The nationality motif also ties Parnell's attitude to the independence and dignity of his country. His symbolic role as King strengthens this bond further while representing Ireland's independence and Parnell's dignity in a special way that draws out the full implications of his attitude. The motif of contempt/disdain/scorn offers the clearest depiction of the central symbol while revealing, through its obvious emotional content, the extent to which the qualities of independence and dignity, which comprise the central theme, are prized by the Myth's authors.

One final item of evidence illustrates how many of these elements reinforce each other. It is an editorial cartoon from the Irish Weekly Independent, published in 1897 (Figure 1). Its caption, "The Dead Lion," recalls both a popular animal metaphor for Parnell, representing the qualities of fierceness and natural dignity, and his symbolic kingship. The subscription, "Every True Irishman Will Remember Him on Sunday, October 10th," identifies him with Irish nationality--indeed makes him a test of Irish nationality. And finally, the inscriptions on the pedestal refer to independence ("Freedom and Liberty of Opinion") and dignity ("He Made England Respect Us"). This cartoon captures the essential message of the Parnell Myth as it existed in the years 1891-99.

**THE DEAD LION.**

EVERY TRUE IRISHMAN WILL REMEMBER HIM ON SUNDAY, OCTOBER 10TH.

Figure 1: from Irish Weekly Independent (Dublin), 2 October 1897.

## Notes to Chapter 4

[1]Throughout this study, I use metaphor in the broader sense, to include both similes and metaphors.

[2]Conor Cruise O'Brien, Parnell and His Party, p. 352.

[3]American priest, quoted in J. B. K., "American Opinions on Mr. Parnell," United Ireland, (Dublin), 12 October 1895.

[4]In the one instance in which Parnell is quoted comparing himself to an animal, he says, "I am hungry as a hawk." The context is not momentous, but the image Parnell chooses is significant, because it conforms so closely to the pattern set by the Myth's authors. Charles Stewart Parnell, quoted in RBOB, 2:290.

[5]J. H. Millar, "The Rebel King," p. 150.

[6]Michael J. Horgan, quoted in RBOB, 2:298.

[7]J. H. Millar, "The Rebel King," p. 149.

[8]J. Louis Garvin, "Parnell and His Power," p. 872.

[9][Henry Labouchere], "Charles Stewart Parnell: Obiit October 6, 1891," Truth, 15 October 1891, p. 772.

[10]Unidentified Irish M.P., quoted in RBOB, 1:349.

[11]Katharine Tynan, "The Green Ivy," Irish Daily Independent (Dublin), 7 October 1892.

[12]Albert Shaw, "Three Fallen Leaders: I. Parnell," p. 420.

[13]"Books: Mr. Parnell," Spectator, 6 July 1895, p. 19.

[14]Tighe Hopkins, Kilmainham Memories (London: Ward, Lock, Bowden, & Co., 1896), p. 365.

[15]The Last Home-coming: A Parable (Dublin: C. W. Gibbs, [1891]), p. 30.

[16]RBOB, 2:38.

[17]Verse on memorial wreath, quoted in "Parnell Anniversary Supplement," Irish Daily Independent (Dublin), 12 October 1896.

[18]TPOC, p. 223.

[19]Katharine Tynan, quoted in RBOB, 2:292.

[20]RBOB, 1:95.

[21]"Parnell and Our Policy," United Ireland (Dublin), 12 October 1895.

[22]Standish O'Grady, The Story of Ireland (London: Methuen & Co., 1894), pp. 210-11, quoted in Lionel Johnson, "The Man Who Would Be King," p. 294.

[23]The Last Home-coming, p. 30.

[24]"Topics of the Day: Banquo's Ghost," Spectator, 15 April 1893, p. 474.

[25][Harold Frederick], "The Ireland of To-day," Fortnightly Review, 1 November 1893, p. 705.

[26]John E. Redmond, speech in Committee Room 15 of the House of Commons, 4 December 1890, reprinted as "The Parnell Crisis [II]," in John E. Redmond, Historical and Political Addresses (Dublin: Sealy, Bryers & Walker, 1898; London: Simpkin, Marshall, Hamilton, Kent & Co., 1898), p. 306; and John E. Redmond, "Fifteen Years in the House

of Commons," speech in New York, 29 November 1896, reprinted ibid., p. 14, delivered again, as part of "Irish Popular Leaders from Swift to Parnell."

[27]Timothy M. Healy, quoted in RBOB, 1:350 and 2:288.

[28]Cartoon, "1890--Dropping the Pilot--The Beginning of the End," Irish Weekly Independent (Dublin), 10 October 1896.

[29]Charles Stewart Parnell, speech in Carlow, 5 July 1891, quoted in "The Last Days of Charles Stewart Parnell," United Ireland (Dublin), 10 October 1896; The Last Home-coming, p. 20; Fenian, quoted in RBOB, 1:146; and Charles Stewart Parnell, speech in Committee Room 15 of the House of Commons, [1 December 1890], quoted in RBOB, 2:283. In the last item, Parnell refers to Timothy Healy's famous Leinster Hall speech urging that Irishmen not speak to the man at the wheel. Oddly enough, O'Brien quotes excerpts from that speech but not the celebrated phrase to which Parnell alludes. See RBOB, 2:244-45.

[30]W. I. P., "Ireland's Leader," United Ireland (Dublin), 31 October 1891.

[31]"The Dead Chief," United Ireland (Dublin), 10 October 1891; The Last Home-coming, p. 14; John Morley, speech to Manchester Reform Club, Manchester, 26 October 1891, quoted in "Mr. Morley at Manchester," Times (London), 27 October 1891; and Ralph D. St. John, "Charles Stewart Parnell," p. 321.

[32]"The Parnell Anniversary," United Ireland, (Dublin), 9 October 1897.

[33]"Liberal Opinion on Leader-killers," United Ireland (Dublin), 24 October 1891; cartoon, "After Death," Irish Daily Independent (Dublin), 6 October 1897; and Patrick Sarsfield Cassidy, untitled poem, quoted in Jeremiah C. Curtain, Thomas C. Luby and Robert F. Walsh, Ireland's Struggle, p. 817.

[34]W. T. Stead, "Parnell the Avenger," p. 599.

[35]John J. O'Shea, review of RBOB, and of "Parnell the Avenger," by W. T. Stead, in American Catholic Quarterly Review, April 1899, p. 57.

[36]RBOB, 1:206.

[37]"Topics of the Day: The Death of Mr. Parnell, " Spectator, 10 October 1891, p. 484.

[38]The Last Home-coming, p. 14.

[39]Robert Buchanan, untitled poem, Echo (London) n.d., quoted in "Englishmen Reproach Irish Ingratitude."

[40]"Too Late," United Ireland (Dublin), 24 October 1891.

[41] [John McGrath], "Done to Death," United Ireland (Dublin), 10 October 1891; and Mac and O', The Parnell Leadership, pp. 26, 30.

[42]U. Ashworth Taylor, untitled poem, United Ireland (Dublin), 31 October 1891.

[43]Richard Staunton Cahill, "In Memoriam," United Ireland (Dublin), 24 October 1891.

[44]Verse on floral shield sent to Glasnevin Cemetery for 1892 Parnell Anniversary, quoted in Irish Daily Independent (Dublin), 10 October 1892.

[45]RBOB, 2:42.

[46]J. H. Millar, "The Rebel King," p. 138.

[47][Archibald Milman], "The Peril of Parliament," Quarterly Review, January 1894, p. 274.

[48]Lionel Johnson, "The Man Who Would Be King," p. 293.

[49]RBOB, 1:105; Timothy Healy, quoted ibid., 1:206; Michael J. Horgan, quoted in RBOB, 1:264; ibid., 2:39; banner legend, quoted in RBOB, 2:42; RBOB, 2:125-26; ibid., 2:228; ibid., 2:301.

[50]Verse on floral shield sent to Glasnevin Cemetery for 1892 Parnell Anniversary, quoted in Irish Daily Independent (Dublin), 10 October 1892.

[51]John Stuart, untitled poem, quoted in Jeremiah C. Curtain, Thomas C. Luby and Robert F. Walsh, Ireland's Struggle, p. 743.

[52]James Bryce, "Charles Stewart Parnell," pp. 330-31.

Notes to Table 6

[a]J. H. Millar, "The Rebel King," p. 139.

[b]Arthur R. Elliot, "Parnell and His Work," pp. 544, 545, 546.

[c]Charles de Kay, "An Intellectual Phenomenon," pp. 731, 731-32.

[d]W. T. Stead, "Parnell the Avenger," pp. 601, 600.

[e]E. G. J., "Parnell, Irish Patriot and Nationalist," p. 74.

[f]Alfred Webb [D. B.], "Parnell.--I.," review of RBOB, in Nation (New York), 9 February 1899, p. 106.

[g]RBOB, 1:342, 41.

[h]John Howard Parnell, interview with R. Barry O'Brien, Avondale, Co. Wicklow, September 1896, quoted in RBOB, 1:55.

[53]The Last Home-coming, p. 22.

[54]W. W. M'Cormack, "Parnell," Chicago Citizen, n.d., quoted in United Ireland (Dublin), 7 November 1891.

[55]W. T. Stead, "Parnell the Avenger," p. 600.

[56]TPOC, p. 54.

[57]"The Dead Chief," United Ireland (Dublin), 10 October 1891.

[58]"The Life of Parnell," Spectator, 26 November 1898, p. 776.

[59]RBOB, 2:8.

[60]John J. O'Shea, review of RBOB, p. 51.

[61]RBOB, 2:8-9.

[62]"What He Was to the Irish Exile," United Ireland (Dublin), 8 October 1892.

[63]J. Louis Garvin, "Parnell and His Power," p. 875.

[64]William E. Gladstone, interview with R. Barry O'Brien, London, 28 January 1897, quoted in RBOB, 2:357.

[65]Ibid., 2:358-59. The story is retold briefly in J. Louis Garvin, "Parnell and His Power," pp. 880-81.

[66]Justin McCarthy, Diamond Jubilee, p. 184.

[67]Lionel Johnson, "The Man Who Would Be King," p. 294.

[68]Justin McCarthy, Diamond Jubilee, p. 81.

[69]Sir Charles Dilke, quoted in RBOB, 1:225.

[70]Charles Stewart Parnell, quoted in Arthur R. Elliot, "Parnell and His Work," p. 568. This review of RBOB repeats a remark Parnell made to Michael J. Horgan, his constituency representative, in Cork in 1887. RBOB, 2:175-76.

[71]John E. Redmond, "Fifteen Years in the House of Commons," p. 11.

[72]William E. Forster, n.p., n.d., quoted in "Parnell and Cork," Irish Daily Independent, 12 October 1897, and in RBOB, 1:349.

[73]J. Louis Garvin, "Parnell and His Power," p. 880.

[74]RBOB, 1:137.

[75]G. H. J. Dutton, A Delineation of the Character and Talents of the Late C. S. Parnell, M.P., and the Right Hon. W. H. Smith, M. P. (Skegness: G. H. J. Dutton, 1891), p. 3.

## Notes to Table 7

[a]Dublin Evening Mail, 16 October 1891, quoting Henry Labouchere in Truth, n.d. The subtitle is the Dublin Evening Mail's own.

[b]Evening Telegraph (Dublin), 6 October 1898.

[c]W. I. P., "Ireland's Leader," United Ireland (Dublin), 31 October 1891.

[d]"The Courage of Parnell," United Ireland (Dublin), 6 October 1894.

[e]Whitehall Review, n.d., reprinted as "Some False Impressions of Mr. Parnell. (By an Irish M.P. in the Whitehall Review)," Irish Times (Dublin), 13 October 1891.

[f]"The Life of Parnell," Spectator, 26 November 1898, p. 777.

[g]J. Louis Garvin, "Parnell and His Power," p. 882.

[h]Arthur R. Elliot, "Parnell and His Work," p. 544.

[i]Lionel Johnson, "The Man Who Would Be King," p. 293.

[j]Jeremiah C. Curtain, Thomas C. Luby and Robert F. Walsh, Ireland's Struggle, p. 609.

[k]J. Stuart, untitled poem, quoted ibid., p. 743.

[l]John E. Redmond, "Fifteen Years in the House of Commons," p. 17.

[m]Charles Gavan Duffy, quoted in RBOB, 2:61.

[n]Irish Daily Independent (Dublin), 6 October 1892.

[o]Albert Shaw, "Three Fallen Leaders: I. Parnell," p. 417.

[p]"Parnell," Harper's Weekly, 17 October 1891, p. 791.

[q]W. T. Stead, "Parnell the Avenger," p. 599.

[r]Ibid, p. 604.

[s]Charles Gavan Duffy, quoted in RBOB, 2:59.

[t]RBOB, 2:341.

[u]Ralph D. St. John, "Charles Stewart Parnell," p. 322.

[v]John J. O'Shea, review of RBOB, p. 55

[w]William E. Gladstone, interview with R. Barry O'Brien, London, 28 January 1897,

quoted in RBOB, 2:363, quoted ibid., p. 57.

[x]William E. Gladstone, interview with R. Barry O'Brien, London, 28 January 1897, quoted in RBOB 2:359.

[y]Ibid., 2:362, quoted in John J. O'Shea, review of RBOB, p. 57.

[z]Sir Henry Thomson, interview with Barry O'Brien, n.p., n.d., quoted in RBOB, 2:161.

[aa]Mrs. Sidney [Constance M. (Lubbock)] Buxton, diary, 19 March 1889, quoted in RBOB, 2:219.

[bb]"The 'King' Is Dead," Harper's Weekly 17 October 1891, p. 795.

[76]Michael J. F. McCarthy, Mr. Balfour's Rule, p. 79.

[77]"Reminiscences of Parnell's Visit to America: By an Exile," United Ireland (Dublin), 12 October 1895.

[78]John E. Redmond, speech in the Academy of Music, New York, 15 June 1892, reprinted in John E. Redmond, Historical and Political Addresses, p. 332.

[79]This is the best place to mention one work, Patrick J. P. Tynan's The Irish National Invincibles and Their Times (London: Chatham & Co., 1894), which departs markedly from this pattern. Its thesis is that Parnell was a founder of the "Nationalist" (extreme separatist) movement but then became timid in the face of British pressure and transformed it into a "Provincialist" (Home Rule) movement. This portrayal is the very antithesis of independence and dignity; it includes the assertions that Parnell's movement sought to compound with the enemy (i.e., accept concessions from Britain) for its crimes (p. 13) and that Parnell betrayed Ireland by denouncing the Phoenix Park murders (p. 537). This book is the most notable exception to the general pattern I discuss.

# CHAPTER 5

## THE PARNELL MYTH 1900-56

The Parnell Myth retained essentially the same characteristics during the first half of this century that it had had during the tumultuous years of the Split. Its central theme continued to be independence and dignity. Its central symbol remained Parnell's attitude, his defiant assertion of those two qualities. Its principal motifs were the same: ancestry, nationality, Providence/destiny/fate, treachery/betrayal and contempt/disdain/scorn. Parnell's kingship remained an important symbol. The metaphors for Parnell, the metaphorical roles assigned to him and the comparisons of him with other great men played the same part in reinforcing the central symbol by illustrating the many sides of its meaning.

I have arrived at these conclusions by constructing a subject index to the approximately 800 pages of notes I took on the evidence published between 1900 and 1956. This index differs considerably from the one I compiled to the evidence from the Split. In making the first index, I was determined to be as inductive as possible, using as many subject headings as the evidence suggested (794) in order to discover whether any patterns existed, and if so, what they were. In constructing the second index, I wanted only to determine whether the patterns I had found in the evidence from the Split were also present in the twentieth century material, so I used a much smaller number of subject headings (57). The result was an index with 9,000 entries (compared to 11,000 for the first index) that confirmed that the same patterns were present in both bodies of material.

My analysis of the Parnell Myth in the twentieth century covers 148 different publications, while my analysis of the Myth during the Split covered 137. As Table 8 illustrates, the twentieth century material includes many more books and magazine articles of Irish authorship and significantly fewer newspaper stories of any authorship than the evidence from the Split. The significance of this changing pattern will be discussed in connection with the history of the Myth. The important point to make here is that the characteristics I have found belong to the evidence as a whole, and not just to particular kinds of publications or to those written by Irishmen.

The metaphors and metaphoric roles for Parnell and the comparisons of him with other great men reinforce the central symbol of the Myth by emphasizing Parnell's importance

TABLE 8

NATIONALITY OF SOURCES FOR THE PARNELL MYTH

| Publications | Irish | British | American | Other |
|---|---|---|---|---|
| | Sources 1891-99 | | | |
| Books and Pamphlets | 17 | 7 | 2 | 0 |
| Magazine Articles | 6 | 25 | 13 | 0 |
| Newspaper Articles | 52 | 7 | 4 | 3 |
| | Sources 1905-56 | | | |
| Books and Pamphlets | 49 | 16 | 8 | 0 |
| Magazine Articles | 34 | 7 | 14 | 0 |
| Newspaper Articles | 18 | 1 | 0 | 0 |

and by clarifying his relationships with other characters in the story. They do not require a lengthy discussion. I have summarized them in Tables 9, 10, and 11 and only the patterns need be pointed out here. The reader will note that, while the list of comparisons (Table 9) is longer than the one based on the evidence from the Split (Table 3), it has a heavier concentration of Irish names on it. This seems to me to reflect two different, but similar, purposes that the later writers had: to emphasize Parnell's stature, by comparing him with the world's great heroes, and to do the same thing for modern Irish public figures, by comparing them with Parnell.

Most of the principal metaphoric roles for Parnell, summarized in Table 10, attribute to him by implication qualities which are part of his symbolic attitude. They are for the most part roles of leadership, guidance and decision-making. There are two significant exceptions. One, the charge that Parnell was a mere figurehead for his lieutenants, undermines the symbol, though it represents only a small minority of items. The second role, that of lover, depicted by Katharine Parnell and picked up by other writers, contributes another facet to Parnell's personality in the Myth but does not affect the central symbol.

The metaphors for Parnell (Table 11) reinforce the central symbol--and reflect the central theme--by graphically representing Parnell as possessing those qualities which make for independence and dignity. The principal inanimate images are of fire (passion), ice (coldness, imperturbability), metal (toughness, strength, hardness), and stone (strength, perseverance, imperturbability). There are many fewer animal metaphors than in the nineteenth century evidence. The most important are the comparisons with big cats and birds of prey (fierceness, natural dignity) and the sphinx (silence). There are also five portrayals of Parnell as a fox in which the connotations (wiliness, untrustworthiness) disrupt the predominent pattern. In all, approximately 240 of the metaphors support the central symbol in the ways I have outlined, while perhaps 35 undermine it.

Mentions of Parnell's ancestry emphasize his heritage of aristocratic leadership and enmity to British dominion. They are also used to explain both positive and negative character traits. Among the positive traits he is said to have inherited are physical courage, strength of character and self-control. The negative traits include a weakness for womanly charms and a tendency to madness under strain. In all, Parnell's ancestry is mentioned 111 times in the evidence.[1] The motif contributes to Parnell's stature by portraying him as an aristocrat entitled by birth and breeding to a leadership role. It also reinforces the tragedy motif by depicting Parnell's fatal weaknesses as the inescapable legacy of his forebears.

## TABLE 9

## PERSONS COMPARED WITH PARNELL 1900-56, WITH THE NUMBER OF COMPARISONS MADE

Characters from Irish History

Brennus (1)
Brian Boru (1)
Issac Butt (18)
Edward Carson (1)
Earl of Charlemont (1)
Michael Collins (3)
Thomas Davis (2)
Michael Davitt (3)
Eamon de Valera (4)
Robert Emmet (8)
Lord Edward Fitzgerald (5)
Oliver Goldsmith (1)
Henry Grattan (13)
Arthur Griffith (2)
Earl of Kildare (8)
J. F. Lalor (1)
Thomas MacDonagh (1)
men of '82 (1)
men of '98 (2)
men of '48 (2)
men of '65 (3)
John Mitchel (3)
Daniel O'Connell (50)
Rory O'Connor (1)
Kevin O'Higgins (2)
Hugh O'Neill (4)
Owen Roe O'Neill (4)
Shane O'Neill (1)
Padraic Pearse (2)
Joseph Plunkett (1)
John Redmond (8)
Sinn Fein leaders (1)
James Stephens (1)
Jonathan Swift (2)
Wolfe Tone (2, 1 ↓)
Duke of Wellington (5)

Other Historical Characters

Alexander (2)
Antony (2)
Asquith (2)
Arthur Balfour (1)
Balzac (1)
Bismarck (5)
Bradlaugh (1)
Bright (1)
Buddha (1)
Julius Caesar (5, 2 ↓)
Casanova (1)
Catiline (3)
Cavour (3, 1 ↓)
Joseph Chamberlain (1)
Charles II (1)
Charles V (1)
Chateaubriand (1)
Lord Randolph Churchill (3)
Cleon (1)
Deak (1, ↓)
Dilke (1)
Disraeli (2)
Edward VII (1)
Bishop England (1)
Foch (2)
Frederick the Great (1)
Gambetta (1)
Garibaldi (1)
Gladstone (7)
Henry George (1)
Goethe (1)
Gordon (1)
Grant (1)
Granville (1)
Hamilton (1)
Hannibal (4)
Hartington (3)
Warren Hastings (2)
Henry VIII (1)
Horatius (1)
Stonewall Jackson (1)
Jefferson (1)
Kossuth (3)
Kruger (1)
Lafayette (3)
Lassalle (1)
Leonidas (3)
Lincoln (2)
Lloyd George (2)
Lohengrin (1)

TABLE 9--Continued

Other Historical Characters

Louis XIV (1)
Madison (1)
Melbourne (1)
Mirabeau (1)
Mohammed (1)
Murat (1)
Napoleon (31, 1 ☋)
Nelson (7)
Palmerston (1)
William Pitt, elder (1)
William Pitt, younger (1)
Pyrrhus (1)
Robespierre (1, 1 ☋)
Marquis of Rochefort (1)
Richard Lion Heart (1)
Rosebery (1)
Rupert (1)
Shakespeare (1)
W. H. Smith (1)
Charles Stuart (1)
Sulla (1)
Warwick (1)
Washington (2)
Kaiser Wilhelm (1)

Biblical Characters

Daniel (1)
David (3)
Esau (1 ☋)
Jesus (6)
Joshua (1)
Lucifer (8)
Moses (6)
Paul (1)
Samson (7)

Characters from Literature

Abelard (3)
Achilles (3)
Ajax (1)
Antonio (1)
Barnardine (2)
Bellerophon (2)
Bobadillo (1)
Edgar of Ravenswood (1)
Ferdinand (1)
Frankenstein (1)
Fury (1)
Galahad (1)
Hercules (1)
Jekyll and Hyde (1)
Mephistopheles (1)
Paolo (2)
Paris (1, 2 ☋)
Romeo (2)
Milton's Satan (1)
Sisyphus (1)
Tristram (1)
Oliver Twist (1)
Ulysses (1)

Note: The symbol (☋) indicates items which say that Parnell was not like the person named or should not be compared with him for some reason.

TABLE 10

PRINCIPAL METAPHORIC ROLES FOR PARNELL 1900-56

| | |
|---|---|
| Champion (6) | Leader (116, 1 ↓) |
| Chief (88) | Lover (21, 1 ↓) |
| Dictator (36, 2 ↓) | Martyr (6) |
| Figurehead (3, 1 ↓) | Patriot (5, 2 ↓) |
| Hero (42, 6 ↓) | Ruler (5) |
| King (113) | Soldier (6) |
| Landlord (5) | Statesman (17) |

Note: The symbol (↓) indicates items which deny Parnell filled the role named.

TABLE 11

PRINCIPAL METAPHORS FOR PARNELL 1900-56

| | |
|---|---|
| Fire (61) | Leopard (1) |
| Ice (30) | Lion (4, 1 ↓) |
| Volcano (6) | Tiger (3, 1 ↓) |
| | Eagle (4) |
| Bronze (2) | Falcon (1) |
| Iron (19, 6 ↓) | Hawk (1) |
| Steel (7) | |
| | Sphinx (6) |
| Flint (4) | |
| Granite (5) | Fox (5) |
| Marble (5) | |
| Stone (5) | |

Note: The symbol (↓) indicates items which deny the metaphor applies to Parnell.

Parnell's story is characterized as tragic by many twentieth century authors. Direct references to "tragedy" occur in 43 of 141 sources.[2] In addition, there are many other places in the material where the writer points out a decisive flaw or presents the events of Parnell's life in a tragic pattern. Maev Sullivan says, for instance, that

> The fatal self-indulgence that caused him habitually to shirk his responsibilities; the fatal vanity that persuaded him that he was undiminished by the process; the egoism that made him take advantage, for his own ends, of the disinterestedness of others were inevitably to betray him in the end.[3]

M. M. O'Hara, though he paints a much more flattering portrait of Parnell, also sees a decisive shortcoming. It was Parnell's "unlimited indifference to the opinion of England that," O'Hara says, "betrayed him into the fatal error which wrecked his leadership and cost him his life."[4]

Most writers emphasize the tragedy of Parnell's misfortune rather than the presence of a tragic flaw. For them, Parnell's story is a tragedy because of the loss that his fall and death meant to Katharine Parnell, to Ireland or to him. The tragedy motif lends Parnell's story dignity and increases Parnell's stature as a hero. It makes the story more emotionally compelling, and it echoes the central theme of independence and dignity. As a motif, tragedy has about equal strength in both the nineteenth and twentieth century bodies of material. Providence/destiny/fate is, on the other hand, a much stronger motif in the twentieth century writing, while treachery/betrayal is somewhat weaker.

The references to treachery/betrayal fall into two separate categories depending on whether Parnell is depicted as the betrayer or as the betrayed. The items that mention Parnell's betrayal of others form no pattern at all. While eight sources accuse him of treachery, a further seven acquit him of it. Eight more refer to charges of treachery made by others in such a way as to cast doubt on them, as when Katharine Parnell and John Cournos quote Captain O'Shea.[5] The items that refer to betrayal of Parnell form a much clearer pattern. Eleven sources contain fifteen items that depict Parnell as betrayed by friends or enemies, while only one item from one source calls that verdict into question. (It is Shane Leslie's reminder that "though it is easy to arraign the anti-Parnellites as traitors, they were anguished at heart.")[6] Although the pattern is distinct, it does not add up to a very strong motif. Twelve sources are many fewer than I have found for the other motifs, and they constitute only a small proportion of the 148 books and articles indexed.

In the twentieth century writing about Parnell, the Providence/destiny/fate motif becomes the destiny/fate motif. Providence, which was mentioned only six times in the nineteenth century evidence (five times in the emotional year of 1891, once in 1892), is referred to only another seven times (in six sources) in the material published in the twentieth century. More important, it is depicted only twice in the traditional, literal sense. The Irish Daily Independent quotes John Redmond's reference to Parnell as "this mighty leader whom God in His favour vouchsafed to Ireland,"[7] and David Marshall concludes that Parnell "may or may not have been a Providential instrument. I rather think he was."[8] Both remarks arrest one's attention, but two instances are far too few to constitute a motif.

In discussing destiny/fate in Chapter 3, I noted that the six strong representations of fate (out of a total of ten) in the nineteenth century evidence appeared in 1893 or earlier. This raised some doubt as to whether the motif had had any continuity of appeal. If it was not picked up and used by subsequent writers, could it be considered a motif at all? The twentieth century evidence answers that question. The words destiny and fate are used fifty-two times in thirty-two sources to describe either a force affecting events or an inevitable course of events. Here are four samples:

> ...the fate which ultimately wrecked his brilliant career and inflicted a ten years' national agony on Ireland and lost us Home Rule for the time.[9]
>
> Yet, just as the game had come so near the winning, Destiny played the card which ruined everything for the Nationalists.[10]
>
> And Parnell was obviously a fated man, or, as the phrase goes, a man of destiny.[11]
>
> It was Parnell's fate to come across men who in the meanness of their natures fawned on him at first, then turned on him in spite: O'Donnell, O'Shea and finally Tim Healy, the greatest and meanest of all.[12]

Destiny and fate are also used to mean "the end result." This happens 21 times in 16 places in the evidence. The distinctions I am drawing here are, however, somewhat arbitrary. While the differences among the end result of events, the course events have followed, and the force that has influenced the events may seem clear enough, they often become blurred when the words destiny and fate are employed to represent them. In fact, seven authors use the words in more than one sense. D. D. Sheehan even does it in a single sentence. Commenting on John Morley's story about the "nullity" sentence in Gladstone's famous letter, he says

> Thus the fate of a great man and, to a very considerable extent also, the destiny of an ancient nation was decided by one of those unaccountable mischances which are the weapons of Fate in an inscrutable world.[13]

Nor is it always clear which meaning is intended. Here are two characterizations of Katharine O'Shea's role in Parnell's life:

> ...the woman with whom his fate had become involved.[14]

> [her] power to help in the making and marring of a destiny.[15]

It seems to me that in the first quotation _fate_ means a course of events, while in the second _destiny_ means the end result of Parnell's career. It is this convergence of meaning which leads me to conclude that all the items in which _destiny_ or _fate_ is employed constitute a single motif. The total number of items supporting the motif is therefore seventy-three, from forty-one sources.

There is one further point about destiny/fate worth making. Nine of the sources that depict destiny or fate also represent Parnell as believing in such an unseen force. T. P. O'Connor, for example, offers six portrayals of destiny/fate in his _Memoirs_, but he also quotes this account by Katharine Parnell of a conversation she had once had with Parnell:

> He spoke of his belief in a personal destiny and fate, against which it was useless for mortals to contend or fight...[16]

These depictions of Parnell's belief in destiny/fate are important. The motif itself complements the tragedy motif, and Parnell's stoic acceptance of fate reinforces the tragedy motif, increases his stature as hero of the story, and enhances our sense of his dignity.

The central symbol of the Parnell Myth, Parnell's _attitude_, is supported by a great many items of evidence. Some explicitly depict him in a public posture in which he asserts independence and dignity, others reflect that posture in different ways. As I pointed out in Chapter 4, Parnell's kingship is itself a symbol and it also reinforces the central symbol. It does this because of the associations--which the authors exploit--of kingship with sovereignty, personal power and a dignified public manner. D. D. Sheehan points out, for instance, that

> The title of 'The Uncrowned King of Ireland' has no frothy exuberance as applied to him--for he was in truth a kingly man, robed in dignity, panoplied in power, with a grand and haughty bearing towards the enemies of his people--in all things a worthy chieftain of a noble race. The one and only time in life I saw him was when he was a broken and a hunted man and when the pallor of death was upon his cheeks, but even then I was impressed by the majesty of his bearing, the dignity of his poise, the indescribably magnetic glance of his wondrous eyes, and the lineaments of power in every gesture and every movement.[17]

A. A. Baumann says simply that "Parnell looked and spoke like a king."[18] The implications that this kingly manner had for the way that Britons and Irishmen customarily regarded each other can be glimpsed between the lines of Mrs. Campbell Praed's description of Parnell's reception in the House of Commons after the verdict of the Special Commission in 1889. She writes that the members cheered loudly

> ...as the man who was called 'The Uncrowned King' waited until the cheers had died down, cold, and apparently unmoved by this spontaneous and wildly enthusiastic exhibition of the British love of fair play.[19]

Parnell's symbolic kingship makes an important contribution to the meaning of the Parnell Myth by linking Parnell's attitude directly to his leadership of his people. It is his nation's independence--as well as his own--that he asserts as King, and his nation's dignity that he reflects. With that "grand and haughty bearing towards the enemies of his people," he is unmistakably "a worthy chieftain of a noble race." The total number of items depicting Parnell as a king or as kingly is 113; they come from forty-five sources in the twentieth century material.

This is a good place to mention the references to Parnell's nationality. There are 161 of them, from sixty different sources. They follow roughly the same patterns as in the nineteenth century evidence. Again, Parnell is represented as being Irish for purposes of national identification, though analyses of his personality tend to ascribe his character traits to an English, American or Anglo-American heritage. Table 12 indicates the curious pattern that results.

TABLE 12

PORTRAYALS OF PARNELL'S NATIONALITY 1900-56

| Nationality | Characteristics | Identification | Descent |
|---|---|---|---|
| Irish | 7, 18 ↓ | 48, 2 ↓ | 4, 4p, 5 ↓ |
| Anglo-Irish | 2, 0 ↓ | 1, 0 ↓ | 3, 1p, 0 ↓ |
| British | 33, 3 ↓ | 1, 6 ↓ | 6, 8p, 0 ↓ |
| American | 9, 0 ↓ | 0, 0 ↓ | 0, 9p, 0 ↓ |

Note: The symbol (p) indicates partial identification with the nationality. The symbol (↓) indicates items which say Parnell did not have that nationality for the purpose named.

The most important point about the references to Parnell's nationality is that he is portrayed as Irish even if he is said to possess qualities characteristic of other nationalities. This identification reinforces the link between Parnell's attitude and the independence and dignity of the Irish people which gives the central symbol much of its power.

Another group of items that contributes to the central symbol is the one that refers to Parnell's silence. In addition to the six comparisons of Parnell to a sphinx already noticed there are fifty-eight explicit mentions of his silence in twenty-eight sources. Parnell's silence is related to both his independence and his dignity. Sir William Butler captures this relationship in his estimate of Parnell's service to Ireland.

> He gave everything to Ireland; his entire fortune; his ancestral home, his time and his pastimes, his thought, his life--all for Ireland.
>
> He did not speak about this service, he did not parade it, or prate of it--this silent, strong-souled man.[20]

It can also be seen in Henry Harrison's description of Parnell's conduct during the trying days of the Split:

> The scandal soared and blazed like a sudden conflagration. Parnell himself, though sorely beset by the political consequences, never flinched from his self-imposed rule of silence. He said to his followers (the writer was present and heard the words): 'I would rather appear to be dishonourable than be dishonourable,' and having said that, he said no more. His courage and his self-possession never failed him. His steadfastness, his constancy of purpose endured unshaken.[21]

In both quotations, Parnell is credited with possessing several admirable qualities that reflect the independence and dignity of his attitude, but the clearest expression of that posture is his silence.

As in the evidence from the Split, the motif most directly related to the Myth's central theme and central symbol is contempt/disdain/scorn. The central theme and symbol find their clearest expressions in the depictions of Parnell's public relationships with other men and groups of men. Many of the most dramatic characterizations of these relationships contain references to contempt, disdain or scorn. The important thing about these references, so far as the central theme and central symbol are concerned, is that Parnell is consistently portrayed as having contempt for others, not as receiving it from them.

In all, contempt, disdain, and scorn are mentioned 124 times in forty-three sources in the twentieth century evidence. In fifty-seven of the items, Parnell is said to have had contempt for the English or for particular Englishmen, in twenty-two for other people, and in fourteen for particular things. (There are no items which deny he had contempt for Englishmen, but three deny he did for other people and three he did for particular things). On the other hand, in only three items is Parnell depicted as the recipient of English contempt, and in only six as the object of others' contempt. In my discussion of contempt/disdain/scorn in Chapter 4, I offered examples taken from depictions of the various confrontations throughout Parnell's career. This time, I want to focus on a particular incident, Parnell's famous reply to the former Chief Secretary for Ireland, William Forster, in Feburary 1883. Forster had charged Parnell with encouraging crime in Ireland for political reasons. In his reply, Parnell refused to answer the charge, saying that he cared only for the opinion of Ireland, nor for that of the House of Commons. That stance is described in terms of contempt/disdain/scorn thirteen times in nine sources, as Table 13 illustrates.

One of those items of evidence, Michael Davitt's evaluation of Parnell's speech, is worth a closer examination because of the light it throws on the interrelationships among independence, dignity, nationality and the motif of contempt/disdain/scorn. Davitt writes that

> This rather brief utterance was, everything considered, the best and noblest speech an Irish leader ever spoke in an English Parliament. It was not brilliant in any sense. There was not a studied expression or sentiment in its composition. But it was superbly dignified and splendidly defiant in its assertion of Irish independence in political thought and action. It struck a note which reverberated through every Irish nationalist heart everywhere; a note of self-reliance; a key-note of nationhood, in a scornful repudiation of his accuser's assumption that the British House of Commons was an international tribunal before which the accredited leader of the Irish race must explain his words and vindicate his actions...[22]

Parnell's "scornful repudiation" is itself an "assertion of Irish independence" at the same time "superbly dignified" and "splendidly defiant."

Other items that depict Parnell's contempt/disdain/scorn also support the central theme and central symbol. Of the fifteen items depicting this attitude, ten, from nine sources, portray Parnell in an independent and dignified posture. Sir Alfred Robbins tells us, for instance, that, unlike many of the Irishmen in Parliament when he arrived there

> ...Parnell took his own haughty, aloof, and inscrutable line from the very first, even, when it suited him, disdaining to reply to personal attacks of the most envenomed description.[23]

And Joan Haslip describes how Parnell led T. P. O'Connor through a hostile crowd in Galway in 1886 "superbly contemptuous of the thousand blackthorns which still menaced

TABLE 13

CONTEMPT, DISDAIN AND SCORN IN PARNELL'S REPLY TO FORSTER 1900-56

| |
|---|
| ....delivered in a cold, careless, almost scornful way,....It was an answer not of defence but of defiance.[a] |
| A smile of contemptuous defiance,....[b]<br>...a scornful repudiation...[c] |
| ...scorn and contempt of [Forster's] lack of control...[d]<br>...he did--not answer--but show his contempt of the whole thing and of the English politicians who had played their hand so badly.<br>...this scornful repudiation of the right of the English to judge him--...,he tore up the accusations and threw them scornfully in the face of the accuser.[e] |
| ...a proud and contemptuous defiance.[f] |
| ...scorn...defiance...[g] |
| ..., saying that he declined to appear as a defendant in any matter at the bar of an English tribunal. Taunting and contemptuous ever of the Briton, he enforced from the controlling government respect and even deference.[h] |
| ..., he simply ignored the accusation,...disdainfully repudiating any interference by Englishmen...[i] |
| He did not affect the scorn he had for these attacks--he felt it in his heart of hearts;...[j] |
| ...contemptuous...[k] |

their safety."[24]

Miss Haslip's description of the confrontation at Galway is a reminder that independence and dignity could be at stake in Parnell's dealings with Irishmen as well as Englishmen. A substantial number of items, twenty-nine, from seventeen sources, mention Parnell's contempt for one or more of his fellow-countrymen. Most of these (twenty-six, from fifteen sources) are compatible with the central symbol. That is, they do not detract from the independence and dignity of his public posture. At the same time, they do not always offer it much support, either. When a man contemns his own people, rather than a powerful opponent, there is often little dignity to be gained. The truth of this can be seen in characterization of Parnell's relationship with his party from a Spectator review:

> ...his supreme contempt for his agents and followers, and the brutality with which he crushed all who crossed his path, partook more of the ruthless despot than of a beneficent reformer.[25]

In this passage Parnell's contemning attitude is excessively independent (i.e., aloof and arrogant) and it undermines both his dignity and that of his people. When, however, the Irishmen he confronts are depicted as formidable or ruthless opponents, the situation changes. George Creel, for example, quotes Timothy Healy's crude taunt about the "mistress of the party"; when he goes on to recount that Parnell called Healy a "contemptible scoundrel" while staring "contemptuously" at the Antiparnellites and that even the crowd in the street afterwards could not affect Parnell's "air of chill disdain,"[26] the contempt bespeaks his dignity rather than his brutal domination. In all, perhaps a third of the 29 items depicting Parnell's contempt/disdain/scorn for Irishmen contribute to the reader's sense of his dignity in this way, while almost all of them are at least compatible with the picture of his independent attitude.

In examining a body of writing for the existence of a symbol, motif, or theme, one looks for a pattern of evidence that constitutes it or supports it. When the writing consists of such a diverse mixture of publications by so many different authors as the Parnell Myth does, it becomes particularly important to distinguish between evidence for a particular characteristic and a clear pattern of support for it. One simply cannot assume consistency in such a varied body of evidence; the existence of two dozen items saying one thing does not rule out the possibility of another two dozen that say just the opposite.

In my second index I recorded all of the portrayals of Parnell's conduct that seemed to me to clearly indicate either a posture of independence and dignity or its opposite. The positive depictions of Parnell's attitude occur 488 times in seventy-seven sources. The negative depictions (those portraying a lack of independence or dignity or both) occur fifty-six times in nineteen sources. This is a strong pattern of support for the central symbol of the Myth. When the individual negative items are examinend, the pattern appears even stronger. Many of the negative items occur in sources in which there are many times more positive items. For example, the largest number of negative items, eleven, occurs in Joan Haslip's Parnell, in which there are also seventy-nine positive items. Table 14 shows the numbers of positive and negative items in several sources that offer similar lopsided proportions of positive items. In sources such as these, the pattern within each publication clearly supports the central symbol.

Three sources exhibit the opposite pattern; the items in them depict Parnell in a posture lacking independence or dignity. Two of them are works by Frank Hugh O'Donnell, his two volume History of the Irish Parliamentary Party and his pamphlet, The Lost Hat. In the former, he offers four negative depictions, all part of his extended commentary on the Kilmainham Treaty and its aftermath. He quotes Freeman's Journal publisher E. D. Grey, M.P., as saying that Parnell's influence in the early eighties was a good deal with the tide and very little against it, then draws the conclusion that Parnell was a figurehead, "a detachable ornament."[27] He describes Parnell as being "so innocently horrified" at the Phoenix Park murders that followed the Treaty "that he almost fainted on the sofa! An uncrowned king!"[28] He confides that "never for a single moment did I mistake him for a Wolfe Tone or a Green Robespierre," explaining that all Parnell really ever wanted to do was to get American dollars and be indispensable to British government majorities.[29] Finally, he describes Parnell as "helplessly and hopelessly beaten" after the Phoenix Park murders and offers this description of Parnell's relationship with Gladstone:

> The grey Premier learned to pity the ruin of this young man, beheld his genuine grief, comforted his despair, and was taught that he was conserving a bulwark of social reconstruction and order in Ireland....Parnell always broke in a crisis. He was imposing till the rout came.[30]

O'Donnell resumes his argument in The Lost Hat, returning to the subject several times. He quotes his own characterization of Parnell (from the History of the Irish Parliamentary Party) as "the acolyte of Gladstone."[31] He remarks with satisfaction that politicians so dissimilar as Ramsay Macdonald and Lord Morley "now agree in recognizing that Parnell was a man full of smallness and dishonour, without ideals or originality--in fact precisely the sort of sham which I described him to be thirty years ago,"[32] and even refers once to Parnell as "this unmanly creature, this Uncrowned King of Ireland."[33] O'Donnell's portrait of Parnell, markedly different from the consensus of Parnell's

TABLE 14

POSITIVE AND NEGATIVE PORTRAYALS OF PARNELL'S POSTURE 1900-56

| Publication | Positive | Negative |
|---|---|---|
| M. Davitt, Fall of Feudalism | 26 | 1 |
| K. Parnell, Parnell | 37 | 3 |
| J. H. Parnell, Parnell | 16 | 1 |
| M. M. O'Hara, Chief and Tribune | 29 | 5 |
| M. MacDonagh, Home Rule Movement | 8 | 1 |
| A. Robbins, Parnell | 16 | 1 |
| T. P. O'Connor, Memoirs | 35 | 5 |
| S. Leslie, Sublime Failure | 12 | 4 |
| J. Haslip, Parnell | 79 | 11 |
| H. Harrison, Parnell, Chamberlain and Garvin | 13 | 2 |

political friends and enemies on many counts, describes a man so limp he hardly has a posture at all, a man of neither independence nor dignity.

The other source that offers a negative depiction of Parnell's posture is an unsigned book review that appeared in two parts in consecutive numbers of the Spectator in 1914.[34] Its emphasis is on the indignities in which Parnell appeared to have acquiesced as the price of his liaison with Katharine O'Shea. The author characterized the affair as "this game of falsehood and degradation" and attributes to the ensuing scandal Parnell's "premature and unhonoured death."[35] He also refers to the "shudder of disgust" which ran "through the whole Nationalist Party" when Captain O'Shea was returned for Galway in 1886.[36]

There is one last source worth examining in some detail. Timothy Healy's memoir Letters and Leaders of My Day, offers the most thoroughly mixed pattern of all the publications I have examined. (See my remarks on this book in Chapter 2.) I have counted nineteen positive and eight negative portrayals of Parnell's posture in it. A few examples will illustrate the ambivalence in Healy's portrait of Parnell. He describes, for instance, the flap in the House of Commons over the Kilmainham Treaty letter. Captain O'Shea read the text of the letter in response to a challenge from ex-Chief Secretary Forster, but when he omitted the sentence in which Parnell offered Irish support to the Liberals, Forster objected. Healy says that "Parnell paled....Parnell stammered that it was possible a paragraph had been omitted." The entire episode dismayed the party, he explains:

> We felt that the Chief had lowered the flag, and had tried to deceive alike his countrymen and the British. His attempt to suppress what Gladstone styled the 'hors d'oeuvre' filled us with disgust.[37]

Another incident that Healy describes happened during the Special Commission hearings. Healy rose to question the potentially dangerous Captain O'Shea:

> Parnell clutched me nervously. 'What are you going to ask? he gulped. I said, 'Don't be afraid!'[38]

In both cases, Healy's very point seems to be Parnell's lack of character, and it is this apparent emphasis of his which makes the more numerous positive portrayals of Parnell's posture all the more remarkable. He quotes, for instance, this letter, which he wrote to his wife during the debate in Committee Room 15:

> Justin McCarthy saw him before twelve, and said he was quite mad, but he has borne himself wonderfully during the meeting, except for one or two interruptions or gestures. He was dignified in the conduct of the proceedings, just as if he had no personal concern in them and laughed at each point as goodhumouredly as anybody

> else, when there was occasion....
>
> ....I cannot conceive any other man going through such an ordeal with so much dignity.[39]

Healy's final estimate of Parnell's character, the most important statement he makes about Parnell in the book, describes Parnell's public posture in positive terms, though it offers only qualified approval of his character as a whole. He says of Parnell that

> In conflict with his Party he achieved his earlier stature, and displayed an astuteness, resolution and courage greater than he had ever shown against the British....
>
> He had long before his death ceased to be an effective force, and during the debates on his deposition every expedient was exhausted by opponents to retain him as figure-head.
>
> Handsome, dignified, and emotionless, he never unduly pressed his view against that of his colleagues. I travelled with him in America, and afterwards worked beside him in Parliament for ten years. Nothing in his personal dealings savoured of arrogance.[40]

Thus the final estimate, along with the evidence from the rest of the book, depicts a man whose public posture exhibits independence and dignity, at least most of the time.

The reader has now seen the most important negative depictions of Parnell's posture. The positive depictions are, as I have said, much more numerous, totalling 488, from seventy-seven sources (as compared to the fifty-five negative depictions, from nineteen sources). They portray Parnell as exhibiting integrity, strength of character, moral courage, self-reliance, pride and self-control, the qualities I sum up as <u>independence</u> and <u>dignity</u>. In many of these items, of course, the question of nationality is involved, and so Parnell's posture of independence and dignity comes to represent the independence (often, the independence of spirit) and the dignity of the Irish nation.

In his article, "Heroes of Democracy," Padraic Colum explains the importance of Parnell's <u>attitude</u> for Irish nationalists.

> His gift to the Irish people was himself, himself as a dramatic character--the proud, firm, combative leader, the type that the Irish imagination needed and without which it could not carry out any revolutionary idea. The spectacle of a proud and confident man bearing down everything in the enemy's citadel, leading in the great dramatic scene of the <u>Times</u> Commission, standing proudly up to the crisis in the O'Shea divorce.[41]

This was true because Parnell's <u>attitude</u> was very closely linked to his sense of nationality. T. P. O'Connor tells us that "the very core of Parnell's being was pride,

Satanic pride, which led to his return of scorn for scorn of the other race which claimed the right to govern--or rather, misgovern--his own race."[42] Describing Parnell's confrontation with Gladstone over the Land Act of 1880, William O'Brien explains how important this could be:

> For the first time in the collisions of the weak and passionate race with the strong and solid one, it was the Englishman who lost his head and the Irishman who went on his way with a calmness too self-restrained to be even contemptuous.[43]

This is why Ruaidhre MacAodha is able to look back and see "an uncrowned king who once stood for the whole Irish race in just demand against England, and who had put spirit into trembling men through the force of his assertion."[44]

The independence and dignity of Parnell's posture are portrayed in the evidence as existing at the core of his personality. Henry Harrison explains that, because Parnell was so hated during his early years in Parliament, "he had need to fall back on his pride and his courage. He remade the surface of his manner so that nothing could shake his calm imperturbability--no sting could gall him, no compliments would melt him."[45] Joan Haslip says that "he owed his ascendency to his strength of will and an iron self-control which banished every human sentiment and feeling from his public life."[46] "With an effort of his will," Shane Leslie writes, "he seemed to place his soul beyond his assailants."[47] T. P. O'Connor describes the same phenomenon too, but he reminds us that there were strong emotions behind that steely manner:

> He had a tremendous sense of his personal dignity, and with all his apparent imperturbability there were very tempestuous depths in his strange soul.[48]

It was not only the British members of the House of Commons who had to face that manner that John Redmond once characterized as "calm, erect and defiant."[49] Irishmen had to cope with it, too. Joan Haslip, who quotes Redmond's characterization, also repeats his description of an election meeting at Enniscorthy in 1880:

> Parnell stood on the platform, calm and self-possessed....he faced the crowd, looking sad and sorrowful but not at all angry; it was an awful picture of patience.[50]

A year before that meeting at Enniscorthy, in 1879, Parnell had addressed one of Michael Davitt's Land League meetings, at Westport. He had gone despite Archbishop McHale's condemnation of the meeting. Telling the story, Davitt explains his elation:

> This was superb. Here was a leader at last who feared no man who stood against the people, no matter what his reputation or record might be; a leader, too, who, though a Protestant, might, on that account, be more politically subservient to a great Catholic prelate on public issues than the Catholic nationalists of Mayo would

> consent to be in such a democratic cause. It was Mr. Parnell's first momentous step in his progress towards the leadership of a race mostly Catholic, and I have always considered it the most courageously wise act of his whole political career.[51]

Years later, during one of the most bitter moments in Committee Room 15, Parnell's independence and dignity were visible again, according to Michael MacDonagh. He describes Parnell just after his retort to Healy's cruel taunt about the "mistress of the party":

> He was breathing heavily through the nostrils, and his thick beard could not conceal the twitching of his lips. He seemed on the verge of an hysterical outburst. The fiery glimmer was quenched in his eyes, though there was no tear in them. It was to himself he was crying--crying as if his heart would break....In the spectacle of that strong and reserved man in his mental agony there was a revelation of the dignity of elemental human nature.[52]

The specific qualities pictured are integrity, courage and self-control, but the elements that all of the portrayals of Parnell' _attitude_ have in common are independence and dignity. The _attitude_ is the Myth's central symbol because it conveys its meaning, and independence and dignity are its theme because they are the values which pervade it.

The Parnell Myth, then, was essentially the same phenomenon in the first half of the twentieth century as it had been in the 1890s. While the motif of treachery/betrayal was somewhat weaker and destiny/fate was notably stronger, the other major characteristics experienced no real change in strength. The function of the characteristics also remained the same. Throughout the Parnell Myth, the ancestry and destiny/fate motifs, as well as the comparisons of Parnell with other great men, served to increase his stature. Parnell's symbolic kingship, the metaphors for him and the metaphorical roles assigned to him contributed to a sense of his independence and dignity. The contempt/disdain/scorn motif, with its numerous depictions of confrontation in which Parnell successfully asserted his independence and defended his dignity, directly supported the central symbol. Since so many of those confrontations involved Englishmen, it also made an important link between Parnell's symbolic _attitude_ and his Irish nationality. Finally, the specific depictions of Parnell's _attitude_ defined the central symbol and carried the values, independence and dignity, which constituted the central theme.

## Notes to Chapter 5

[1]The sources are divided among Irish, British, and American authors in proportions roughly the same as for the evidence as a whole.

[2]I had originally intended not to index references to tragedy in the twentieth century evidence but changed my mind when I ran across several of them early in the compilation. In the end, I indexed all but 7 of the 148 publications for the word tragedy.

[3]Maev Sullivan, No Man's Man (Dublin: Browne & Nolan, 1943), pp. 38-39.

[4]M. M. O'Hara, Chief and Tribune: Parnell and Davitt (Dublin: Maunsel & Co., 1919), p. 239.

[5]KOSP, 2:80, 81, 83, 95, 95n; John Cournos, A Modern Plutarch: Being an Account of Some Great Lives in the Nineteenth Century, Together with Some Comparisons between the Latin and the Anglo-Saxon Genius. (Indianapolis: Bobbs-Merrill Co., 1928), pp. 172, 173.

[6]Shane Leslie, Studies in Sublime Failure (London: Ernest Benn, 1932; reprint ed., Freeport, N.Y.: Books for Libraries Press, 1970), p. 106.

[7]John E. Redmond, speech in Dublin, 1 October 1911, quoted in "Parnell's Memory: The Statute Unveiled," Irish Daily Independent (Dublin), 2 October 1911.

[8]David Marshall, "Parnell after Fifty Years," Commonweal, 24 October 1941, p. 6.

[9]Michael Davitt, The Fall of Feudalism in Ireland: Or the Story of the Land League Revolution (London: Harper & Bros., 1904), p. 207.

[10]Rosa C. Praed, ed., Our Book of Memories, p. 208.

[11]John Cournos, A Modern Plutarch, p. 170.

[12]Joan Haslip, Parnell: A Biography, p. 55.

[13]D. D. Sheehan, Ireland since Parnell (London: Daniel O'Connor, 1921), p. 26.

[14]T. P. O'Connor, "The Life Drama of the Parnells," p. 781.

[15]KOSP, 1:137.

[16]T. P. O'Connor, Memoirs, 2:238.

[17]D. D. Sheehan, Ireland since Parnell, p. 15.

[18]Arthur A. Baumann, The Last Victorians (Philadelphia: J. B. Lippincott Co., 1927), p. 312.

[19]Rosa C. Praed, ed., Our Book of Memories, p. 175.

[20]William Butler, "Parnell," lecture, n. p., 1908, published in The Light of the West with Some Other Wayside Thoughts 1865-1908 (Dublin: Gill & Son, 1909), p. 76.

[21]Henry Harrison, Parnell, Joseph Chamberlain and Mr. Garvin (London: Robert Hale, 1938), p. 217.

### Notes to Table 13

[a]James Bryce, "Charles Stewart Parnell," in Studies in Contemporary Biography, p. 235.

[b]Michael Davitt, The Fall of Feudalism, p. 457.

[c]Ibid., p. 461.

[d]KOSP, 2:56

[e]Ibid., 2:57.

[f]John Howard Parnell, Charles Stewart Parnell: A Memoir (London: Constable & Co., 1916), p. 208.

[g]M. M. O'Hara, Chief and Tribune, p. 242.

[h]Melville E. Stone, "Things Seen," Collier's: The National Weekly, 26 June 1920, p. 38.

[i]Alfred Robbins, Parnell: The Last Five Years (London: Thornton Butterworth, 1926), p. 196.

[j]T. P. O'Connor, Memoirs, 1:281.

[k]Shane Leslie, Studies in Sublime Failure, p. 87.

[22]Michael Davitt, The Fall of Feudalism, p. 461.

[23]Alfred Robbins, Parnell: The Last Five Years p. 196.

[24]Joan Haslip, Parnell, p. 299.

[25]"Books: Charles Stewart Parnell (Communicated.)," review of KOSP, in Spectator, 6 June 1914, p. 954.

[26]George Creel, "Love of the Leader," Mentor, September 1929, p. 60.

[27]Frank Hugh O'Donnell, A History of the Irish Parliamentary Party, 2 vols. (London: Longmans, Green & Co., 1910), 2:166-67.

[28]Ibid., 1:252.

[29]Ibid., 1:145.

[30]Ibid., 1:123.

[31]Ibid., 1:152, quoted in Frank Hugh O'Donnell, The Lost Hat, p. 15.

[32]Ibid., p. 7.

[33]Ibid., p. 28.

[34]"Books: Charles Stewart Parnell," Spectator, 30 May 1914, pp. 912-14, 6 June 1914, pp. 953-54.

[35]Ibid., p. 913.

[36]Ibid., p. 954.

[37]Timothy M. Healy, Letters and Leaders, 1:161-62.

[38]Ibid., 1:299.

[39]Timothy M. Healy to his wife, 1 December 1890, quoted ibid., 1:331.

[40]Timothy M. Healy, Letters and Leaders, 1:366-67.

[41]Padraic Colum, "Heroes of Democracy," Catholic World, November 1946, p. 129.

[42]T. P. O'Connor, Memoirs, 1:118.

[43]William O'Brien, The Parnell of Real Life, p. 20.

[44]Ruaidhre MacAodha and Séan ÓhÉagcearteigh, Parnell (Dublin: Craobh na hAiseirghe and Dublin Wicklowmen's Association, 1941), p. 7.

[45]Henry Harrison, "Memories of an Irish Hero," Listener, 22 March 1951, p. 455.

[46]Joan Haslip, Parnell, p. 118.

[47]Shane Leslie, Studies in Sublime Failure, p. 87.

[48]T. P. O'Connor, Memoirs, 1:119.

[49]John E. Redmond, quoted in Joan Haslip, Parnell, p. 234.

[50]Ibid, p. 120.

[51]Michael Davitt, The Fall of Feudalism, pp. 153-54.

[52]Michael MacDonagh, The Home Rule Movement (Dublin: Talbot Press, 1920). p. 221.

# CHAPTER 6

## THE PARNELL MYTH AND SOME TRADITIONAL ASSUMPTIONS

### Assumptions Derived from the Term Parnell Myth

The Parnell Myth I have just described differs in several important aspects from "the Parnell myth" of conventional usage. The phenomenon that tradition has described (and to which I refer for clarity's sake as "the Parnell myth") is a much narrower thing. It is based, not on Parnell's entire career, but on the Split and the arguments surrounding it. In it, Parnell is the tragic hero hounded to death by English Liberal hypocrites and their allies, spiteful or weak Irish politicians and narrow-minded Irish priests. He is supported by a few Irishmen who have the courage of their convictions and by the Fenians, who admire his extreme nationalism and who share his distaste for clerical dictation.

The most thought-provoking descriptions of "the Parnell myth" and its influence come from the pens of F. S. L. Lyons and Conor Cruise O'Brien. I would like to discuss their assumptions and conclusions about "the myth" in some detail because of the light that will throw on the Parnell Myth, its structure and its relationship to historical reality. I have chosen their work as the vehicle for this discussion because what they have had to say is important and because it represents assumptions many of us have shared.

In their writing, they have been interested not so much in establishing the existence of "the Parnell myth" or in identifying its characteristics as in understanding its effects. Since "the Parnell myth" has always been somewhat tangential to their central concerns, their conclusions about it have been based more on general observations than on extensive research and analysis. The purpose of my discussion of their work is not, therefore, to criticize writings that have appeared over a period of many years and that have never claimed to represent systematic research, but to indicate what relationship my findings have to the traditional assumptions that Lyons and Cruise O'Brien articulate.

What is "the Parnell myth" they describe? No single passage from the work of either man contains all of their assumptions and conclusions, but this paragraph from Lyons's Fall of Parnell sums up much of what they have had to say:

> Time, however, dealt more kindly with Parnell than with his opponents. The idea of the lonely, heroic figure, deserted by his party, fighting to the end against overwhelming odds, had a nobility which made an irresistible appeal to those--such

> as John O'Leary, for example--who saw the issue primarily in terms of the ancient struggle against England; to others, like Yeats, whose pity and indignation were stirred by the spectacle of greatness overthrown by mediocrity; and to such as Joyce, for whom the fall of Parnell symbolised the triumph of all that was disgusting and degrading in Irish life. There had, of course, already been a Parnell legend while Parnell himself was still alive, but from the day he died it was assured of immortality. And as he receded further into the past, the sharp outlines of memory were blurred, the real man became merged in the legend, and the legend in its turn exerted a powerful influence upon a fresh generation, which knew little of the rights or wrongs of the split, but was ready to interpret it in the light of its own hopes and aspirations.[1]

Neither historian defines a specific canon for "the Parnell myth," but, since both see the Split as the main story line of "the Parnell myth,"[2] they regard Parnellite and Parnellite/republican writing as forming its own core. Both historians name some important retailers of "the Parnell myth." Though their lists are different, both of them have William Butler Yeats and James Joyce at the top. Lyons also mentions Arthur Griffith, Padraic Pearse, James Connolly and Sinn Féin and Irish Parliamentary Party speakers during the 1918 election campaign.[3] Cruise O'Brien lists categories of people rather than individuals. They include teachers, writers, parents, dramatists, singers and filmmakers. The only individual he mentions, besides Yeats and Joyce, is Michael Davitt.[4]

The two historians both see "the Parnell myth" as having had real existence. Cruise O'Brien says that, "true or false, becoming part of our national consciousness, it is now part of the historical record,"[5] while Lyons warns that "it would be wrong to underestimate its influence, for a myth can often be as potent as reality, may itself, indeed, be a kind of reality."[6] The difference is that Cruise O'Brien regards "the Parnell myth" as essentially static,[7] while Lyons sees it as changing, darkening its republican tint in response to the 1916 Rising.[8]

It is important to understand the assumptions that underlie what these two historians have had to say about "the Parnell myth." The first one is, of course, that there is a "Parnell myth" at all, that the material written about Parnell--or, at least, that part of it written from a Parnellite point of view--forms a whole. The second is that it exists in the popular mind and is accurately reflected in the printed work. The third is that "the Parnell myth" is Parnellite, that the writers who have contributed to it have written from that political perspective. (Lyons also assumes that many of those writers, especially in the twentieth century, have also been republicans.) The fourth assumption is that individual books, pamphlets and periodical articles can be regarded as representative of "the myth" as a whole, or of its line of development. The fifth assumption, which follows from the fourth, is that there is no difference with respect to "the myth" among writings of a political, journalistic, literary or other nature and that, therefore, Yeats and Joyce accurately represent it in their works. Many of these assumptions constrast sharply with my findings.

I have, of course, concluded that a Parnell Myth did exist in the years I surveyed. The patterns that emerged in the two indexes confirmed not only that the material exhibited certain characteristics when viewed as a whole but that it also possessed the unity and coherence of an integrated whole. My analysis extended only to a political, journalistic and historical unity. I excluded literary works, printed ballads and the stories in the Irish Folklore Collection after deciding, as I have explained, that they possessed somewhat different, if analogous, characteristics and that analysis of them would require a different methodological approach.

I have not assumed, as both Lyons and Cruise O'Brien seem to have done,[9] that the publications I have examined are evidence of some picture of Parnell which once existed among the Irish people generally. In the first place, many of the writers whose work I have analyzed were not Irish and did not write for an Irish audience. In any case, even if the material had been all "Irish" in some way or other, it need not have reflected the Parnell stories circulating among the common people. In fact, if the stories about Parnell in the Irish Folklore Collection are any indication--and they are virtually the only evidence we have--it did not.[10]

Both historians assume that "the Parnell myth" is the Parnellite interpretation of the Split, and Lyons also assumes that it has a distinctly republican coloring. One must distinguish here between a school of historical interpretation, such as, for instance, the Irish republican school, in which there is basic agreement about why events unfolded the way they did, and a broader phenomenon like the Parnell Myth, in which diversity of interpretation, even about the hero's politics, need not preclude an underlying unity of meaning. The evidence I have examined exhibits a strong interest in many different phases of Parnell's career, not just the Split. It does show a Parnellite tendency when referring to the Split, but it is by no means uniformly Parnellite in point of view. I have found approximately 160 items of evidence, from fifty sources in the twentieth century evidence, that make Parnellite arguments, as opposed to eighty items, from twenty-five sources, that make Antiparnellite arguments. More important, I have also found 157 items, from forty-nine sources, that refer to issues of the Split but do not themselves make partisan points. This indicates to me that the arguments surrounding the issue of the Split are less important in the Parnell Myth, in the twentieth century evidence, than they have been generally assumed to be. The important point about the Parnell Myth is not that it exhibits a consensus of political opinion but that it has unity. I have included in this study the work of writers of three different nationalities who look at Parnell from several mutually hostile political points of view (including Parnellite, Antiparnellite, Liberal, Unionist and republican). Despite the diversity of their political interpretations, these sources share many important characteristics, including their portrayal of Parnell's public attitude. That is, while they interpret Parnell's motivations variously, they agree on what public posture he adopts, and they tend to use the same motifs and symbols in telling his story.

An important element in "the Parnell myth" is a negative characterization of the clergy's role in Parnell's fall from power and subsequent death. Actually, the twentieth century evidence tells a much fuller story about Parnell's relationship with the clergy. While 117 items from forty-four sources discuss the relationship in terms of the Split, the total number of items describing it is 223, from fifty-four sources. In other words, while the Split is of major concern--and it is the sole concern in twenty sources and the predominant concern in four others--Parnell's relationship with the clergy throughout his entire career commands about as much interest. This is additional evidence that "the Parnell myth" of traditional usage is too narrow a conception. The Split is important for the Parnell Myth, but so are the other major struggles of Parnell's career.

The Parnell Myth is not a republican parable. The twentieth century evidence does not portray Parnell as either a separatist or a believer in physical force. Seventeen sources maintain that Parnell was against separation from Britain, while only eleven say he favored it. The pattern is even stronger in regard to Parnell's attitude towards physical force. Only one source says unequivocally that he favored it; four more say that he would have if he had thought an armed rebellion could have succeeded or if he had been pushed to the wall. Twenty-two sources conclude that he opposed physical force, though many of these add that he did so because he believed it a hopeless policy. Only Timothy Healy's daughter Maev Sullivan connects the questions of the Split and Parnell's "republicanism" the way Lyons describes saying that Parnell denounced physical force before the Special Commission but appealed to Robert Emmet and Wolfe Tone during the by-election campaigns of 1891.[11] How do republicans I have indexed portray Parnell's attitudes on these two questions? They are divided on separation: Padraic Pearse, M. M. O'Hara, R. M. Henry and J. J. Horgan say he was for it, and John Denvir, Padraic Colum and Ruaidhre MacAodha claim he was not. They all agree Parnell was against the use of physical force, though Denvir and O'Hara argue he would have resorted to it if he had thought it could have been successful.

There are three more republican authors whose writing I have indexed but whose views are much harder to pin down. P. S. O'Hegarty says that "Parnell was a constitutional separatist" who "knew that separation was possible only by physical force, and...that an insurrection had no hope of success." It had therefore to be approached by degrees.[12] I do not think that when O'Hegarty calls Parnell "a constitutional separatist" he is referring to policy but rather to an attitude or spirit. Later in the same book he says:

> Davitt has written of Parnell that he never went farther in thought or in act than Henry Grattan. That is probably true in the strictly literal sense, but the historical impression which it conveys is not true. Ireland to him was not a colony, and not a dominion, but a Nation....
>
> ...The effect of Parnell was a Separatist effect. His appeal was to Separatist sentiment and his support came from Separatist sentiment.[13]

Nora Connolly and Dorothy Macardle are a little more elusive on this point, but I think they refer to the same attitude or spirit. Miss Connolly writes that

> Parnell used to say to the British House of Commons: If you do not listen to me, there is a large band of physical force men, with whom I have no influence, and upon [whom] I have no control, and <u>they</u> will compel you to listen to them....
>
> [John Redmond] knew also, that, as in the days of O'Connell, Butt and Parnell, the people firmly believed that all the talk and show of constitutionalism was a blind, merely a throwing of dust in the eyes of the English Government...[14]

Miss Macardle says:

> Parnell had received from the most ardent patriots in Ireland that homage which they render only to insurgent leaders as a rule. It was, perhaps, because they recognized that Parnell shared their wholehearted detestation of English rule, and knew that the modesty of his demands at Westminster was no measure of his ambition for Ireland. He did not regard the British Parliament as the proper arena for Ireland's struggle and believed that the sending of members to the House of Commons should be a temporary expedient. 'No man,' he had said, 'can set bounds to the march of a nation,' and, with a gesture, gathered Republicans as well as moderate Home Rulers under his banner. For a decade, the two currents of the Irish struggle flowed as one.[15]

In all three cases, the writers feel more of a kinship with Parnell that with other constitutional politicians, and they cite his uncompromising spirit as the reason. Clearly, they want to believe that Parnell is with them, but they cannot bring themselves to claim that he was a republican in practical politics. The uncompromising spirit they describe is, I think, fundamentally the same as the attitude that is the central symbol of the Parnell Myth.

Lyons and Cruise O'Brien assume that individual works can be taken as representative of "the Parnell myth" as a whole. Both of them use the writings of William Butler Yeats and James Joyce in this way.[16] (So, of course, do many other modern writers.)[17] One problem with that assumption is the diversity of sources. In a large body of material with many different authors, the existence of a sizable number of items saying one thing does not preclude the existence of an equally large number indicating just the opposite. That is why I began my analysis with an index. I wanted to know what the patterns in the evidence were and how many items conformed to or deviated from each one. In that first index, I used as many subject headings as the material seemed to suggest (794), because I was looking for the Myth's characteristics. The second index was much shorter (57 headings), because I was testing only to see whether the characteristics I had found in the material from the 1890s were also present in the twentieth century evidence. When the same patterns appeared, I was confident that they represented characteristics that were true of the evidence as a whole.

A critical look at a recent study of the popular imagination underlines the crucial significance of this admittedly imperfect empiricism. The study is The Great War and Modern Memory, by Paul Fussell. It has a great deal that is interesting to say about the literature of World War I, but it exhibits one of the pitfalls that threaten studies of popular opinion. When Fussell discusses the effect "the ridiculous proximity" of the front to the comforts of home had on the English soldiers, he says:

> The absurdity of it all became an obsession. One soldier spoke for everyone when he wrote home, 'England is so absurdly near.'[18]

He quotes four other examples and moves on. The examples illustrate his point, but they cannot be said to establish it. Did that soldier really speak for everyone? Did the soldiers from the West of England and from Wales also feel themselves to be ridiculously close to home? There is no way to know, given the evidence the reader has seen. Conclusive evidence would have to include the numbers of soldiers who expressed feelings each way. Negative evidence is bound to be crucial in any study of this kind that makes general statements about the tendencies within the products of a large group of independent individuals.

A second problem with assuming that the writing of Yeats and Joyce can be taken as representative of the subject matter of "the Parnell myth" is that it involves the further assumption that the writings of politicians, journalists and literary men share the same characteristics with respect to "the myth." Two things can be said on this question. One is that the values that constitute the central theme of the Parnell Myth, independence and dignity, and the image which is its central symbol, Parnell's public attitude, can clearly be found in the writing of Yeats and Joyce and a number of other authors, including Seán O'Faoláin. The other is that the emphasis of the literary material as a whole seems different--focused, like Yeats's poems and Joyce's novels, on the independence and dignity of Parnell's posture in a more personal sense, perhaps reflecting the artists' concern with individual integrity more than national pride and self-respect.

As we have seen, Lyons and Cruise O'Brien have followed Yeats and Joyce in laying emphasis on the Split and the apparent extremism in Parnell's last campaign as the basis of "the Parnell myth." Because of this emphasis, they conclude that "the Parnell myth" misses Parnell's main achievements, though they disagree to a certain extent about which of Parnell's accomplishments were most important. Cruise O'Brien, who lists the revolution in land tenure, the conversion of the Liberal Party to Home Rule and the tradition of democratic government as Parnell's greatest political contributions,[19] says of "the Parnell myth" that

> As for the leader, he survives most vividly not by the memory of his constructive acts, but by the mark which his romantic image in the last struggle made, and continues to make, on young imaginations. The young saw him as Samson pulling down the pillars of the temple--and forgot that it was a temple he himself had planned and built for his own people.[20]

Lyons agrees that "the Parnell myth" is not good history. He writes of it that

> In all of this, it is necessary to insist, there was little enough resemblance to the real Parnell. Or rather, myth and symbol fastened only upon one facet of his character, one aspect of his career, to produce a portrait which, while recognizable, was manifestly distorted....
>
> To say this ["that Parnell was neither a creative thinker nor a radical innovator"] is not to minimize his achievement--it is rather to define it more precisely by emphasizing, in a way the Parnell myth conspicuously fails to do, that the greatness of the achievement lay in Parnell's ability to realize his potential despite the limitations inherent in his own character and in the Irish context within which he had to work. The essence of what he did can be summed up in a single sentence. He gave his people back their self-respect.[21]

I do not see such a difference between the Parnell Myth and Parnell's real achievement. I agree with Lyons that a significant part of that achievement--though not the whole of it, certainly--lay in Parnell's contributions to Irish self-respect. It seems to me, however, that the public image through which Parnell built up Irish self-respect was very similar to his symbolic attitude in the Myth, that, in fact, the symbol was an extension of his public image. A passage from United Ireland that I quoted in Chapter 4 discusses what Parnell meant to Irish self-respect in terms of that very attitude:

> Who that ever saw him in the House of Commons proudly confronting the representatives of Great Britain, the rulers of the British Empire, meeting their scorn with a kinglier scorn, their hatred with a loftier hate, calm and implacable whilst the storm seethed around him--who that saw him so, as he often was to be seen, did not feel a thrill of joy at finding that this country could boast of having for a champion such a ruler of men?[22]

The writer is saying that Parnell projected independence and dignity in his confrontations with Englishmen, that he did so as the Irish leader, and that Irishmen identified closely with him as a result. This suggests to me that Parnell's symbolic attitude in the Parnell Myth not only was an extension of Parnell's public image but that it performed the same function, bolstering the self-respect of the Irish people, after his death. I will explore this point in my history of the Myth in Chapters 7 and 8.

My conclusions about the Myth are actually quite compatible with much of what Lyons and Cruise O'Brien have had to say about Parnell himself. In Parnell, Lyons writes that "at different times Parnellism had meant different things to different people." To the reunited Irish Parliamentary Party (after 1900) it "represented the most sustained and vigorous of all nineteenth-century attempts to solve the Irish problem by peaceful persuasion," and the Party took comfort from the fact that Parnell himself had remained the constitutional politician to the end.

> But to those who looked back to the Parnell of the land War, or to the Parnell of the split, the constitutional politician seemed less important, less fundamental, than the potential revolutionary.[23]

Cruise O'Brien says that it was politically necessary for Parnell to seem constitutional and revolutionary at the same time:

> To use again Pareto's useful terms, Parnellism was a system in which the emotional 'residues' of historical tradition and suppressed rebellion could be enlisted in the services of parliamentary 'combination' of a strictly rational and realistic character. But the driving force of the 'residues' could be successfully directed in the sense of the 'combinations' only under one condition. This was that ambiguity of the system must be crystallized in terms of personality.[24]

Lyons is writing about "the Parnell myth," Cruise O'Brien about Parnell's real career. They both recognize Parnell's strong appeal for people of very divergent politics.

Parnell's politics were undeniably ambiguous.[25] This explains why they did not alienate many people across the wide spectrum of Irish politics. But why were so many attracted to his leadership? Ambiguity is not a strong attractive force. The answer is that, though Parnell's politics were hard to decipher, their basis was not. It lay in his strong emotional commitment to the independence and dignity of the Irish nation, and it could be seen in a political posture--clearly visible in the House of Commons and on political platforms--which defiantly exhibited those qualities. The Irish Independent once called that posture "the inexorable attitude of Independence from which no power on earth could move him."[26] The appeal of the attitude was instinctive; it operated at a level more fundamental than questions of political goals or tactics. This was how Irish nationalism became "crystallized in terms of personality." If "he gave his people back their self-respect," this was because his successes were specifically identified, thanks to his attitude, with the independence and dignity of the nation.

For Lyons, the symbol in "the Parnell myth" is Parnell himself. Since he sees "the Parnell myth" as the Parnellite/republican interpretation of Parnell's career, he sees Parnell as "the symbol, not of the limited independence he had actually sought, but of the independence which would only be satisfied by freedom in the widest and most absolute terms."[27] This follows consistently from the tendency, which Lyons has observed, "to picture him as one of the archetypal figures of nineteenth-century Irish nationalism, leading yet another forlorn hope against the connection with Britain, and brought low, like so many before him, by a combination of English guile and Irish weakness."[28] He draws the conclusion, therefore, that "myth and symbol fastened only upon one facet of his character, one aspect of his career, to produce a portrait which, while recognizable, was manifestly distorted."[29]

The evidence I have analyzed indicates something different. If all of the political writing about Parnell is considered, and not just the Parnellite material, it cannot be characterized as a Parnellite/republican creation. It is much broader than that. The Parnell of the Myth, too, is a far more complex person and politician that the tragic hero. It is possible to identify in him many qualities that he may be taken to represent. The man himself is just too complex to be a symbol, though an individual writer, drawing on the Myth for resource material, may use him in a symbolic way.[30] He is, however, presented as behaving in a particular way in political situations, especially confrontations. The consistent pattern is that of the attitude I have described. There is not, as I have already explained, any similar pattern establishing a connection between Parnell and extreme politics. The attitude Parnell adopts in his public relationships is the central symbol of the Myth. That is because it is represented in many sources in the evidence, and because it focuses the Myth's meaning.

Comparison of the Parnell Myth with "the Parnell myth" of conventional usage yields several insights into the Myth itself and into the methodology necessary for studying it. It illustrates the advantages of analyzing writing from across the political spectrum and the disadvantages of adopting uncritically traditional assumptions about the meaning of "the Parnell myth." Above all, it demonstrates the value of considering both the positive and negative evidence in searching for the Myth's characteristics. The Parnell Myth which emerges from such an analysis has unity, coherence and power. The unity and coherence can be seen in the Myth's structure. The power shows up in the visible influence the Myth and its central symbol have exerted on Irish politics.

## Assumptions Derived from the Term *Myth*

In addition to the traditional assumptions about the "Parnell myth," there is a second set of preconceptions surrounding the use of the term *myth* itself. The natural tendency is to employ it as a generic term, in thought as well as discourse, but it should not be used that way. It has no consistent meaning. This means that the two natural questions, "Is the Parnell Myth a true myth?" and "What kind of myth is it?" are inappropriate. The inadequacy of myth as a generic term is, unfortunately, not readily apparent--it certainly was not apparent to me when I began this study--and so it is necessary to examine the various meanings of the word as they relate to the Parnell Myth. Happily, this examination is more than an exercise in semantics, revealing facets of the Myth that might otherwise have been overlooked.

Every literate person has assumptions about myth. Except in rare instances, they are not derived solely from scholarship but rather reflect, at least partially, the meanings the word has acquired in popular usage. Many people assume that myths are the very opposite of reality. The common expression, "the myth versus the man," illustrated by Figure 2, reflects this assumption. A variant is the idea that myths are "untrue," factually inaccurate. It underlies the conversation in Figure 3. Following directly from it is the natural assumption that the content of a myth need not be taken too seriously, that the specifics do not much matter--as they do not matter to the female character in Figure 4. Popular assumptions about myth range from these relatively simple notions to the more sophisticated ideas in Table 15. Their diversity is a reminder that, when we talk about *myth* in ordinary conversation, speaker and listener can have quite different things in mind. The same is true of scholarly discourse, except that specialists in directly related disciplines readily acknowledge that they disagree.

Figure 2: cartoon by Stan Hunt, New Yorker, 6 June 1977, p 47.

Figure 3: cartoon by Charles M. Schulz, Chicago Tribune, 25 October 1975.

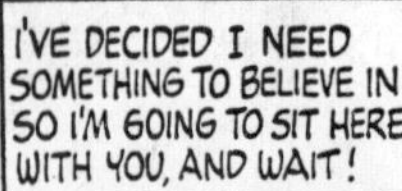

Figure 4: cartoon by Charles M. Schulz, Chicago Tribune, 31 October 1977.

TABLE 15

EXAMPLES ILLUSTRATING THE USE OF THE WORD MYTH IN POPULAR DISCOURSE

---

Myth does not mean something fictitious: Levi-Straus and the new anthropologists have taught us that a myth is the true, hidden meaning of an event in any culture...This is why the movie gets under your skin and excites you--behind the scrabbling style of the reporters lies a world of moral meaning.[a]

---

...what are myths except dramatic organizations of the varieties of human life?[b]

---

..., if myth is history transformed into a body of work one can permanently refer to, which grows out of and transcends the limits of its crator and touches perimeters so wide that the generic begins to take the place of the specific:...[c]

---

Campbell says in his preface that the 'argument is, briefly, that through dreams a door is opened to mythology, since myths are of the nature of a dram, and that, as dreams arise from an inward world unknown to waking consciousness, so do myths: so, indeed, does life.' This idea was introduced by Jung in relation to his theory of the 'universal unconscious,' but it has never before been given such a clear and splendid demonstration.[d]

---

There is no consensus among scholars about what myths are, what characteristics they have, or what functions they perform. This is true partly because the question of the nature of myth has recieved scholarly attention only recently and partly because myths are studied by specialists whose disciplines vary widely in methodology and subject matter. Anthropologists, classicists, historians of religion, psychologists, folklorists and others study the stories told by peoples of a wide variety of ancient and modern cultures. The result is a jumble of theories from competing schools which overlap but do not coincide based upon evidence which, because particular disciplines tend to study particular cultures, often does not overlap at all.

Needless to say, the theoretical literature on myth has not provided a model for the Parnell Myth. Neither the literature as a whole nor the theory of any individual scholar I have encountered fits the evidence very closely. One can, however, extract from the literature propositions that are pretty generally accepted and can be utilized in reflecting on the evidence. What role has the literature about myth played in influencing this study? It has suggested possible solutions to problems presented by the evidence, it has confirmed my intuitions, and it has warned me away from pitfalls in thinking. In order to clarify the relationship between my conclusions and myth theory, I will describe some of the characteristics commonly ascribed to myth and discuss their applicability to the Parnell Myth. This will amplify and sharpen some of my conclusions about the Parnell Myth.

The principal sources for myth theory in the discussion that follows are a book by G. S. Kirk, Myth: Its Meaning and Functions in Ancient and Other Cultures,[31] and a series of lectures entitled "The Dimensions of Myth," which Theodor H. Gaster delivered at the University of Chicago in April, 1977.[32] Kirk discusses the theories of a variety of scholars, analyzing them in terms of actual myths from many different cultures. While he does not, in my opinion, offer a successful synthesis, he presents a very useful critical overview of the work others have done. Gaster's lectures presented a more coherent theory of myth, emphasizing its role as a mediator between everyday reality and the world of ideas.

Some of the widely accepted general propositions about myth have little or no applicability to the Parnell Myth. They include the following:

(a) myths deal with the sacred;

(b) myths are set in the timeless past;

(c) myths are a form of dream, they exhibit a dream's internal logic;

(d) myths explore the meaning of life thorough the release of fantasy about the distant past;

(e) myths are reenactments of a creative and determinative past;

(f) myths are solemn narratives played out in conformance to immemorial patterns;

(g) myths usually describe the creation of the world as we know it.

Obviously, these propositions do not describe the Parnell Myth. It deals with political values, not religious ones. It is set in real historical time, not in some time-out-of-mind. It exhibits the logic of human events, of political argument, rational analysis and sentimental recollection, not the logic of dreams. It concerns a unique historical person, not the incarnation of an archetype; it relates actual historical events, not the incidents in a ritual drama. It concerns the struggle for Irish independence and dignity, not the creation of the world.

The statements about myth that follow in italics are much closer to the characteristics of the Parnell Myth.

Myths are stories. The commonly accepted definition is that myths are stories and not the unspoken ideas in people's minds which give rise to them. At an early stage in my thinking, I was forced to decide what the ultimate subject of this study would be: the written evidence I had collected, the spoken stories (which the published material might be considered to have represented), or the people's unarticulated ideas and feelings about Parnell. I concluded that the only thing that the evidence reliably represented was itself, so I would focus on that. The stories in the Irish Folklore Collection seemed to indicate a divergence between the published material and the oral tradition. There was, moreover, no sure way to tie particular elements of published pieces to what was in the minds of the people, or even to demonstrate who had read what.

Myths are products of the collective unconscious. Denis Ireland described the effect of Parnell's memory on the Irish people this way:

> ...a haughty aristocratic presence at the mere breath of whose a name it was still, fifty years on, as if somebody had exploded a battery of depth-charges deep down amongst the black sea caves and sunken wreckage of the Irish mind.[33]

His assumption is, of course, that there exists a shared unconscious and that it contains a residue of deeply-held values and half-forgotten memories ready to be stirred up by the action of a myth. Whatever its intrinsic value, this theory is not necessary for understanding the Parnell Myth. In fact, the values that constitute the Myth's central theme, independence and dignity, have been in the forefront of Irish consciousness for some time, and the Irish people have been the Myth's principal audience. A related postulate is that a myth's symbols are universal and that its characters are archetypes. Parnell's attitude does not reflect any universal symbol I know of, and the Myth's characters, derived from history, do not conform to archetypes. Even though there are "universal" elements in the Myth--the kingship symbol and the motifs, for instance--explaining the evidence does not require the positing of a collective unconscious, either Irish or universal.

Myth is intimately connected with ritual. Some writers claim that myth is necessarily connected with ritual; when the ritual ceases to exist, the myth becomes something else. They have in mind the recitation or acting out of a narrative in conjuction with a ceremony. Ritual can be political as well as religious--the annual republican pilgrimage to Bodenstown is a good example--and there has been a substantial amount of ritual connected with the Parnell Myth. Ritual practices have included the observance of Ivy Day, the use of ivy as a badge, and the anniversary march to Glasnevin. These practices are acts of homage but not reenactments of Parnell's story. While the anniversary speakers have sometimes recalled Parnell's exploits, they have tended to focus on the topics of the day--and the perfidy of the Antiparnellites--instead. Very little of the text of the Parnell Myth consists of anniversary speeches, partly because the remarks that were reported touched only briefly on Parnell. There is, however, one anniversary practice which gave rise to moderately large chunks of Parnell Myth text, the newspapers' anniversary stories. Voluminous at first, they dwindled as the years wore on, but increased in number again at the important anniversaries, especially 1911 and 1941. The anniversary celebrations have made one other contribution to the Myth: their speaker's platforms have offered some politicians the perfect opportunity to claim Parnell's legacy, a phenomenon I will discuss in Chapter 8.

Myths follow a sequential line of development. Scholarly studies of the "myths" surrounding Constantine, Napoleon and Robert E. Lee,[34] for instance, each analyze a series of biographies in chronological order as if the books were successive versions of the myth. Whatever the general merits of this approach, two of the assumptions which must necessarily underlie it are not true of the Parnell Myth: each of the Myth's authors does not repeat the whole story--some, in fact, only relate anecdotes or make brief characterizations--and many authors show little acquaintance with what was published earlier. (It is often possible to infer what an author has read about Parnell from what he writes about, and, while authors such as William O'Brien, T. P. O'Connor, and Timothy Healy were widely acquainted with the material on Parnell, many read very little.) Except for the sequence of publications I outlined in Chapter 2, which began with William O'Brien's article in the Cork Free Press (1913) and ended with his book The Parnell of Real Life (1926), the individual works do not build on each other very much. The important publishing events for the Parnell Myth are only two: the appearance of Barry O'Brien's biography in 1898 and of Katharine Parnell's memoir in 1913. The various works comprising the myth cannot be considered versions of it in sequence, and the full-length biographies do not constitute the entire Myth.

A myth consists of all its versions. I have based my analysis of the Parnell Myth on the characteristics that the evidence exhibits when examined as a whole. Three influences led me to do that. One was the suspicion, derived from my initial reading of the evidence, that the material had some sort of essential unity. Any test for unity had to involve all of the evidence. The second was the need to anticipate my conclusions in a paper delivered in 1974.[35] Preparing it started me asking a series of basic questions: was there a myth, what were its characteristics, what was its significance, etc. The third influence was a brief passage from the correspondence of University of Chicago anthropologist Robert Redfield:

> I have, on the whole, found it my experience that preliminary definitions of procedure are of limited value in the accomplishments of research. Stating a significant question in a precise way seems to me the natural point of beginning. After that the investigator develops his procedures as they are dictated by his question and its refinements.[36]

This passage encouraged me in the practice of taking the evidence as a given and concentrating on refining the questions to be asked about it. Since the indexes were my tool for dissecting the evidence to answer those questions, and since they covered the entire body of the evidence, they also reinforced the tendency to conceive of the evidence as a whole. Once I had concluded that the Myth possessed an essential unity, I was, of course, bound to continue to treat the evidence as a whole in asking questions to test that conclusion.

The alternative approach would have been to examine each work in turn, commenting on its significance. Such a method would necessarily have excluded much material from this study because of its sheer volume. It would also have meant reliance on some sort of preexisting conceptual framework for examining the evidence. If I had used the traditional assumptions about the "Parnell myth" discussed in the first part of this chapter, I would have identified it with the works of Yeats and Joyce, gone in search of antecedents, parallels and the like, and probably have missed the essential characteristics of the Myth that I have outlined.

It is important to understand that I have invented much of the methodology which I have employed. Fairly early on in the work, it became obvious that there were no acceptable models to follow, as one would, say, in writing a biography. The studies of similar popular phenomena which I examined suffered from the conceptual and methodological inadequacies which I have described. My own discipline, history, had little to offer methodologically in dealing with this type of evidence. I made up my method, therefore, as I went along, shaping it to fit the evidence, while trying to keep it simple and compatible with the methodology of my discipline. This insistence on approaching the problem as an historian would have prevented me from making very much of myth as a generic term even if there had been a consensus among theorists, because of the historian's tendency to treat historical phenomena individually, as unique problems.

Myths change when written down. They acquire formal consistency (that is, a logical relationship among the events in them), as well as artistic language, and they lose much of their fanciful element. Before encountering this concept, I had already concluded, as I have said, that the "oral" traditions about Parnell, the stories in the Irish Folklore Collection, differed from the published material. The former consisted of brief stories or characterizations of Parnell narrowly focused on a single, usually local, incident. Two were actually stories about other Irish patriots (one fleeing British soldiers in 1798, the other winning a court case) that had somehow been connected to Parnell. I decided that published stories differed considerably from those which had circulated orally: some kind of editing process had taken place to insure that they would be plausible, if not historically true. The evidence even contained what seemed to be an example of the process. It was a romantic tale, told by a gossip columnist, in which the future Katharine O'Shea Parnell saved the Chief from Fenian assassins as he left a party given by her mother, Lady Hatherly.[37] In an article entitled, "A Ludicrous Story," Dublin's Daily Express commented

> Mrs. Parnell is not a daughter of Lady Hatherly; and as she married Captain O'Shea in 1867, eight years before Mr. Parnell was heard of in the political world, the story of their meeting at Lady Hatherly's is mere nonsense.[38]

The Dublin Evening Mail pointed out that the incident was to have occurred "as far as we can calculate on the not very specific date of the event given, before he was twenty-one years of age." It concluded that

> 'Miranda' hailing as she does from Dublin, ought to have known better.[39]

Published stories were obviously much more vulnerable to this sort of public contradiction, and that very vulnerability must itself have served to discourage implausible inventions. It is not surprising, therefore, that the published material exhibits diversity in interpretation but not often in the presentation of the basic facts of the story.

A myth is affected by widespread literacy or sophisticated values in its audience. The Parnell Myth developed in a society that not only read, it read newspapers. Ideas were disseminated widely and quickly. Irish newspapers regularly printed items of interest that appeared in their British counterparts, and, occasionally, major stories from the North American, Australasian and Continental press. British and American publications were less apt to reciprocate--reflecting the relative impact of Ireland on their consciousness--but they did so from time to time. The existence of this newspaper culture meant that much of the Myth's audience encountered the same material about Parnell at the same time. The readership of magazines and books was smaller, but many books were reviewed in newspapers and some of them--along with some magazine articles--were reprinted there. The effect of this accessibility was that the Myth actually had an audience, a group of readers who experienced it virtually simultaneously and who sometimes registered their reactions through the newspapers' letter columns. And the text of what they experienced remained consistent, because they read it for themselves or heard it read aloud. (Compare this, for instance, with a priest speaking from a sacred text, explaining and embellishing the story as he goes along. The story heard by each segment of its audience will vary from telling to telling and from priest to priest.)

The Irish portion of the Myth's audience was not only literate, it was also predominantly Roman Catholic. While the value system promulgated by the Roman Catholic Church was certainly sophisticated, the important factor for the Myth lay in its separateness rather that in its sophistication. In primitive cultures, myths reflect many of a society's values and are a principal means of their transmission. In Irish society, the Parnell Myth supported the ideals of independence and dignity, values of a nationalist tradition quite distinct from, and, in some respects, in conflict with, Roman Catholic moral teaching. And, of course, Parnell's personal conduct itself deviated from the Church's standards. This meant that the Myth's Irish audience could interpret Parnell's career on the basis of the Myth's own values, or Roman Catholic values, or some combination of both. It is not surprising, therefore, that as the Myth developed, its central symbol, which had to possess a consistent meaning--reflecting an underlying consensus among the Myth's diverse authors--came to be Parnell's defiant attitude and not the man himself. It allowed the authors to differ in their judgments of the man while agreeing on the meaning of the symbol.

Myths organize reality. The Parnell Myth links characters and events and accounts for the occurence of events, as any story would. It has unity and coherence. It does so, not because the material comprising it would tell a single story economically when read from start to finish--obviously, it would not--but because its underlying structure endows it with these qualities. The Parnell Myth is "organized" around independence, dignity and nationality.

Myths reflect a society's concerns; they mirror incompatibilities in the culture. A myth presents its audience with a paradigm of the audience's situation. The Parnell Myth, as I will argue in Chapters 7 and 8, reflects its audience's concern for the fundamental independence and dignity of the nation. In it, especially in the representations of Parnell's confrontations with British politicians, one can feel the tension which resulted from the nation's unrealized aspirations, tension which persisted until the middle of this century. Every day, nationalist Ireland experienced affronts to its pride, and it often vented some of its frustration by recalling Parnell's exploits. Parnell, confronted by British power in the House of Commons and in the countryside, had been in the same situation that nationalists believed themselves to be in, and his defiant attitude had set the example that they wished to emulate. The Myth went beyond representing the problem, however, because it also offered a solution.

Myths employ the release of fantasy to solve problems; a myth can be a model for overcoming a contradiction. The message of the Parnell Myth, and Parnell's message during his career, was that the essential need for Irishmen was for a fundamental independence of spirit, not just legal independence. While this goal was, in many respects, more difficult to attain than political independence, political independence was not necessary in order to achieve it. What was needed was the strength of character epitomized by Parnell's attitude in the Myth.

Myths represent the punctual in universal terms, the universal in punctual terms. Myths employ symbols that can transcend the story itself. Although it reflects Irish nationalist concerns, the Parnell Myth is not itself a symbol. Rather, it makes use of symbols. The Myth carries a message, its central theme, but it is the central symbol, Parnell's attitude, that actually represents the values of independence and dignity. The symbol's meaning has, moreover, become so widely accepted that the mere evocation of Parnell's attitude, independent of the specifics of the story, conveys it. That is why the legacy phenomenon, which I will discuss in Chapter 8, works so well: it is not even necessary to tell the story, just call up the image.

Symbols need not be concrete things, they can be relationships between things (e.g., between earth and sky). Some cultures conceive of the potency or effectiveness of a thing (e.g., the warming power of the sun) as itself a being. One of the most important conclusions of this study is that it is Parnell's attitude that constitutes the central symbol of the Myth and not the man himself. The attitude is unambiguous in its meaning, while the man is not only too complex to be a symbol but is also interpreted differently by the Myth's different authors. They agree on the independence and dignity of his attitude but disagree markedly about his methods, motives and abilities. It is his attitude, therefore, that serves as the symbol.

Myths possess significance through their structures. The Parnell Myth is not composed solely of narrative but of many disparate elements including poems, personality profiles and character studies. The Myth's narrative structure does, nevertheless, convey meaning. The often charged confrontations between Parnell and British political leaders do not just add drama, they also provide a context for Parnell's attitude. This clarifies its representation of independence and dignity while linking it unmistakably to the question of nationality. It is not the Myth's structure per se (i.e., the fact of the confrontations) that conveys the message that Parnell's attitude stands for independence and dignity--although some anthropologists would expect this--but rather it is the descriptions of Parnell's demeanor and of the nature of the confrontations. Similarly, it is the combination of these elements with the narrative structure which indicates that nationality lies at the basis of the conflict. The Myth's narrative structure does not, however, reveal the richness of the Myth: the motifs, Parnell's metaphoric roles, the other metaphors and the kingship symbol play important roles.

Myths exist to solve problems. When I began thinking about the meaning of the Parnell Myth, I assumed that it, like any historical phenomenon, had existed for a reason, but not necessarily to solve problems. I did, however, attempt to relate its core values of independence, dignity and nationality to historical events. Certain post-1922 gestures of independence had long puzzled me--why were they necessary?--and this led me to develop the thesis I discuss in Chapters 7 and 8. In those chapters, I argue that the primary reason for the Myth's existence was that its central symbol met needs for leadership on the national question, the independence-and-dignity-of-the-nation question, that were not being met by Parnell's ertswhile successors. There would, of course, have been much interest in Parnell's memory independent of this need, especially in the first years after his death: he had dominated the Irish political stage, his fall had stirred up great political passions, his story had been dramatic and romantic, and he had died young. But the Parnell Myth, with its unity, coherence and power, is more than a disparate collection of memorial writings about a great leader, and any historical explanation for it must account for those characteristics as well as for the existence of simple memories of the man.

Heroic myths offer hope as well as a memory. The Parnell Myth is crucial for an understanding of Irish politics during the years 1891-1956, not because it chronicles the successes of earlier years, but, as I argue in Chapters 7 and 8, because it played a role in sustaining the nation's spirit. Although it consisted of writing about the past, it was concerned with one of the most pressing concerns of the present: the unfulfilled aspirations of the Irish people to national independence and dignity. Whatever daily vicissitudes the nation encountered, the Myth presented, in Parnell's attitude, a sign of what could, of what ought to be. As United Ireland's correspondent once wrote:

> We imagined his standing there with folded arms like a marble man....In him there was not only success, there was National self-respect embodied.[40]

The purpose of this brief review has not been to assess the validity of the various propositions about myth--or even to list them exhaustively--but rather to use them as points of comparison to clarify and expand upon my conclusions about the characteristics of the Parnell Myth.

Both parts of this chapter illustrate what cumbersome baggage the term Parnell Myth has proven to be. Students of Irish politics have speculated about the meaning of the "Parnell myth" or "Parnell legend" since 1891. Virtually everyone has preconceived ideas--and different preconceived ideas, at that--about the word myth itself. Why, then, have I labelled this particular phenomenon the Parnell Myth? I actually considered using another term,[41] but changed my mind. There are good reasons for remaining with the traditional Parnell Myth. It implies that the phenomenon discussed here is the same one that has been commented on for generations--and it is, with the crucial qualification that this study does not extend to Parnell in literature. That qualification, moreover, does not constitute a reason for using some other term. Quite the opposite. Commentators have seen a "Parnell myth" in the work of Yeats and Joyce precisely because they have assumed it to be representative of nationalist writing about Parnell. This study examines nationalist writing and the writing of a much wider political spectrum as well. In that sense, it is revisionist and should employ the traditional term to underline its revisionism: the Parnell Myth I discuss in these pages is not what political commentators, scholars--or I--would have predicted. A second benefit of using the term Parnell Myth is that it has required this chapter for explanation of just what it does and does not mean. The result is a much fuller, and more precise, statement of my conclusions than would otherwise have seemed necessary.

## Notes to Chapter 6

[1]F. S. L. Lyons, The Fall of Parnell 1890-91 (London: Routledge & Kegan Paul, 1960), p. 309.

[2]Lyons says that "the myth" also looks back to the Parnell of the Land War. See F. S.

L. Lyons, Parnell, p. 35. Cruise O'Brien disagrees; he maintains that all the stress is laid on Parnell's last great fight. See Conor Criuse O'Brien [Donat O'Donnell], "Parnell's Monument," Bell, October 1945, p. 573.

[3]F. S. L. Lyons, Charles Stewart Parnell (New York: Oxford University Press, 1977), p. 608, and Parnell, p. 35.

[4]Conor Cruise O'Brien, "Parnell's Monument," pp. 567, 573.

[5]Ibid., p. 573.

[6]F. S. L. Lyons, Parnell, p. 35. Italics are his.

[7]Conor Cruise O'Brien, "Parnell's Monument," pp. 567, 573.

[8]F. S. L. Lyons, Charles Stewart Parnell, p. 610.

[9]Ibid.; Conor Cruise O'Brien, Parnell and His Party 1880-1890, pp. 352, 355-56, and "Parnell's Monument," p. 567.

[10]There are 26 stories that mention Parnell. They exhibit characteristics, including folktale motifs (such as identity transference), not present in the published material.

[11]Maev Sullivan, No Man's Man, p. 157.

[12]P. S. O'Hegarty, A History of Ireland under the Union, 1801-1922 (London: Methuen & Co., 1952), p. 513.

[13]Ibid., p. 597.

[14]Nora Connolly, The Unbroken Tradition (New York: Boni & Liveright, 1918), p. xv.

[15]Dorothy Macardle, The Irish Republic (London: Victor Gollancz, 1937; paperback ed., London: Transworld Publishers, 1968), p. 55.

[16]F. S. L. Lyons, The Fall of Parnell, p. 309, and Charles Stewart Parnell, p. 611; Conor Cruise O'Brien, Parnell and His Party, pp. 355-56.

[17]See Denis Ireland, "October Afternoon at Glasnevin," Threshold 3 (Winter 1959-60): 35; Tom McGuirk, "Ivy Day in the E.E.C.," Irish Times (Dublin), 12 October 1973.

[18]Paul Fussell, The Great War and Modern Memory (Oxford: Oxford University Press, 1975; paperback ed., 1977), p. 64.

[19]Conor Cruise O'Brien, Parnell and His Party, pp. 353-54.

[20]Ibid., p. 355.

[21]F. S. L. Lyons, Charles Stewart Parnell, pp. 611, 616. Italics are his.

[22]"The Dead Chief," United Ireland (Dublin), 10 October 1891.

[23]F. S. L. Lyons, Parnell, pp. 34-35.

[24]Conor Cruise O'Brien, Parnell and His Party, p. 350. Italics are his.

[25]"I wonder what are Parnell's real politics!" his faithful friend J. G. Biggar once mused. RBOB, 1:362.

[26]Irish Daily Independent (Dublin), 7 October 1893.

[27]F. S. L. Lyons, Charles Stewart Parnell, p. 608.

[28]F. S. L. Lyons, Parnell, p. 35.

[29]F. S. L. Lyons, Charles Stewart Parnell, p. 611.

[30]Virginia Woolf does this in The Years. Whenever young Delia feels frustrated, she

daydreams of speaking on the same platform as Parnell, "in the cause of Liberty,...in the cause of Justice." Virginia Woolf, The Years (London: Hogarth Press, 1937; paperback ed., London: Penguin Books, 1968), pp. 20-21. See also pp. 70, 92-95, 97-98.

Notes to Table 15

[a]Jack Kroll, "Behind the Front Page," review of All the President's Men, directed by Alan J. Pakula, in Newsweek, 5 April 1976, p. 85.

[b]Michael J. Arlen, "The Air: Waiting for the Storyteller," New Yorker, 21 April 1975, p. 108.

[c]Howard Moss, "Great Themes and Connections," review of Cavafy, by Robert Liddell, in New Yorker, 1 August 1977, p. 67.

[d]Winthrop Sargeant, "Books: Plus Ca Change," review of The Mythic Image, by Joseph Campbell, in New Yorker, 21 July 1975, p. 86.

[31]G. S. Kirk, Myth: Its Meaning and Functions in Ancient and Other Cultures, Sather Classical Lectures, vol. 40 (Cambridge: Cambridge University Press, 1970; Berkeley: University of California Press, 1970; Ann Arbor: Campus, 1973).

[32]Theodor H. Gaster, "The Dimensions of Myth," American Council of Learned Societies Lectures in the History of Religions for 1976-77, Divinity School of the University of Chicago, Chicago, Illinois, April 25-29, 1977. Individual lecture titles were "The Nature and Function of Myth," "Ritual and Heroic Myth," "Myth and History," "The Techniques of Myth," and "Myth Today."

Other sources include: Encyclopedia of the Social Sciences, (1968 ed.), s.v. "Myth and Symbol," by Victor W. Turner, pp. 576-581, and Dictionary of the History of Ideas, s.v. "Myth in the Nineteenth and Twentieth Centuries," by Mircea Eliade, pp. 307-18; Thomas Mann, "Freud and the Future," in Essays, trans. H. T. Lowe-Porter (New York: Vintage Books, n.d.), pp. 303-24; Robert Redfield, "The Santo and the Veterano," chapter 11 of Tepoztlan: A Mexican Village: A Study of Folk Life (Chicago: University of Chicago Press, 1930, Midway Reprint, 1973), pp. 194-204; Leon Edel, "Walden: The Myth and the Mystery," American Scholar 44 (Spring 1975): 272-81.

[33]Denis Ireland, "October Afternoon at Glasnevin," p. 35.

[34]Vacher Burch, Myth and Constantine the Great (London: Oxford University Press, 1927); Abert Leon Guérard, Reflections on the Napoleonic Legend (New York: Charles Scribner's Sons, 1924); Thomas L. Connelly, The Marble Man: Robert E. Lee and His Image in American Society (New York: Alfred A. Knopf, Borzoi Books, 1977).

[35]William Michael Murphy, "Symbol and the Meaning of the Parnell Myth," paper presented at joint session of American Committee for Irish Studies and American Historical Association, Chicago, Illinois, 28 December 1974.

[36]Robert Redfield to W. B. Dutcher, a student at Columbia University, 16 April 1943, quoted in [Albert M. Tannler], One in Spirit (Chicago: University of Chicago Library, 1973), pp. 106-7.

[37]Miranda, story in Ladies Pictorial, n.p., n.d., quoted in Dublin Evening Mail, 17 October 1891.

[38]"A Ludicrous Story," Daily Express (Dublin), 19 October 1891.

[39]Leading article, Dublin Evening Mail, 19 October 1891.

[40]"What He Was to the Irish Exile," United Ireland (Dublin), 8 October 1892.

[41]In one of the papers I gave anticipating my conclusions, I spoke about the "Parnellian Tradition." Parnellian was meant to forestall assumptions that the phenomenon was Parnellite; Tradition was supposed to avoid the problems raised by the term myth. William Michael Murphy, "The Parnellian Tradition," paper presented at the

17th annual meeting of the American Committee for Irish Studies, James Madison University, Harrisonburg, Virginia, 26 April 1979.

# CHAPTER 7

## THE POLITICAL CONTEXT

This chapter is an outline of the political context of the Parnell Myth. It is a brief history of the national question--that is, the independence-and-dignity-of-the-nation question--in Irish politics after the death of Parnell. This question is increasingly being seen by historians as having been a significant factor in Irish politics during the first half of the twentieth century.[1] Since it was based on the same values which constituted the central theme of the Parnell Myth, those values tied Myth and context together and allowed them to influence each other. I will describe that influence in Chapter 8. In this chapter, my purpose is to demonstrate the continuity of the national question and to examine the various forms which it took. In it, I quote extensively from the comments of Irish historians in order to demonstrate that the national question has not only been important but has been perceived to have been important by Irish observers.

Very shortly after Parnell's death on October 6, 1891, the Antiparnellites made overtures for a reconciliation. The Parnellites angrily turned them down. Not only had the struggle of the previous nine months been an extremely bitter one, but a reunion of the old Party immediately after Parnell's death would have been an admission that the disagreement had been over one man's leadership and not over political principle. And the Parnellites were convinced that by supporting the Chief they had been fighting for principle. "The man himself," their organization in Britain had asserted a few days after his death, "was, indeed, a principle--the principle of self-reliance and of an independence which nothing could sap."[2]

Their refusal to come to an agreement cost the Parnellites dearly at the polls a year later. Only nine were returned in 1892, compared to seventy-two Antiparnellites. Gladstone formed the new government after this election, and both nationalist factions supported it. Within two years, however, Gladstone's second Home Rule Bill was rejected by the House of Lords. Shortly afterwards, he resigned, to be succeeded by Lord Rosebery. Rosebery's support for Home Rule was far less enthusiastic than Gladstone's had been. Shortly after he took office, he delivered his famous "predominant partner" speech in the Lords, declaring that England had the right to be conviced of the "justice and equity" of Home Rule before it passed. The main body of Antiparnellites continued to support the government despite Rosebery's position, but the Parnellites, and Timothy

Healy's personal following, took a more critical stance. They attempted to judge each proposed measure on its merits, giving the government only this qualified support.[3]

The return to power of the Conservatives in 1895 allowed all three Irish nationalist factions to return to the more congenial position of formal opposition. The Parnellites continued, however, to take an independent line within the Irish camp. From time to time they consulted with, even cooperated with, the Conservative government in forwarding legislation of which they approved. This basic political alignment continued until 1900.

Party politics was not the only arena in which the theme of independence was significant in the 1890s. In fact, among some of the groups which turned their attention away from the bitter squabbles of the politicians, the value of independence was held very high indeed. The journalist D. P. Moran was, for instance, one of those most dissatisfied with the party politicians, but he continued to preach the need for independence. Brian Inglis tells us that in Moran's many newspaper articles "he urged that true nationhood is not necessarily the product of <u>political</u> independence: it is the reflection of an independent attitude of mind which may not be reflected in, and may even be obscured by, victories in the political field."[4] During the 1890s, that independent attitude of mind resulted in the self-conscious revival of the Irish language, in the national literary movement, and in the growth of the agricultural cooperative movement. It also contributed to the widespread interest in the "native sports" which were played under the aegis of the Gaelic Athletic Association. As Conor Cruise O'Brien explains, the playing of these sports encouraged a hardy sense of independence. "In the 90's, and early 1900's," he writes, "the G.A.A. built on the ground cleared by the Land League: that is to say that it organized with faith and enthusiasm the replacement, among the young in many parts of the country, of what had been a servile spirit by a spirit of manliness and freedom."[5]

The Boer War helped reunite the Irish Parliamentary Party in 1900. At the same time, however, it helped weaken some of the Party's support in the country. That happened because, while the Party opposed the War, it did not take so extreme a position as more militant nationalist groups. (It could not do so because part of its task was to convince its Liberal allies and their supporters of Ireland's friendliness to Britain and fundamental loyalty to the Empire.)[6] This was of continuing importance because both English parties were more than ever determined that no Irish settlement should weaken the United Kingdom.[7] Nevertheless, with the Conservatives in power, the Party found no apparent difficulty in maintaining an independent posture, until the Liberals came to power in 1906.

Then, it seems to me, its independent policy began to give way. The Party consistently supported the Liberal government,[8] even though the government was pledged not to bring in a full Home Rule Bill during the life of that Parliament. And it was no salve to the national dignity that the Irish votes were not even needed. When, after a few years, the elections of 1910 gave the Party the balance of power, it did manage to extract a Home Rule Bill from the Liberals, but the long-ignored Protestant and Unionist community in Northeast Ulster (ignored, that is, by the Party and the Liberals) revolted, and then the onset of war in Europe threw everything into suspension. After two more years, there followed the 1916 Rising, the reprisals in its aftermath and the anti-conscription campaign. By this time, the Party was finished. The election of 1918 finally and permanently swept it from the political stage.

Unquestionably, the high value the Irish people put on the nation's independence and dignity played a large part in the Party's demise and in Sinn Féin's remarkable victory in 1918. Sinn Féin benefited from an association (in the popular mind, at least) with the Rising, from its superior handling of the conscription issue (almost all nationalists opposed the extension of conscription to Ireland, but Sinn Féin got the credit), from its more attractive political goals, including total separation from Britain, and from its general tone of intransigence. After its election victory, Sinn Féin took independence a step further than any of its predecessors by actually forming a government and setting up an Irish judiciary and civil service sanctioned only by its parliament, Dáil Éireann.

When, after three years of intermittant fighting, Irish and British representatives sat down to negotiate a permanent settlement, the question of independence was not only the topic of the negotiations but a complicating factor as well. Not only had the members of the Dáil taken an oath of allegiance to the Irish Republic in 1919, but they had elected Eamon de Valera President of that Republic in 1921.[9] (Up to that time, de Valera had been President of Dáil Éireann--that is, premier.) The first factor meant that many members of the Dáil considered themselves oath-bound to accept only a treaty that was based on an independent republic with no ties to Britain (and especially with no Crown, the _sine qua non_ for British negotiators). The second insured that de Valera, as head of state, would not be among the delegation sent to London to negotiate the treaty.[10]

De Valera laid down guidelines for the negotiators and was adamant on the question of allegiance to the King. "If war is the alternative," he wrote to the Irish delegation at one point, "we can only face it."[11] In the event, of course, the negotiators disagreed with this judgment and accepted dominion status rather than face a renewal of the fighting. Dominion status was, as Lloyd George noted, much more that Ireland had ever been offered before, but it was not complete independence.

The Dáil debates on the Treaty (which a majority of de Valera's cabinet had accepted but which he had not) turned mainly on the question of independence. Both proponents and opponents of the Treaty hoped by their positions to win for Ireland as much independence as was possible. I will discuss some of the speeches against the Treaty in Chapter 8 because they specifically invoked Parnell. At this point, it is worth taking note of at least one pro-Treaty speech because of the emphasis the speaker, Michael Collins, put on the question of independence. F. S. L. Lyons describes the speech this way:

> He recommended acceptance of the Treaty, he said, because it gave freedom, 'not the freedom that all nations aspire and develop to, but the freedom to achieve it.'...She would remain a weak country for a long time to come, however, and for him this was the chief justification of membership of the Commonwealth with the same status as the other dominions. The very fact of being associated with Canada, South Africa and the rest, would safeguard the Irish position.[12]

In the end, the Dáil accepted the Treaty (64-57), and this decision was ratified by the electorate shortly afterwards.

The results of that election--as well as those of the election of 1892--demonstrate that, while the electorate generally supported the widest possible measure of independence (as it had in 1885 and 1918), it did not do so indiscriminately. When the anti-Treaty republicans--or the Parnellites--seemed to endanger the national position by reaching for too much, they could not carry the voters with them.

Neither the establishment of the Irish Free State nor the end of the Civil War that followed (1922-23) put to rest the question of independence. In the years between these events and the outbreak of the Second World War, however, successive Irish governments made considerable progress in widening both the real extent and outside acceptance of Irish independence. The administrations of William T. Cosgrave (1922-32) concentrated on enlarging dominion rights within the Commonwealth, while those of Eamon de Valera (1932-48) emphasized the redefinition of Ireland's fundamental relationship to the Commonwealth. Cosgrave's government worked hard to establish equality of status with Britain. To that end, it joined the League of Nations and the International Labor Organization, and in 1924 it took the further step of registering the Treaty with the League, just as it would have any other international agreement. Two years later, at the Imperial Conference of 1926, it joined South Africa in pushing hard for a definition of dominion status. The result of this effort was the Conference declaration that Britain and the dominions were "equal in status, in no way subordinate one to another in any aspect of their domestic or external affairs, though united by a common allegiance to the Crown and freely associated as members of the British Commonwealth of Nations."[13] Three years after this remarkable declaration, the Irish government announced that it would submit all its international disputes, including those with Commonwealth countries, to the Permanent Court of International Justice. Commonwealth relations were to be an external, not an internal, matter.

The climax of this development toward full statehood within the Commonwealth was reached in the Imperial Conference of 1930 and the Statute of Westminster of 1931. The Statute provided that the Parliament of the United Kingdom could legislate for the dominions only with their specific consent. Further, it said that the dominions were free to legislate in areas previously reserved to the United Kingdom Parliament and to repeal legislation previously enacted by that Parliament.[14] F. S. L. Lyons calls this Statute "the coping-stone" of the Cosgrave government's efforts to enlarge Irish rights within the Commonwealth. Within a year, however, the election of 1932 had swept Cosgrave from power and allowed Eamon de Valera to form his first government.[15]

De Valera began proposing constitutional changes almost as soon as he came to power. He wanted, he said, to remove

> any form or symbol that is out of keeping with Ireland's right as a sovereign nation...so that this state that we control may be a Republic in fact: and that, when the time comes the proclaiming of the Republic may involve no more that a ceremony, the formal confirmation of a status already attained.[16]

In order to do this, he proposed that the oath of allegiance to the King that Dáil deputies were required to take--certainly the most emotional issue of the Civil War for anti-Treaty republicans--be abolished. The Dominions Secretary in London objected, claiming that abolition of the oath would be a violation of the Treaty, but de Valera remained adamant, resting his case, as Nicholas Mansergh says, "in the last resort upon indefeasible national sovereignty."[17] The act eliminating the oath finally passed in 1933. That same year, legislation was enacted abolishing the Governor-General's discretionary functions and ending the citizen's right of appeal to the Privy Council.[18]

Three years later, Edward VIII's abdication crisis presented the opportunity to delete the King from the Constitution, and de Valera seized it. On the day that Parliament, acting with the consent of and on behalf of the other dominions, declared a demise of the Crown in favor of the next in line (11 December 1936), Dáil Éireann passed a constitutional amendment deleting all references to the King and the Governor-General from the Constitution. The following day it passed the Executive Authority (External Relations) Act. This accepted King Edward's abdication, but, instead of naming a successor, it merely authorized the King recognized by Britain and the dominions to act on the Irish government's behalf for certain diplomatic (that is, entirely external) purposes. Vincent Grogan explains the legal result:

> The Irish Free State had ceased to be one of His Majesty's Dominions. It had become an Associated State, republican in form, without a titular Head.[19]

It got that titular head the following year when de Valera's new Constitution was adopted. The new Constitution provided for both a head of government (Taoiseach) and a head of state (President), although the King continued to be authorized--by statute only, he was not mentioned in the Constitution--to act for Ireland, on the Irish government's advice, in foreign affairs.

Political independence, however, was not enough. As early as 1928, Fianna Fáil party spokesman Séan Lemass had described the party's economic goals in terms of independence:

> We believe that Ireland can be made a self-contained unit, providing all the necessities of living in adequate quantities for the people residing in this island at the moment and probably for a much larger number.[20]

"Here, in a sentence," says F. S. L. Lyons, "was the germ of a new departure, looking to the creation of an Ireland that would be both politically and economically freer of the British connection than the men of the Treaty had ever been able to make her."[21] The success of the drive for self-sufficiency, once Fianna Fáil came to power, was something less than complete, but the attempt itself was an important exercise of independence.

Shortly after taking over the reins of power, de Valera's government began withholding the annuities that Irish farmers paid to the British Exchequer in return for the very-long-term loans that had been extended under the various Land Acts between the 1880s and the First World War. The British government retaliated by placing high duties on some Irish agricultural products to recoup the lost revenue, and the Irish government, in turn, raised the tariffs on some British goods. This legal and commercial dispute, called the Anglo-Irish Trade War, continued for five years. The reaction of the Irish Labour party, which supported de Valera's government without joining it, is instructive. The party was at first very critical of the government's handling of the annuities dispute, but, when the British retaliated, "Labour immediately declared that the British Government had challenged the Irish people on a political as well as an economic issue. The question it said was one of subjugation or independence, equality or subordination."[22] Cosgrave's party, Cumann na nGaedheal, took a different stand but one that was also founded on a concern for the nation's dignity. During the election campaign of 1933, Cumann na nGaedheal criticized Fianna Fáil for violating the national honor by illegally withholding the annuities and by altering the Constitution outside the limits of the Treaty. Fianna Fáil's reply, that it was acting on the rights of a small nation to free itself from imperial ties, found more favor with the voters, however, and de Valera was given his first overall majority in the Dáil.[23] The electorate chose, as it had in 1885 and 1918, the party that sought the widest measure of independence.

The Trade War was not so much a departure from Fianna Fáil's overall tariff policy as an exaggeration of it. The government had two goals in mind. It wanted to lessen Ireland's commercial dependence on Britain, but it also wanted to increase the area under tillage at the expense of grazing land. Self-sufficiency meant more and stronger home industries, more home-grown grain, increased employment and decreased emigration, as well as greater independence of British economic and political policy.

Three Anglo-Irish treaties concluded the Trade War in April 1938. One settled the annuities dispute, another provided for much freer trade between Britain and Ireland while still protecting the developing Irish industries, and the third abrogated the articles of the Treaty of 1921 that had given Britain control over three Irish naval bases (the "Treaty ports") and the right to claim additional facilities in an emergency. The return of the Treaty ports made a policy of real neutrality possible for the first time,[24] and the measure of self-sufficiency achieved during the Trade War--especially the enormous increase in tillage[25]--helped Ireland weather the wartime shortages.[26] Though F. S. L. Lyons feels that "the effect of the quarrel seemed to be to emphasise economic interdependence rather than economic separateness,"[27] and I would have to agree (imports from Britain fell from 75 percent to 54 percent of Irish trade, but exports to Britain continued at over 90 percent),[28] the Trade War itself was a kind of reassertion of independence, and its successful conclusion with the three agreements of 1938 must have greatly increased national self-confidence.

There are, however, different kinds of independence. Writing in 1925, the Irish poet George Russell (AE) predicted that, just as Ireland had reacted against the idealism of the war of independence and Civil War with "an era of materialism," she would eventually turn away from materialism to "a new fight for spiritualism."[29] Francis MacManus makes some interesting comments in assessing that prediction:

> So spoke the prophet who was, as we can tell after the events, both right and wrong. He was wrong in his expectation of a spiritual fight fifteen years or more hence. True enough, there were fights for intellectual liberty against censorship; and for an Irish mind against the disappearance of the Irish language; and for more autonomy in Irish economics against British control. Yet, all those reactions weren't part of any general 'fight for spiritual freedom.'[30]

If those efforts did not add up to MacManus's definition of a fight for spiritual freedom, they certainly did represent struggles for different types of independence.

One kind of independence still eluded the Irish. In a description of Irish society in the 1930s, Terence de Vere White says:

> England was too much on the national mind. If some hankered after the old and were unable to throw off social subservience to England, others had only to know what was done in England to prescribe the opposite. It was necessary to forget England, and that would take time.[31]

That kind of independence was the hardest for Irishmen to acquire, and it was not won during the period between the Wars. It required too much self-confidence. Only the successful maintenance of neutrality during the Second World War would bring it about.

The effort to keep Ireland neutral was, indeed, a success. Several factors were responsible for this. The return of the Treaty ports and the increased self-sufficiency of the Irish economy were, as I have said, two of the most crucial. John Murphy, who points out both of them, finds a third factor still more important. "Above all," he says, "neutrality was sensed as the acid test of real independence and what saw it through to eventual success was, in the first place, a remarkable consensus of popular determination."[32] The evidence seems to bear out this assessment. I do not mean to suggest that a self-conscious striving for independence-through-neutrality existed. Rather, I would agree with David Grene's assessment, written in 1941:

> In the present conflict the Irish are not interested. Even if the newspapers were not censored until no item of conceivable political importance is left, it is doubtful if the political turmoil would rage around the issues of this war. But the Irish do look with truly pitiable earnestness and faith to Eamon de Valera not to get them into the war.[33]

The point is, however, not that the consensus for neutrality was based on acute political perception but that it represented feeling that was both widespread and very strong.[34]

In his article, Grene emphasized de Valera's crucial role in maintaining Irish neutrality. (His next sentence was, "All roads in Irish feeling lead back to de Valera.")[35] This was no exaggeration of the Taoiseach's role. Joseph Carroll, for instance, calls de Valera's effort "a considerable diplomatic and political triumph."[36] It was a distinctly personal triumph, and the independence Ireland exhibited through neutrality was colored by de Valera's own distinctly personal brand of independence. This is how the American minister to Ireland, David Gray, described the Taoiseach in a dispatch written early in 1941:

> His whole power is based on his genuis for engendering and utilizing anti-British

sentiment. His administration otherwise is generally unsuccessful. He is probably the most adroit politician in Europe and he honestly believes that all he does is for the good of his country. He has the qualities of martyr, fanatic and Machiavelli. No one can outwit, frighten or blandish him. Remember that he is not pro-German, nor personally anti-British, but only pro-de Valera.[37]

The anger and frustration with de Valera--and especially, the incomprehension of him--evident in this assessment reflect the great extent of his true independence of the points of view of all the belligerents.

The most significant threats to Irish neutrality during the War were the Anglo-American efforts to get Ireland to cede use of the Treaty ports to Britain and the "American note" demanding expulsion of the Axis diplomats from Dublin. After the War, Winston Churchill explained British policy on the Treaty ports:

> It is true that in the end we survived without the ports. It is also true that if we had not been able to do without them we should have retaken them by force rather than perish by famine.[38]

The British Representative in Dublin, Sir John Maffey, sounded out de Valera on the ports in 1939. The Taoiseach expained then that Irish public opinion would tolerate no departures from neutrality. If any government were to depart from the policy, he maintained, it could not stand.[39] The British, on the other hand, felt that the Irish were living in a "world of illusion,"[40] if they thought that the War would really not touch Ireland. Their response to the Irish refusal was to reduce the volume of imported goods available to Ireland--most of them carried in British bottoms, in British convoys--so that Ireland would at least feel the shortages caused by the War. The result was that shipments of coal were greatly reduced, and that those of fats, sugar and wheat were cut off completely.[41]

A memorandum which the Dominions Secretary wrote to the war cabinet outlined the British policy. It explained that

> The bubble of Irish complacency had effectively and we may hope finally been pricked. The Southern Irish now know that England is not dependent on them and that on the contrary, it is Ireland that is dependent on England....To-day Southern Ireland is very uncomfortable, and she is going to become progressively more uncomfortable.[42]

The next British action was, in fact, a drastic reduction in the amount of tea shipped to Ireland.[43] Through all of this, de Valera's government remained resolute, but it could exert very little counter-pressure. In fact, the only pressure it did exert was the threat to withhold supplies of Guinness stout from the United Kingdom.[44]

There were two principal reasons why Ireland survived the economic squeeze as well as she did. In the first place, Britain's actual policy was to keep "Eire's economy going on a minimum basis," not to starve her.[45] In the second, the small factories which had sprung up during the push for economic self-sufficiency, along with the greatly increased area under tillage, allowed Ireland to meet more of her own needs.[46]

The second great threat to Irish neutrality was the "American note," a message from the United States government in early 1944 requesting the Irish government to expel the diplomatic representatives of the Axis powers. The Americans wanted this done, they said, to ensure the security of their plans for the invasion of France from German espionage. David Gray, the American minister, presented the note to de Valera on February 21, 1944. In a report to Sir John Maffey, Gray described de Valera's reaction. The Taoiseach, he said, stopped reading the note at one point to ask if it was an ultimatum, and Gray assured him that it was not.

> He then finished reading the Note and said in substance, 'We have done all we can do and will do no more. As long as I am here my answer to this request must be--no.'...The Prime Minister was at all times extremely courteous.[47]

The next day, it was Maffey's turn. He presented a much shorter note that said simply that the British government supported the American request, to which the Irish government had not yet formally replied. This note received a much stronger reaction from de Valera than Gray's note had gotten:

> After perusing it, he turned to me, white with indignation, and exclaimed, 'This is an ultimatum. This is an outrage.' I pointed out that it was none of these things and that he was taking up an unreasonable attitude to a most reasonable and justifiable request....He professed to see nothing in the proceedings, nothing but an attempt to push him into the war and to deprive Eire of the symbols of neutrality and independence. It was obvious that he attached immense importance to this symbolic factor.[48]

He certainly did. The presentation of the American note gave de Valera an opportunity to reaffirm his, and Ireland's, attachment to neutrality, and he took full advantage of it.

The morning after he had seen Maffey, de Valera summoned the Canadian High Commissioner, John Kearney. Though he had been assured by both Gray and Maffey that the notes had not constituted an ultimatum, de Valera behaved as if they had. Here is Maffey's report of the account Kearney gave him of the interview:

> Mr. de Valera, very emotional and stubborn, complained that the notes were merely a political move, that they implied a direct threat to which Eire would react, that interference with the sovereignty of Eire would be resisted, and that the army and

> the country would fight, and were even now preparing for eventualities. He intended to summon the Dáil and receive their endorsement of this renewal of the old struggle, this time against England, against America, against anybody.[49]

As the political situation continued to develop, and as it became obvious that the incident would eventually become public, de Valera continued to press home his advantage.

On February 26, the Irish minister in Washington called on an official of the State Department's European section. The official confirmed to him both that the American note had not constituted an ultimatum and that the American non-invasion pledge of 1942 still stood.[50] The Taoiseach was, nevertheless, breathing defiance when he spoke in Cavan the next day. His audience had not yet learned of the diplomatic exchanges, but it had heard plenty of invasion rumors in the previous few weeks. De Valera did nothing to still the rumors. Instead, he assured his audience that

> At any moment the war may come upon us and we may be called to defend our rights and our freedom with our lives. Should that day come we will all face our duty with the traditional courage of our race.[51]

Though this outburst must have seemed grossly unnecessary to the diplomats and politicians familiar with the true state of affairs, it was in fact well calculated. De Valera knew that the affair could not be kept quiet forever, and he wanted the Irish government's stand on record in a way that would reflect Irish independence.

The story of the American note finally broke in the world's press in March. Joseph Carroll explains what the incident meant to Irishmen:

> After almost five years of sombre neutrality, cramping censorship, high emigration and unemployment, food shortages and transport difficulties, here suddenly was Ireland back in the world's headlines and in the pose that appealed to every Irish person--standing up fearlessly to the big fellows....De Valera had refused to let himself be pushed around and if in the rest of the world admiration was grudgingly accorded, it was unbounded in Ireland.[52]

De Valera had not only stood up to the great powers, he had done it successfully. Neutral nations quite often suffer in great conflagrations, but they very rarely win victories in them. De Valera had indeed won one for Ireland, and George Bernard Shaw--of all people--gave voice to Ireland's emotional response:

> Howbeit, that powerless little garden called Ireland wins in the teeth of all the mighty Powers. Erin go Bragh![53]

In the course of maintaining Ireland's neutrality throughout the War, de Valera overplayed his hand only once. He made a major political mistake in calling at the

German legation in Dublin to express his condolences on Adolph Hitler's death in May 1945. He later argued that this was only proper, since he had made a similar gesture on Franklin Roosevelt's death a few weeks earlier, but most observers remained unconvinced. He even explained to his minister in Washington that such formal acts of protocol were never meant to indicate approval or disapproval of a particular government's policies, but such careful distinctions were overwhelmed by the ghastly stories of the German extermination camps that were just being revealed in the world's press. And the fact that de Valera felt he had to explain his action to his own diplomatic representatives was a sign that even Irishmen found it difficult to understand this act of formal neutrality.[54]

Fortunately for de Valera, Churchill almost immediately offered him the opportunity to recover his position. On May 13, 1945, the Prime Minister delivered a major speech on the Allied victory in Europe. In it, he castigated de Valera for Irish neutrality, which, he said, had cost Britain the use of Irish ports and airfields against German submarines and which had allowed "the de Valera government to frolic with the Germans and later with the Japanese representives to their hearts' content." Lauding his own government's forebearance in not seizing the ports and airfields--"a restraint and poise to which, I say, history will find few parallels"--he declared that, if Britain had thought it necessary for her survival, she would have taken what bases she needed.[55]

The Taoiseach waited three days before making his reply to what Joseph Carroll has called "Churchill's contemptuous sneer."[56] Exhibiting great restraint, he described Britain's "forebearance" from the Irish point of view:

> Mr. Churchill makes it clear that in certain circumstances he would have violated our neutrality and that he would justify his action by Britain's necessity.
>
> It is indeed fortunate that Britain's necessity did not reach the point when Mr. Churchill would have acted. All credit to him that he successfully resisted the temptation which, I have no doubt, many times assailed him in his difficulties and to which I freely admit many leaders might have easily succumbed. It is indeed hard for the the strong to be just to the weak...By resisting his temptation in this instance Mr. Churchill, instead of adding another sordid chapter to the already bloodstained record of the relations between England and this country, has advanced the cause of international morality an important step...

Then drawing a parallel between British and Irish displays of fortitude, he reminded his audience that Ireland, too, had a reason to be proud:

> Mr. Churchill is proud of Britain's stand alone after France had fallen and before America entered the war. Could he not find in his heart the generosity to

> acknowledge that there is a small nation that stood alone not for one year or two but for several hundred years against aggression,...a small nation that could never be got to accept defeat and has never surrendered her soul?[57]

It was, after all, by means of the very neutrality for which Churchill castigated her that Ireland had maintained her "independent soul."

De Valera's address was, in John Murphy's words, "a notable speech: sincere, reasoned, ironical, chiding, magisterial and statesmanlike. It made both an immediate and lasting impression on those who heard it."[58] By the time de Valera left the Radio Éireann studio, a crowd had gathered in the street outside. It cheered him as he got into his car and drove off. The telephone, his secretary later reported, rang all night. "Never," say Longford and O'Neill, his biographers, "had he spoken so clearly for the nation and never had the nation been so proud of him."[59]

The War had been a trying time for Ireland, but neutrality had done more than any other thing in the State's short history to confirm and enlarge its independence. Neutrality was so significant for Ireland that it is worthwhile quoting at some length the assessments of it that two eminent Irish historians have offered. John Murphy writes that

> More than any other event since independence, neutrality put a stamp on the state and underlined its homogeneity. The success of the policy not only saved the country from the ravages of war, it did much to emphasise the the consciousness of sovereignty, renew a sense of national confidence, heal the wounds of the Civil War through a common dedication to a national purpose and at the same time, paradoxically, sublimate anti-British hostility. The success and popularity of neutrality laid the basis for the development of an independent foreign policy at a later date.[60]

F. S. L. Lyons addresses the question of independence explicitly. He writes that

> ...neutrality, after all, was not just the instinctive reaction of a small power to keep clear of the quarrels of big powers, it was the outward and visible sign of absolute sovereignty. To be free to choose between peace and war was the mark of independence, to be free to choose between peace and a British war demonstrated to all the world just how complete that independence really was.[61]

Neutrality proved that Ireland was a truly sovereign, independent state, and, as John Murphy points out, it laid the basis for an independent foreign policy after the War. It did not, however, put an end to the question of independence. For a small nation, that question is never really settled. But it did mean that Irish independence would be maintained with a greater self-confidence than ever before.

The next blow for independence was not struck by de Valera's Fianna Fáil government but by the inter-party government which succeeded it in 1948. That year, the Tánaiste (deputy premier), William Norton, told the Dáil that "it would do our national self-respect good both at home and abroad if we were to proceed without delay to abolish the External Relations Act," which authorized the King to act for Ireland in foreign affairs. De Valera immediately promised no opposition.[62] The government, however, handled the matter clumsily, and, in the event, the Republic of Ireland Act which finally resulted made less popular impact than the manner and timing of its announcement. Somehow, the final decision to repeal the External Relations Act was leaked to the press while the Taoiseach was abroad, and John Costello wound up making the formal announcement in reply to a reporter's question at a press conference in Ottawa.

The Republic of Ireland Act declared Ireland to be a republic and formally took her out of the Commonwealth. F. S. L. Lyons has pointed out, however, that, despite the claim of absolute sovereignty embodied in the Act, its effects were not entirely under Ireland's control but

> Whatever the reaction in Ireland--and there was, of course, some enthusiasm along with a good deal of indifference--the ultimate success of the government's policy depended not just on its own unilateral action, but upon the response of Great Britain and the other Commonwealth countries.[63]

Ireland, he says, was "most vulnerable" in the areas of citizenship and trade. In the first, the British decision was to treat Irish citizens as British subjects when they were in Britain. (Ireland would reciprocate this treatment for British subjects in Ireland.) In the second, Britain decided to continue the preferential trade agreements, and these were held not to conflict with the General Agreement on Tariffs and Trade of 1947. So Ireland kept the advantages of Commonwealth membership while breaking that "last tenuous link that bound her to Britain."[64]

The Republic of Ireland Act was not, however, a complete success. Costello had hoped, as he had said, that it would "take the gun out of politics" by giving the republicans their republic, but the gun, and many of the romantic illusions which facilitated its use, stubbornly remained. The Act did not help relations with Northern Ireland, either. In 1949, the year in which the Act took effect (on Easter Monday, in keeping with republican pieties), the nervous Unionist government in Northern Ireland persuaded the British government to push through Parliament the Ireland Act. This measure provided that no part of Northern Ireland would cease to be part of the United Kingdom without the assent of the parliament of Northern Ireland. These results notwithstanding, both John Murphy and F. S. L. Lyons believe that the Republic of

Ireland Act was a necessary and useful step, and their reasoning is instructive.

Murphy, who concedes that "it would appear at first sight that the declaration of the Republic was unnecessary, precipitate and fruitless," points out that India became a republic while remaining within the Commonwealth the same year that Ireland seceded, and did it through the Irish device of external association. Nevertheless, he says, the cases were not comparable:

> In the case of Ireland, the decision to adopt such a status was bound up with the intangible, though none the less real, factor of national honour and self-respect, heightened perhaps by the experience of neutrality. In the last analysis, Ireland's very closeness to Britain and the past relationship between the two countries made Irishmen feel that even the most shadowy constitutional connection suggested a position of subordination and made an adoption of formal sovereignty imperative, whatever the consequences.[65]

Lyons's emphasis is slightly different from Murphy's, but his conclusions are similar. He wonders if the Irish example does not demonstrate "that not even the most imaginatively conceived association of states can fulfil the inner demands and compulsions of a passionate sense of nationality." Then, drawing on the Irish case, he states the general problem of nationality and independence as he sees it:

> If the Commonwealth should disappear--and recent prime ministers' conferences have brought this within the realm of possibility--it will disappear because it will have been proved that political independence is not enough. Just two months before the Easter Rising Patrick Pearse expressed this fundamental truth in words that go far beyond the immediate Irish context in which he wrote them. 'Independence,' he declared, 'one must understand to include spiritual and intellectual independence as well as political independence; or rather, true political independence requires spiritual and intellectual independence as its basis, or it tends to become unstable, a thing resting merely on interests which change with time and circumstance.[66]

The problem of this analysis is, of course, that, twenty-four years after the Republic of Ireland Act came into effect, Ireland joined a new super-state, the European Economic Community, 83 percent of those voting having indicated their approval in a referendum the year before.

What does Ireland's entry into the EEC tell us about the question of independence in Irish politics? It identifies the values that have been associated with independence, and it indicates how sophisticated the electorate has been in measuring gains in this area against their cost. This is how a Fianna Fáil foreign minister explained the entry decision a few years after it took place:

> Remember, as a country with only recent independence, we were conscious to a certain extent of the effect which membership would have on our sovereignty, but we also knew that by becoming members of the Community we were being enabled for the first time to influence decisions which would influence us anyway. Therefore, we were contributing to a pooling of sovereignty to enable us to have a more enriched sovereignty.[67]

The key differences between the attitudes apparent in this statement and those which helped take Ireland out of the Commonwealth are an appreciation of the necessarily limited nature of Irish independence and a confidence that agreeing to limit of the nation's sovereignty would not necessarily imperil its essential independence, or its dignity.

If the principal political events of the second quarter of the twentieth century, especially the Anglo-Irish Trade War and the Second World War, had confirmed that Irish independence was genuine, they had also demonstrated that it had limits. But once independence had been successfully asserted, the limitations to it could be accepted realistically without threatening the nation's dignity. The Commonwealth had been unacceptable because of the vestiges it had contained of Britain's old predominant partnership, but a new community, voluntarily entered into, free of associations with an ascendency class, coercive administration or the suppression of the national culture, presented no threat to the nation's dignity.

Since the Irish electorate formed a large proportion of the audience for which the authors of the Parnell Myth wrote, it is worth discussing briefly the sophistication that that electorate demonstrated. It consistently rewarded with its support those politicians who exhibited the dignity-based independence which it valued, but it repudiated them when they pursued independence at too great a price. Thus, it supported Sinn Féin against the Irish Parliamentary Party on the question of separation in 1918, but it refused de Valera a majority against the Treaty four years later. When de Valera made his peace with the new order of things, it eventually gave him its confidence again, supporting his thrust for greater independence in association with the Commonwealth, sustaining his governments, despite the sacrificial cost, in the Anglo-Irish Trade War. The electorate also gave consensus support, at arguably less cost, to his neutrality policy. When, however, de Valera's successors in the inter-party government declared the Republic and withdrew from the Commonwealth, it was not sufficiently impressed with that action either to sustain them in office or to allow them (or the Clann na Poblachta party from among them) to supplant Fianna Fáil as the preeminently nationalist party. In fact,

Fianna Fâil remained so confident of its position as the party of independence that it eventually led the way in the campaign for EEC membership.

## Notes to Chapter 7

[1]John Murphy confirmed this point in a conversation in Chicago in April 1977. He agreed that the continuing question of independence (after 1921) had been a major theme in his and F. S. L. Lyons' histories of twentieth century Irish politics and said that, if he were to write Ireland in the Twentieth Century over again, he would give it even greater emphasis. John A. Murphy, Ireland in the Twentieth Century, Gill History of Ireland, vol. 11, general eds. James Lydon and Margaret MacCurtain (Dublin: Gill & Macmillan, 1975); F. S. L. Lyons, Ireland since the Famine, rev. ed. (London: Collins/Fontana, 1973).

[2]Manifesto of the central executive of the Irish National League of Great Britain, n.d., quoted in National Press (Dublin), 12 October 1891.

[3]F. S. L. Lyons, John Dillon: A Biography (Chicago: University of Chicago Press, 1968), pp. 161-62.

[4]Moran's articles began appearing in the New Ireland Review in 1898 and in the Leader after 1900. Brian Inglis, "Moran of the Leader and Ryan of the Irish Peasant," Thomas Davis Lectures, Radio Éireann, Dublin 1955-56, in The Shaping of Modern Ireland, ed. Conor Cruise O'Brien (Routledge & Kegan Paul, 1960; Routledge Paperback, 1970), pp. 109-10.

[5]Conor Cruise O'Brien, "1891-1916," in The Shaping of Modern Ireland, pp. 15-16.

[6]Conor Cruise O'Brien, States of Ireland (London: Hutchinson & Co., 1972; New York: Random House, Pantheon Books, 1972; Vintage Books, 1973), p. 67.

[7]Patrick O'Farrell, England and Ireland since 1800 (Oxford: Oxford University Press, 1975), p. 100.

[8]I do not mean to imply that this consistent support meant the neglect of Irish interests. The Party successfully resisted the application to Ireland of educational and social welfare legislation that it thought inappropriate.

[9]John A. Murphy, Ireland in the Twentiety Century, pp. 27-28.

[10]He himself said it would not be appropriate for him to go. John A. Murphy, Ireland in the Twentiety Century, p. 30; F. S. L. Lyons, Ireland since the Famine, pp. 428, 429n.

[11]Quoted in F. S. L. Lyons, Ireland since the Famine, p. 432.

[12]F. S. L. Lyons, Ireland since the Famine, p. 444.

[13]Report of the Inter-Imperial Relations Committee (Cmd. 2768), p. 14, quoted ibid., p. 508.

[14]Winston Churchill objected to his last provision, pointing out that the Dáil would be empowered to repeal any part of the Treaty that it wanted; Cosgrave replied in a letter to the British government that the Treaty was not a legislative enactment but a mutual agreement based on good faith. In the event, de Valera realized Churchill's fears by persuading the Dáil to abolish the oath of allegiance mandated by the Treaty three years later. In 1935, the Judicial Committee of the Privy Council ruled that the Statute of Westminster had indeed given the Dáil the right to abrogate the Treaty or parts of it. F.

S. L. Lyons, Ireland since the Famine, pp. 509-10, 517.

[15]This account of the Cosgrave Commonwealth policy follows John A. Murphy, Ireland in the Twentieth Century, pp. 65-66, and F. S. L. Lyons, Ireland since the Famine, pp. 509-10, 515-17.

[16]Quoted in John A. Murphy, Ireland in the Twentieth Century, p. 87.

[17]Nicholas Mansergh, "Ireland: External Relations 1926-39," Thomas Davis Lectures, Radio Éireann, Dublin, 1962, in The Years of the Great Test, ed. Francis MacManus (Cork: Mercier Press, 1967), p. 130-31.

[18]Vincent Grogan, "Towards the New Constitution," in The Years of the Great Test, p. 167.

[19]Ibid., pp. 167-68.

[20]Séan Lemass, Dáil Éireann, February 1928, quoted in F. S. L. Lyons, Ireland since the Famine, p. 610.

[21]F. S. L. Lyons, Ireland since the Famine, p. 610.

[22]Donal Nevin, "Labour and the Political Revolution," in The Years of the Great Test, p. 61.

[23]John A. Murphy, Ireland in the Twentieth Century, p. 78.

[24]Ibid., p. 95.

[25]The area devoted to wheat increased from 21,000 acres in 1932 to 230,000 in 1938 to 640,000 in 1944. Joseph T. Carroll, Ireland in the War Years (Newton Abbot: David & Charles, 1975; New York: Crane, Russack & Co., 1975), p. 88.

[26]F. S. L. Lyons, Ireland since the Famine, p. 557.

[27]Ibid., p. 613.

[28]Ibid.

[29]George W. Russell to Van Wyck Brooks, summer 1925, quoted in Francis MacManus, "The Literature of the Period," in The Years of the Great Test, p. 115.

[30]Francis MacManus, "The Literature of the Period," pp. 115-16.

[31]Terence de Vere White, "Social Life in Ireland 1927-1937," in The Years of the Great Test, p. 27.

[32]John A. Murphy, Ireland in the Twentieth Century, p. 101.

[33]David Grene, "Ireland and the War," University of Chicago Magazine, April 1941, p. 16.

[34]The British Representative in Dublin reported to the Dominion Secretary that "The policy of neutrality commands widespread approval among all classes and interests in Eire. It is remarkable how even the 'pro-British' group, men who have fought for the Crown and are anxious to be called up again, men whose sons are at the front today, loyalists in the old sense of the word, agree generally in supporting the policy of neutrality for Eire." John Maffey to Anthony Eden, 23 October 1939, quoted in Joseph T. Carroll, Ireland in the War Years, p. 30.

[35]David Grene, "Ireland and the War," p. 16.

[36]Joseph T. Carroll, Ireland in the War Years, p. 172.

[37]David Gray, report to U. S. State Department, November 1940, quoted ibid., p. 101.

[38]Winston S. Churchill, The Second World War, vol. 1: The Gathering Storm, p. 248, quoted in Joseph T. Carroll, Ireland in the War Years, p. 26.

[39]John Maffey to Anthony Eden, 21 October 1939, in British War Cabinet minutes, CAB 66, 2, quoted in Joseph T. Carroll, Ireland in the War Years, p. 29.

[40]Lord Cranborne, memorandum to War Cabinet, 19 March 1941, CAB 66, 15, quoted in Joseph T. Carroll, Ireland in the War Years, p. 84.

[41]Joseph T. Carroll, Ireland in the War Years, p. 84.

[42]Lord Cranborne, memorandum to War Cabinet, 19 March 1941, CAB 66, 15, quoted ibid., p. 85.

[43]Joseph T. Carroll, Ireland in the War Years, p. 85.

[44]Ibid., p. 92.

[45]Committee of the War Cabinet, quoted ibid., p. 92.

[46]Joseph T. Carroll, Ireland in the War Years, p. 87.

[47]David Gray to John Maffey, [21 or 22 February 1944], quoted ibid., p. 142.

[48]John Maffey, report, Foreign Office political correspondence, FO 371, 42679, quoted in Joseph T. Carroll, Ireland in the War Years, pp. 142-43.

[49]Ibid., p. 143.

[50]Joseph T. Carroll, Ireland in the War Years, p. 146.

[51]Eamon de Valera, speech in Cavan, 27 February 1944, quoted ibid., p. 146.

[52]Joseph T. Carroll, Ireland in the War Years, pp. 158-59.

[53]George Bernard Shaw, interview in Forward, n.p., n.d., quoted ibid., p. 159.

[54]Joseph T. Carroll, Ireland in the War Years, pp. 160-61.

[55]Winston S. Churchill, speech on BBC Radio, London, 13 May 1945, reprinted in New York Times, 13 May 1945, reprinted as "Review of War, Pledge for Future: De Valera Denounced," in Vital Speeches of the Day, 1 June 1945, pp. 482-83.

[56]Joseph T. Carroll, Ireland in the War Years, p. 163.

[57]Eamon de Valera, speech on Radio Éireann, Dublin, 16 May 1945, reprinted as "International Morality: Answer to Churchill," Vital Speeches of the Day, 1 June 1945, p. 485-86.

[58]John A. Murphy, Ireland in the Twentieth Century, p. 107.

[59]Frank Pakenham [Earl of Longford] and Thomas P. O'Neill, Eamon de Valera (Boston: Houghton Mifflin Co., 1971), p. 414.

[60]John A. Murphy, Ireland in the Twentieth Century, p. 107.

[61]F. S. L. Lyons, Ireland since the Famine, p. 554.

[62]William Norton, speech, and Eamon de Valera, interjection in reply, Dáil Éireann, August 1948, quoted in John A. Murphy, Ireland in the Twentieth Century, p. 125.

[63]F. S. L. Lyons, Ireland since the Famine, p. 568.

[64]Ibid., p. 569. It is significant that, though F. S. L. Lyons does not much like Parnell or his (supposed) rhetoric, he chooses to echo one of Parnell's most notorious statements in this connection. I discuss the tendency to connect Parnell with the question of independence in contemporary politics in Chapter 8.

[65]John A. Murphy, Ireland in the Twentieth Century, pp. 128-29.

[66]F. S. L. Lyons, Ireland since the Famine, p. 570.

[67]Michael O'Kennedy, interview with John Cooney, "No Wish for 'Constant Mendicant' Role," Irish Times (Dublin), 1 August 1977. I am indebted to Prof. Edna M. McGlynn for this reference.

## CHAPTER 8

## THE RELATIONSHIP OF MYTH TO CONTEXT

The relationship between the Parnell Myth and its political context was cemented during the first years after Parnell's death. Parnell had fought his last campaign on the issue of independence, and the years 1893 and 1894 saw political developments which underlined both the validity and importance of this issue. In 1893, Gladstone's second Home Rule Bill passed the House of Commons but failed in the Lords. While the Liberal government was deciding what to do next, John Redmond reminded a Parnellite audience in Dublin that the Antiparnellites had claimed that Parnell was the sole remaining obstacle to Home Rule, and he contrasted Parnell's political strategy with theirs:

> Mr. Parnell's greatest achievement was that he converted the Irish question into an impassable barrier between the English democracy and the achievement of English reforms...The people were told that all that was necessary to obtain Home Rule was to dislodge Mr. Parnell from the leadership of Ireland (groans) ....Mr. Parnell was dead and gone, but had they got Home Rule, or had the year 1893 seen the end of the struggle as Mr. Dillon said it would?[1]

This was Parnellite rhetoric, of course, but Redmond was right in his intuition that the "impassable barrier" had disappeared. The next year brought many things: Gladstone resigned; the Liberals decided not to risk a second election on Home Rule; the new Prime Minister, Lord Rosebery, laid down his "predominant partner" policy; and the Antiparnellites decided to continue to support the government, which was still dependent on their votes, anyway.

The Antiparnellites' position stung the pride of at least some nationalists. Here is one stanza of a song sung at an Irish nationalist gathering in New York in 1895 (the speaker in it is meant to be the Liberal Chief Secretary for Ireland, John Morley):

Oh, then, Paddy, dear, and won't you wait
    For twenty years or so,
Till we end or mend the House of Lords
    And lay the Churches low?
Our Bill can lie upon the shelf
    While reform goes marching on;
For Rosebery's but half convinced

And Parnell--he is gone.[2]

Clearly, the author of these lyrics felt that some part of the nation's independence had been surrendered and that its dignity had suffered thereby.

The political events of 1893-94 contradicted the Antiparnellites' interpretation of Parnell's last year. They had claimed that Parnell's leadership (after Gladstone's letter and Parnell's manifesto) was an obstacle to Home Rule and that his warning about the threat to the country's and the party's independence was mere electioneering rhetoric. The failure of the Home Rule Bill and the Antiparnellites' subsequent support of Rosebery's government weakened the persuasiveness of this interpretation. These factors did not turn the Parnell Myth into a Parnellite parable--the wide spectrum of opinion represented by contributors to the Myth ensured that that would not happen--but they did remove the main obstacle to the emergence of Parnell's attitude as the Myth's central symbol. So long as Antiparnellite skepticism remained about Parnell's warnings of the threat to Irish independence, Parnell's attitude could not have an unambiguous enough meaning to be a powerful symbol. After 1894, Parnell's motivation in assuming his independent posture could be questioned, but not the validity of the posture itself or the need for a leadership which assumed it.

It was precisely because Parnell had attached such importance to Irish independence of English party politics and had warned that the Liberals were not to be trusted that his memory had an increasing relevance for contemporary politics after 1894. In the autumn of 1896, United Ireland described one facet of that relevance. When the Liberals had started going back on their pledges, it said, there had at first been silence in the Antiparnellite camp, then faint praise for the dead Chief. Finally, after the Tories had returned to office in 1895, the Antiparnellites "discovered that Parnell was, indeed, a great statesman." Parnell's legacy, United Ireland noted, was becoming a valuable political commodity.

> Indeed, latterly it has become quite customary with these consistent politicians [the Antiparnellites] to insinuate that they, and only, they, are the true followers of Parnell's principles.[3]

It was a sure sign that Parnell--or, rather, the memory of him--was growing in popular estimation.

Events encouraged this growth. The wrangling during the Split gave an impression of drift and impotence. (William O'Brien wrote of this time that one-man power had been replaced by eighty-man powerlessness.)[4] After the old Irish Parliamentary Party was reunited in 1900, the bitter faction fights between the main body under John Redmond and John Dillon and the splinter groups led by Timothy Healy and William O'Brien did nothing to improve the Party's reputation. The lack of unity was embarrassing--humiliating, when it stimulated English ridicule--and the endless rain of charges and counter-charges made parliamentary politics appear squalid in the eyes of many young Irishmen.[5]

Nationalist M.P.s faithfully tried to represent Irish aspirations in the years 1891-1918, but they were only modestly successful. The long period of Tory rule (1895-1905) was extremely frustrating for the nationalists despite real progress in land purchase and local government reform. The Party's political position eroded during that time, moreover, and the election campaign of 1906 illustrated just how far. During that campaign, even though a Liberal government dependent on Irish votes seemed the likely outcome, the Party was unable to extract a Home Rule pledge from the Liberals. In fact, the Liberals ran pledged not to bring in a full Home Rule Bill during the life of the next Parliament. When, in the event, the new Liberal government had no need of Irish support--but got it anyway--the nation's dignity suffered as much as its independence. Nor did things greatly improve under the Liberal government. True, the practical preparation for self-government was completed: the Party was conceded the right to review proposed legislation as well as a wide measure of control over patronage and civil service appointments. But practical power was not the only question. When, in 1914-16, the Party acceded to suspension of the Home Rule Act for the duration of the War, admitted that temporary partition of the country might be necessary, and supported the government's recruiting drive, it seemed to be making concessions from weakness. When it then failed to react satisfactorily to the government's mishandling of the Rising and to the threat of conscription, it lost the consensus support it had enjoyed for thirty-three years and was crushed at the polls by Sinn Féin.

Two things about this period are important for the Parnell Myth's relationship to its political context. The first is that the Party's performance was disappointing to many Irish observers, at least in terms of its mission to represent national aspirations, and the second is that those who expressed disappointment with it often invoked Parnell's name in doing so. When, for instance, Bishop O'Dwyer, of Limerick, criticized the Party's handling of the education question in 1906, he used these words:

> Oh, for a touch of the vanished hand. Did they think that Parnell, if he was alive, would ask the Irish nation to abandon the interest of religion and allow the Catholic schools to be trampled upon?[6]

Five years later, Arthur Griffith's newspaper, Sinn Féin, took the opportunity to evaluate the Party's progress in a leading article on the unveiling of the Parnell monument. It said:

> Twenty years ago they laid Parnell in the grave at Glasnevin--'the last obstacle to Home Rule'--and on Saturday Mr. John Redmond told the people--'We have got back at long last to the point to which Parnell led us'.[7]

The combination, present in these two quotations, of dissatisfaction with the present state of affairs and a nostalgic backward look at Parnell tended by implication to depict the period of Parnell's ascendancy as a kind of Golden Age, a time that, if it was not ideal, was markedly better than the writer's own. The Golden Age phenomenon, as it might be called, was one specific link between the Parnell Myth and its context.

A second connection was the widespread perception of a leadership vacuum which existed for a long time after Parnell's fall. The reference to the Golden Age of Parnell's ascendancy implied the existence of such a vacuum because Parnell's leadership was usually assumed to have been the crucial difference between the successful 1880s and the present, but there were many specific references to it as well. The crucial fact was that Parnell had no real successor. None of the three party leaders of the 1890s was really national leader, and, even when John Redmond assumed the leadership of the reunited Party in 1900, he did not succeed to Parnell's full position of national leadership. Other movements had grown up during the 1890s, and the Party and its affiliated institutions no longer monopolized public attention as they once had. Moreover, there was the question of personality. Whatever one could say of Redmond's considerable abilities, or of John Dillon's, neither was a Parnell. Neither man was as militant on the national question or as strong-willed, neither was as sensitive to issues involving the nation's independence and dignity, and neither was perceived to have been as successful. The Sinn Féin editorial on the unveiling of the Parnell monument put it this way in assessing Parnell's brilliant former lieutenants:

> If they had been soldiers of Napoleon most of them would have become generals. But all of Napoleon's generals put together could never equal Napoleon himself.[8]

There are several contrasts of Redmond with Parnell in the material comprising the Parnell Myth. Taken together, they exhibit a number of characteristics in common. All but one find Redmond lacking in comparison with Parnell. The exception is the book, Redmond's Vindication, written by the Rev. Robert O'Loughran and published in 1919, which describes Redmond as a more formidable politician that Parnell.[9] The other contrasts come from sources hostile to the Irish Parliamentary Party (Unionist, Sinn Féin and republican). The Unionist source is an Irish Times editorial on the unveiling of the Parnell monument that was published in 1911. It complained that

> It would not have been possible for a Liberal Government to hold Parnell in the humiliating servitude in which, for five years, Mr. Redmond has been content to

remain.[10]

Nine years later, Sinn Féin sympathizer R. M. Henry asserted that, while Home Rule under Parnell would not have offered many more practical advantages than Home Rule under Redmond, the difference between the two men was nevertheless significant. The reason, he explained, was that Parnell "would have obtained it in a different way and would have accepted the concession with a gesture of independence."[11] Three republican authors, whose books were published over a span of thirty-four years, also found Redmond lacking. Nora Connoly (in 1918),[12] Dorothy Macardle (in 1937)[13] and P. S. O'Hegarty (in 1952)[14] agreed that Redmond had not been nearly as militant as Parnell would have been. For these observers, if the scale was independence and dignity, Redmond simply did not measure up to Parnell's stature. That is why I have referred to a "leadership vacuum": in terms of the leader's duty to assert the nation's independence and safe-guard its dignity, neither Redmond nor anyone else succeeded Parnell until well into the 1930s.

Eamon de Valera seems to have understood very early in his political career that this function of the leader was essential, and it was his successful performance of it that eventually enabled him to succeed to Parnell's leadership role. In 1921, he refused to travel to London for the negotiations that led to the Treaty, and it appears that a major reason for his refusal was directly related to his sensitivity about the nation's independence and dignity. He had been elected President of the Republic (that is, head of state) just before the negotiations started--he had been merely President of Dáil Éireann (head of government) before that--and he was unwilling to take part in the negotiations in that capacity.[15] The wisdom of his decision aside, his concern for the nation's independence and dignity demonstrated his appreciation of the leader's special role and his responsibilities in this regard.

Had de Valera continued to lead the Irish government after the Treaty, especially in the new state's formative years, it is possible that he would have established himself then as Parnell's full successor. As it was, he did not--and yet his adamant position on the republic prevented any of his gifted opponents from succeeding Parnell in his stead. When he returned to power in 1932 and again assumed the initiative on the national question, in the practical form of moves against the oath to the King and the land annuities, he moved much closer to the special postion Parnell had occupied. The election of 1938, after the successful conclusion of the Trade War, demonstrated the popular support his leadership enjoyed. His special position as heir to Parnell was further strengthened and finally made impregnable by his skillful preservation of Irish neutrality and his masterful reply to Churchill at the close of the War. That is not to say that he became quite the "dictator" he has sometimes been called--he did, after all, lose two general elections after 1945--but that he came to represent Irish national aspirations in the same special way in which Parnell had done it before him.

I have described a leadership vacuum on the national question between Parnell's fall and the mid 1930s. The primary unsatisfied need for leadership was for a symbol of the nation's independence and dignity. The central symbol of the Parnell Myth was a response to that need. Parnell was no longer there to assert his nation's independence and safeguard its dignity, and no political leader succeeded him fully in that function for over forty years. It was the central symbol of the Myth, therefore, that substituted until a flesh-and-blood successor emerged. This means that it was the central symbol itself that served as the most important connection between the Parnell Myth and its political context. The values that the symbol represented, independence and dignity, underlay both the Myth and the politics of the time. They constituted the central theme of the Myth and the basis of the national question in politics. This enabled the Parnell Myth to play a significant role in Ireland's political culture in those years.

The perceptions of both the Golden Age and the leadership vacuum complemented and reinforced each other, and they defined the central symbol's role in the political culture. Some of the best evidence for both perceptions is found in the group of entries in my index under the subject heading "Ireland after Parnell." This includes seventy-eight items from forty-two sources in the twentieth century evidence.[16] The preponderant number of these, sixty-two, from thirty-three sources, describe Ireland as being much worse off without Parnell. Only three, from two sources, maintain the opposite. (They come from a book by Sir Horace Plunkett and a friendly review of that book that both maintain that Parnell's fall released the Irish people from their preoccupation with politics and allowed them to make practical, constructive efforts in other directions, such as Plunkett's cooperative movement.)[17] The more numerous negative characterizations of Ireland after Parnell were not confined to observers from one period of time or a single political point of view. In 1931, Henry Harrison quoted in Parnell Vindicated this passage from Sir Algernon West's Diary for 1891:

> He was the chosen representative of the loftiest aspirations of his countrymen, and his death left a void indescribable.[18]

This assessment is reflected in the comments of three Irishmen with three different political orientations. The Ulster Unionist St. John Ervine wrote in 1925 that

> When we are tempted to doubt the ability or greatness of Parnell, we need only test him in one way: what was the state of the Irish Party before he took command of it, what was its state during the eleven years he led it, and what was its state for

> thirty years after its death?[19]

Five years earlier, William O'Brien had recalled to his readers the advice that the Pall Mall Gazette had given to the Antiparnellites in 1891 to make quick work of Parnell:

> 'A bubble and a squeak and all is over', was the cheerful summary of the situation by the principal organ of the English Liberal Party, and the war cry was noisily caught up in Ireland. Thirty years have gone and no doubt 'all is over'--with the Parties, English and Irish, which compassed his destruction. Mo náire! all is not over, even yet, with the anarchy into which the disappearance of Alexander plunged his luckless generals and their country.[20]

P. S. O'Hegarty's assessment, written in 1952, was similar, even though it reflected distinctly republican sympathies. Here is how he described the political situation in the years after Parnell:

> The Home Rule movement, the Home Rule Party, went on, but like an automaton, went on with the motion that had been imparted to it by Parnell. It had no motion of its own, and it had no fresh accession from the people to give it such a motion. The young ceased to take any interest in it, and the old went on automatically. It was the pale proud fierce ghost of Parnell that sustained it.[21]

In this passage, the idea of a previously-existing better time is present by implication in the description of its dull, disappointing aftermath, and the leadership vacuum--partially filled by Parnell's proud, fierce ghost--is definitely evoked.

The ghost to which O'Hegarty referred, the spirit of Parnell leading his people from beyond the grave, is a good example of another phenomenon that connected the Parnell Myth to its context. I have indexed it under the subject heading "Parnell's legacy." It includes both descriptions of Parnell's posthumous influence (thirty-one, from twenty-four sources) and invocations of his name in support of contemporary policies (eighty, from fifty-two sources).[22] These characterizations of Parnell's legacy are of interest because they made specific connections between Parnell's story and the political context within which it was told and because they often reinforced the portrayals of the Golden Age and the leadership vacuum.

The references to Parnell's legacy that most clearly reflected the perception of the leadership vacuum after his death were those that described his posthumous influence. Not surprisingly, they were concentrated in the first twenty years after his death (twenty-three from seventeen sources in the years 1891 to 1911, eight from seven sources between 1912 and 1956), although they continued to appear into the 1950s. Indeed, William O'Brien called Parnell "an even more powerful factor" in 1925 than a generation earlier,[23] and Margaret Leamy wrote that Parnell's memory was "a vital force" in the Ireland of 1936.[24] As we have seen, O'Hegarty used the image of Parnell's ghost to evoke this influence. William Butler Yeats utilized the even more dramatic image of the burning pillar in a poem he wrote for United Ireland to rally his fellow Parnellites just after Parnell's death. He wrote:

> Mourn--and then onward, there is no returning
> He guides ye from the tomb;
> His memory now is a tall pillar, burning
> Before us in the gloom![25]

Descriptions of Parnell's posthumous leadership were used to justify as well as to exhort. At the Parnell anniversary demonstration in 1892, J. J. O'Kelly replied to the charge that the Parnellites were animated mainly by vengeance by describing the influence that Parnell's memory exerted:

> If motives so base entered and controlled their minds the spirit of the great leader who was gone would rise up to chide them and lead them back to nobler aims.[26]

Sometimes the evocation of Parnell's posthumous leadership was tied to specific policies. The most remarkable example of this was an article published in United Ireland in October 1893. Entitled "From beyond the Grave," it consisted of nine passages from nine different speeches Parnell had delivered in 1891. One dealt with the Boulogne negotiations between Parnell and William O'Brien, the rest with topics of immediate political interest in 1893: the plight of the Plan of Campaign tenants, redistribution of seats in the House of Commons, amnesty for Fenian prisoners, and the need for self-reliance and for independence of English parties.[27]

It was nothing unusual for Parnell's authoritiy to be appealed to in this way. Even the Antiparnellites did it. In June 1892, for example, the Weekly Freeman published a leading article, "Mr. Parnell's Fundamental Principle," which quoted, approvingly, a letter from the Roman Catholic Archbishop of Dublin to an Antiparnellite M.P. The letter said in part that

> Whatever some few constituencies here and there may do towards the abandonment of the fundamental principle of Mr. Parnell's public life [by supporting the Parnellites], that principle has taken root too deeply to leave any possibility of its being displaced even under cover of the most specious appeals to the sayings and doings of Mr. Parnell during the unhappily over-clouded closing year of his life. To that principle, the principle of national unity, the Nationalist constituencies of Ireland mean to hold fast.[28]

In later years, Parnell's name was invoked by a national teacher against the Royal University (in 1895),[29] by William O'Brien in defense of the Land Conference of 1903 (in

1905),[30] and by the Irish Times against new taxes (in 1911).[31]

Parnell's many enigmatic sayings made perfect raw material for those who wished to claim his legacy. The most popular of them was his dictum that no man could set bounds to the march of a nation.[32] Ruiadhre MacAodha wrote of this saying that, when Irish hopes were finally realized, the Irish people would come to understand "that Parnell's refusal to set bounds to the march of the Irish nation was the headline for all intervening Irish statesmen who would speak for a united Irish race."[33] It certainly was a headline for Eamon de Valera. The peroration of his speech against the Treaty in the Dáil debates of 1921 concluded with the warning that

> As far as you can, if you take the [Treaty] you are (cries of 'No' and 'Yes') presuming to set bounds to the onward march of a nation (applause).[34]

When, some weeks later, de Valera launched his public campaign against the Treaty, he again made use of Parnellian associations. The first speeches of the campaign were delivered from a platform in O'Connell Street. "There," wrote Mary Bromage, "under the shelter of Parnell's statue, de Valera...issued his challenge to a street crowd."[35]

Parnell's legacy was claimed by individuals from across the political spectrum. We have seen this done by spokemen for the Parnellites, Antiparnellites, anti-Treaty republicans, Unionists and Roman Catholic bishops. Even the rebels of 1916 "proclaimed themselves," in R. M. Henry's words, "followers of Tone and Mitchel and Davis and Parnell."[36] Indeed, Padraic Pearse wrote a pamphlet entitled Ghosts, published in 1916, which quoted at length from Parnell's "march of a nation" speech and which identified Wolf Tone, Thomas Davis, James Fintan Lalor, John Mitchel and Parnell as the bearers of the tradition of separatism, which Pearse espoused.[37] No wonder that, a few years later, amidst the political confusion of 1919, M. M. O'Hara could explain that he had written his study of Davitt and Parnell because

> Both Parnell and Davitt are being appealed to daily by the protagonists in the raging struggle. I have hopes that my book, while treating of a bygone time, may help to throw light on some of the political problems and controversies of the present.[38]

The claimants to Parnell's legacy represented a wide variety of political opinions, but does that indicate that the claims themselves were merely cynical rhetoric? Even if they were, of course, the fact that Parnell was appealed to at all would be important--because each appeal was a specific connection between the Myth and its political context--but if Parnell's legacy was taken seriously it would be evidence that the Myth had some influence on the political context. It seems to me that Parnell's legacy, as it related to specific policies, was taken very seriously indeed. Bishop O'Dwyer, de Valera and the national teacher who opposed the Royal University all quite obviously felt that Parnell would have stood with them had he lived. Far from cynicism, there seems to have been a geniune respect for Parnell's authority on almost any question. Perhaps the most striking example of this is an anecdote, written by a United Ireland reporter in 1895, about an incident that happened during the Carlow by-election in 1891. When a party of politicians and reporters stopped at a clergyman's house, the young man's editor leaped over a three foot tall garden gate and chided him for not following suit.

> The Chief, a long frock-coat flapping about his legs, suddenly, and without word, moved out from the group, took three or four quick strides along the gravel, cleared the gate, opened it, walked through, closed it again, and, without uttering a syllable on the subject, rejoined the party....Was it merely the act of an essentially simple and boyish nature, or was it a sermon on the text, 'Deeds, not words?'[39]

Not all observers searched Parnell's words and actions so closely for direction, of course, but most repected his authority. And the enigmatic character of many of his political pronouncements gave them room to believe that he agreed with them.

Many instances of the legacy phenomenon were, as we have seen, appeals to Parnell's authority in support of particular policies. "Charter myths" have as their principal function the legitimization of the status quo. Does the legitmizing function which these invocations of Parnell's legacy performed indicate that the Parnell Myth has been a charter myth for the modern Irish state? The answer is no, for two reasons. First, the claims made to Parnell's legacy in the Myth were on behalf of policies, not institutions, and charter myths are usually associated with institutions. More important, the dissatisfaction with the political present often stated or implied in the references to Parnell's legacy, especially in the references to his posthumous leadership, is the exact opposite of the fundamental assumption behind a charter myth. Charter myths legitimize; they explain why an institution or practice is satisfactory, not unsatisfactory. The Parnell Myth described a time better than the present, a Golden Age.

If it was not the basis of a charter myth for the Irish State, Parnell's legacy was a valuable political commodity in Ireland during the first half of the twentieth century. Just how valuable it was can be seen in the genesis of the style and office of the Irish premier. De Valera greatly admired Parnell and, as we have seen, claimed his legacy when opposing the Treaty. He also seems to have valued the Parnellian associations his followers evoked by calling him by Parnell's old title, "Chief." When, therefore, he was constructing the Constitution of 1937, he called the premier (whose office was fashioned after his own style of leadership) Taoiseach, a term evocative of chieftainship.[40] He did this deliberately, I think, in order to place Taoisigh in the line of leaders that went back beyond the Presidents of the Executive Council of the Irish Free State to Parnell, and, through him, to Daniel O'Connell and, perhaps, Henry Grattan. There was a special kind of legitimacy in this line of succession. Arland Ussher recognized it when he wrote of de Valera in 1950 that "he is, in spite of all, of the line of Grattan and Parnell and Swift--the Uncrowned Kings of Ireland."[41] (The list of chiefs or kings would, of course, vary with the political and cultural affiliations of its composer.)

In Chapter 7, I outlined the political context, the national question in Irish politics from 1891 to 1956. My purpose was to demonstrate that the values that constituted the central theme of the Parnell Myth, independence and dignity, also underlay the national question in the years under study. In this chapter, I have discussed the specific connections that existed between the Myth and its context, the Golden Age phenomenon, the perception of a leadership vacuum on the national question, and the legacy phenomenon. Taken together, these three elements indicate (1) that part of the appeal of Parnell's story was that it described a better time than the unsatisfactory present; (2) that that time was better because Parnell provided strong, successful leadership on the national question; (3) that contemporary leaders (before de Valera's success on that question between 1933 and 1945) were found lacking; and (4) that Parnell was still looked to for a kind of leadership, to represent the nation's aspirations to independence and dignity in a way that his successors (before de Valera, at least) had failed to do. In fact, it was the central symbol of the Parnell Myth, Parnell's attitude as portrayed in the stories told about him, that performed this representational function.

This role of the symbol was of crucial importance. We have already seen that the central theme and central symbol gave the Myth its unity and coherence. By having effect on the political culture in which the Myth existed, the central symbol added another dimension. It gave the Myth emotive power. The Myth, the collection of compatible, consistent stories published about Parnell, gave the central symbol its meaning. The central symbol, in turn, came to affect people's attitudes and actions outside of the telling and retelling of Parnell's story, to exercise influence on Irish politics and culture. And, whenever it acted in this way, whenever the image of the proud, defiant Irishman was evoked for some immediate purpose, the meaning of the symbol was reinforced (because it always stood for independence and dignity) and the unity and coherence of the Myth were strengthened. Parnell's symbolic attitude transcended the Parnell Myth, serving as the vehicle through which Myth influenced its political context and enabling the Myth to be reinforced by that context.

## Notes to Chapter 8

[1]John E. Redmond, speech in the Rotunda, Dublin, 9 October 1893, quoted in Weekly Freeman (Dublin), 14 October 1893.

[2]"The Shamrock and the Ivy," Irish Weekly Independent (Dublin), 12 January 1895.

[3]"The Whigs As Prophets," United Ireland (Dublin), 10 October 1896.

[4]William O'Brien, An Olive Branch in Ireland and Its History (London: Macmillan and Co., 1910), p. 67.

[5]See Conor Cruise O'Brien, "Timothy Michael Healy," in The Shaping of Modern Ireland, p. 172.

[6]Edward O'Dwyer, Irish Catholic, 20 June 1906, quoted in David W. Miller, Church, State and Nation in Ireland 1898-1921 (Dublin: Gill & Macmillan, 1973; Pittsburgh: University of Pittsburgh Press, 1973), p. 159.

[7]"Parnell," Sinn Féin (Dublin), 7 October 1911.

[8]Ibid.

[9]Robert O'Loughran, Redmond's Vindication (Dublin: Talbot Press, 1919), pp. 44-45, 170-71, 194, 210.

[10]Leading article, Irish Times (Dublin), 2 October 1911.

[11]R. M. Henry, The Evolution of Sinn Fein (New York: B. W. Heubsch, 1920), p. 40.

[12]Nora Connolly, The Unbroken Tradition, p. xiv.

[13]Dorothy Macardle, The Irish Republic, p. 55.

[14]P. S. O'Hegarty, A History of Ireland under the Union, p. 682.

[15]F. S. L. Lyons, Ireland since the Famine, pp. 428-29, 429n.; John A. Murphy, Ireland in the Twentieth Century, pp. 27-30; Earl of Longford and T. P. O'Neill, Eamon de Valera. p. 146.

[16]I indexed only the twentieth century evidence for characterizations of "Ireland after Parnell."

[17]Horace Plunkett, Ireland in the New Century (London: John Murray, 1904), pp. 5, 79; Gilbert Parker, "The New Ireland," review of ibid., in National Review, June 1904, p. 600.

[18]Algernon West, Diary (n.p., n.d.), quoted in Henry Harrison, Parnell Vindicated, p. 77.

[19]St. John Ervine, Parnell, p. 269, quoted in Mary T. Hayden, review of ibid., Studies 14 (September 1925): 489.

[20]William O'Brien, Evening Memories, p. 68.

[21]P. S. O'Hegarty, A History of Ireland under the Union, p. 605.

[22]Six items from four sources deny that a contemporary policy has anything to do with Parnell or his principles. Twelve items from eleven sources note that politicians are appealing to Parnell's legacy in some way.

[23]William O'Brien, "Parnell and Afterwards," review of Parnell, by St. John Ervine, in

English Review, October 1925, p. 522, reprinted in William O'Brien, The Parnell of Real Life, p. 209.

[24]Margaret Leamy, Parnell's Faithful Few, p. 213.

[25][William Butler Yeats], "Mourn--and Then Onward!" United Ireland (Dublin), 10 October 1891.

[26]J. J. O'Kelly, oration at Parnell anniversary demonstration, quoted in Weekly Freeman (Dublin), 15 October 1892.

[27]"From beyond the Grave," United Ireland (Dublin), 7 October 1893.

[28]William J. Walsh to David Sheehy, n.d., quoted in "Mr. Parnell's Fundamental Principle," Weekly Freeman (Dublin), 24 June 1892.

[29]J. T., "Another Reminiscence of Parnell," United Ireland (Dublin), 12 October 1895.

[30]William O'Brien, Recollections (London: Macmillan & Co., 1905), p. 333.

[31]Leading article, Irish Times (Dublin), 2 October 1911.

[32]I have found 40 quotations of this saying and 9 other references to it in the evidence.

[33]Ruaidhre MacAodha, Parnell, p. 15.

[34]Ireland, Dhail Éireann, Debate on the Treaty between Great Britain and Ireland, 19 December 1921, p. 27, quoted in Mary C. Bromage, De Valera and the March of a Nation, p. 153. Erskine Childers followed de Valera in the debate and he, too, quoted Parnell's dictum. Debate on the Treaty between Great Britain and Ireland, 19 December 1921, p. 41.

[35]Mary C. Bromage, De Valera and the March of a Nation, p. 162.

[36]R. M. Henry, The Evolution of Sinn Fein, p. 35.

[37]Padraic Pearse, Ghosts (Dublin: Wheland & Son, 1916), pp. 12-13.

[38]M. M. O'Hara, Chief and Tribune, pp. v-vi.

[39]J. M'G., "A Day at Carlow," United Ireland (Dublin), 5 October 1895.

[40]While Taoiseach is more frequently translated as leader, I have also seen it rendered as chief. The association of Taoiseach and chief certainly exists. Brian Farrell, for instance, entitled his study of the Taoiseach's role in Irish government Chairman or Chief?. Brian Farrell, Chairman or Chief? The Role of Taoiseach in Irish Government, Studies in Irish Political Culture, no. 1 (Dublin: Gill & Macmillan, 1971).

[41]Arland Ussher, The Face and Mind of Ireland (New York: Devin-Adair, 1950), p. 67.

# CHAPTER 9

# CONCLUSION

My principal conclusions about the Parnell Myth can be summarized briefly. The central theme, independence and dignity, and the central symbol, Parnell's attitude projecting those qualities, give it unity. The Myth also exhibits coherence: the various elements comprising it fit together well. They include the motifs--ancestry, Providence/destiny/fate, treachery/betrayal, tragedy, nationality, and contempt/disdain/scorn--as well as the metaphors, the metaphoric roles assigned to Parnell, the kingship symbol, the comparisons with other great men, and the speculations on What Might Have Been. These elements give the myth color, add to its appeal as a story, and support and enrich the central theme and central symbol. Parnell's symbolic attitude focuses the meaning of the Myth and endows it with great emotive power. This power enabled it to play a significant role in filling the leadership vacuum following Parnell's death. Two manifestations of the symbol's power are the legacy and Golden Age phenomena, which link the Myth with its political context.

I first became interested in the Parnell Myth through reading Yeats and Joyce. I wanted to know what it was that had so completely captured their imaginations. When I began to work on this study, I planned to examine the use of Parnell as a symbol in literature, after first analyzing how he was presented in the political writing read every day by both the literary artists and their audiences. The point of studying the political writing was to fill in as much as possible of the background against which the literary artists wrote. As my work proceeded, however, I began to suspect that some characteristics were true of the material as a whole, regardless of the political orientations of individual authors. This meant that the political writing, what I have called the Parnell Myth, required its own explication, and that an analysis of it, and of its relationship to its historical context, would itself require a full-length study. Furthermore, since the political writing greatly affected the context within which the artists worked, it needed to be studied first.

That was a fortunate decision. It probably prevented me from confining my analysis of the political writing to a search for antecedents of characteristics in the literary material, which would, of course, have led to very different conclusions about it. Instead, I was forced to examine the material on its own merits, and the sheer volume of evidence led me to adopt an inductive approach, in the form of the two indexes. Though flawed--ideally, the indexes should have been based on the original material rather than on my notes--this method enabled me to avoid the pitfalls described in Chapter 6, especially the questionable practice of basing conclusions about heterogenous material on what seem to be representative examples.

Parnell Myth is not a new term. In Chapter 6, I discussed the "Parnell myth" described by F. S. L. Lyons and Conor Cruise O'Brien, the shape of which they extrapolated from the works of Yeats, Joyce and certain Irish political writers. They were not, however, the first commentators to discuss a "Parnell myth" or "Parnell legend." In fact, the terms had been invented before Parnell was in the grave. The first number of United Ireland to appear after his death declared, in verse, that

> No, they will not forget him,
> 'They'll talk of him for years to come,
> In cottage, chronicle, and tale;
> When for ought else renown is dumb
> His legend shall prevail!'[1]

A year later, the Gladstonian Pall Mall Gazette cautioned that

> Legends don't always grow. They are sometimes made, and the manufacture of a Parnell legend which shall enshrine his memory as an intransigent is, as everyone knows, being carried on very briskly in Ireland.... Mr. [J. J.] O'Kelly industriously circulated the legend yesterday, and spoke of Mr. Parnell as if the object of his life had been to make cooperation with an English party impossible, and as if alliance with Mr. Gladstone had been to him as the accursed thing. This, of course, is a mythical Parnell, as everyone may see for himself by recalling Mr. Parnell's utterances.[2]

Gladstonian Liberals were not the only ones worried about the manufacture of a Parnell legend. Dublin's Unionist Daily Express warned in 1894 that

> If the efforts of the Parnellite Press were crowned with anything like success, it might be predicted that there would grow up a Parnell legend comparable with the Napoleonic legend and the half dozen or half score legends whereby certain portions of history are reduced to something little better than chaos. Already both enemies and friends are ascribing to the dead leader qualities he never possessed, only in a limited and qualified degree.[3]

Five years later, the same newspaper had to admit that

> The demonstration which took place in Dublin, however we may regard it, unquestionably furnished striking evidence of the hold which the Parnell legend

possesses on the popular mind in Ireland.[4]

That hold continued. Here is a sampling of comments publish

1948:

> ...Parnell's life--in which, as in the lives of so many r
> any number of legends.[5]

> For Parnell is already a legend, and though Mr. [William] O'Br ...ew book rightly scorns the 'transpontine drama' picturization of biographies like Mr. St. John Ervine's, a legend he will remain.[6]

> The legend of each [Parnell and Padraic Pearse] still persists.[7]

Finally, there is Denis Ireland's description of a Parnell Anniversary celebration, published in 1959, but, on internal evidence, probably written several years earlier. It concludes:

> As if we had ever forgotten. As if he was not always there, haunting the pages of A Portrait, in the hearts of the Irish people, in odd ballads still sung at country fairs, in the imagination of young dramatists seated at battered typewriters in shabby attic rooms--a haughty aristocratic presence at the mere breath of whose name it was still, fifty years on, as if somebody had exploded a battery of depth-charges deep down amongst the black sea caves and sunken wreckage of the Irish mind.[8]

That "haughty aristocratic presence" still remains, and it is literature, more than any other influence, that will not let us forget it. The Parnell of Parnellite Party rhetoric, the solitary hero battling both the priests and former colleagues afraid to stand up to English dictation and clerical intimidation, has captured writers' imaginations in a way that no other Irish political leader has done for centuries. It is partly the romantic story of the forbidden love and tragic fall, partly the compelling personality of the hero, partly the fact that some of Parnell's most conspicuous opponents also posed a threat to artistic freedom in subsequent years. For these and other reasons, artists have identified themselves with him and his final struggle, and made him their hero. The Parnell Myth obviously has a different focus from this literary Parnellism,[9] but there is one important similarity which should be noted. Independence and dignity are as crucial for the literary artist as for the authors of the Myth. Those values are, after all, basic constituents of the artist's integrity. An important difference between the Myth and literary Parnellism is that, while Parnell's attitude is the central symbol of the Myth, it is the man himself who seems to represent independence and dignity in the artists' work. This allows the artist to identify more closely with him. The artist admires Parnell's independence and n the face of familiar adversity, and often sees himself as acting out Parnell's y, living Parnell's myth, in his own career as an artist.

The Parnell Myth is important, even crucial, to an understanding of twentieth century Irish politics, but it is not the only popular phenomenon to play such a vital role. To place the Myth in proper historical perspective, it is necessary to recall the other "myths" and personality cults influential in Irish political life. First, of course, is Parnellism itself. Ever since Parnell's tragic last campaign, there has been a Parnellite myth--the creation that nineteenth century leader-writers warned against and Denis Ireland celebrated--and it persists to the present day. Among the tenets maintained by its adherents are that Parnell was the indispensable leader, the only one who could have secured Home Rule; that Home Rule was the last, best chance for a united, self-governing Ireland; that Parnell was brought low by a depressing combination of clerical intolerance, political cowardice, personal jealousy and Irish disunity; and that Ireland has still not recovered from the blow. This myth has had a powerful effect on individual Irish imaginations, many of them literary.

In States of Ireland, Conor Cruise O'Brien quotes a famous passage from Yeats's Nobel Prize acceptance speech and comments on its significance:

> 'The modern literature of Ireland, and indeed all that stir of thought which prepared for the Anglo-Irish war began when Parnell fell from power in 1891. A disillusioned and embittered Ireland turned from parliamentary politics and the race began, as I think, to be troubled by that event's long gestation.'
>
> The event was one thing, the way the event was imagined another thing, and more powerful. And there were men and women who lived through the event, and through the imagining of the event. Their lives, marked by this double experience, marked mine. And both the event and its imagining, and the consequences of the way in which it was imagined, helped powerfully to shape what happened in Ireland in the early twentieth century, and what is happening now.[10]

Note that, while Cruise O'Brien distinguishes between Parnell's fall and "the imagining of the event" and Yeats does not, both of them focus on the fall of Parnell, while the Parnell Myth centers on the great political confrontations of Parnell's career. This is the major difference between the two myths, and it leads to differences in the lessons to be drawn for contemporary politics. The Parnellite myth teaches that Irish politicians should resist clerical influence, stand up to the respectable middle class, and keep all English politicians at arm's length. The message of the Parnell Myth, different because it conveys meaning on a more fundamental level, is that independence of spirit is the essential thing and that it should be maintained above all.

A second potent political myth surrounds the 1916 Rising, with its saintly martyrs, antecedents in the Gaelic Revival, and idealistic Proclamation of the Republic. This myth, and not one of the ones centering on Parnell, is the charter myth for the modern Irish state. It explains the origin of the state, provides a suitable pantheon of heroes, and describes revolutionary ideals that are recalled on appropriate public occasions. Closely related to this myth, and to the events of 1916-23, are three potent personality cults, each celebrating an individual and the ideal he is taken to represent: Padraic Pearse (Gaelic culture), James Connolly (socialism) and Michael Collins (the strong leader, the Big Fellow). These personality cults focus on What Might Have Been had the careers of their heroes not been cut short, and they, along with the myth of the 1916 Rising, and its corollary, the myth of the first Dáil, also encourage a legacy phenomenon. Policy is still often justified in terms of them. The Parnell Myth coexists with these and other popular phenomena, and, together with them, constitutes the rich political culture of the modern Irish state.

My thesis about the Parnell Myth is based on the close relationship between the Myth and its Irish audience. But why should the Myth have been so responsive to the Irish portion of its audience when both its authors and their readers were drawn from people of three different nationalities? The evidence as a whole does, after all, exhibit the same characteristics as the Irish part of it. The answer is that the Parnell Myth was the product of a conflict based on nationality. As parties to the conflict, Irishmen and Englishmen knew very well what was at stake. Americans, as outside observers, seem to have accepted the frame of reference of the participants. (Irish Americans, of course, often counted as participants.) The motif of contempt/disdain/scorn is the key to understanding the dynamic: dignity and self-respect were at stake on the Irish side, while a sense of superiority and the right to rule were at stake on the English side. British rule in Ireland was supported by an ascendancy class and institutions of control (army, judiciary, police), all of which had English trappings. English imperialists justified this rule in terms of their natural superiority (demonstrated by their political institutions and commercial success as well as by the power of the British Empire) and Irish unfitness for self-government (as evidenced by chronic poverty, endemic agrarian crime and the secular power of the Roman Catholic clergy in Ireland). English and Irish participants did not merely recognize the issues at stake in their confrontations, but felt them deeply. It was not difficult for them, or even for American observers, to sense the meaning of Parnell's symbolic _attitude_ or its representation of Irish aspirations.

Examination of the Parnell Myth throws light on a number of historical questions. One of the most important conclusions to be drawn from it is that dignity was as important a constituent value of Irish nationalism as independence. The Irish, in other words, resisted not only English dominion but English contempt. The depth of emotion involved is obvious in the passages constituting the motif of contempt/disdain/scorn. Parnell's genius, as those passages testify, lay in his ability to turn the tables of contempt, to emerge from confrontations more the contemner than the contemned, and the Myth records those triumphs. Being a constitutional politician was for Parnell, in this respect, an advantage. As such, he operated in the House of Commons, the very seat of British imperial power, and his triumphs were, for that reason, all the more significant. The dignity component in Parnell's attitude was of crucial importance to the Irish nationalist.

So, of course, was the independence component. The Parnell Myth offers a significant insight into it as well. Parnell's independence existed on a more fundamental level than the traditional nationalist disagreements about means and ends. It was a radical independence of spirit, a total disregard of English opinion. In the Myth, it is most explicitly portrayed in Parnell's reply to Forster's indictment, an incident that looms much larger in the Myth than it would in a conventional biography. It was, on the face of it, merely a statement of principle, a refusal to justify his actions to a predominantly English assembly. The ordinary people back home, however, thrilled at Parnell's declaration that their opinion alone mattered to him, because, in making it, he placed them above their contemptuous rulers, did it in the House of Commons, and did it successfully. That is exactly the kind of independence his attitude represents in the Myth.

For a number of years now, historians have been trying to elucidate the system of unwritten rules which underlies Irish politics. The work done at the University of Chicago, for instance, suggests that the foundations of the modern Irish state were laid in the mid-1880s when Parnell formed a political alliance with the Roman Catholic bishops, created a formidable electoral machine as well as a disciplined parliamentary party, and began a gradual nationalist takeover of the adminstrative machinery, judiciary and local government of Ireland.[11] The history of the Parnell Myth reveals still more about that system. It demonstrates that the question of the nation's independence and dignity continued to be a significant factor in Irish politics long after the apparently decisive events of 1921-23 and until the new state's experiences in the 1930s and 1940s had confirmed that Ireland's independence, if limited, was also real.

The Myth also offers significant insight into the nature of the leadership that Parnell exercised during his lifetime. As the metaphorical roles assigned to him indicate, it consists of two distinct functions, direction and representation. Because the portion of the Myth's audience that could remember the living Parnell--or, at least, the press's representation of him--remained considerable throughout the Myth's formative years, it follows that the Parnell of the Myth must have been roughly consistent with the living Parnell's public image. This means that it must have included the same qualities of independence and dignity, and the same identification with Irish nationality, as his symbolic attitude in the Myth. The public image of the living Parnell must, therefore, have represented Irish nationalist aspirations in much the same way as his attitude does in the Myth.

This deduction leads to further conclusions about the leadership of nationalist Ireland.[12] F. S. L. Lyons says that Parnell gave the Irish back their self-respect. Others would argue that Daniel O'Connell had already done that. In either case, it is pretty obvious that O'Connell before Parnell, like de Valera after him, represented nationalist Ireland's highest aspirations to independence and dignity. This suggests the solution to a puzzling problem. The intuition that O'Connell, Parnell, and de Valera were special leaders, different in kind as well as degree from such worthy individuals as Isaac Butt, John Redmond and William T. Cosgrave, is a common one. Following this line of thought one step further, I would contend the first three leaders were different not because of the skill with which they guided the nation but because of the peculiar way in which they represented, even came to embody, its aspirations. The kind of independence they represented was different, too, because it went beyond constitutional formulas--on which they differed considerably--to an independence of spirit grounded in national self-respect.

The Myth also offers a key to understanding Parnell's historical contribution. It is far from the last word on the subject--not least because it emphasizes the national question at the expense of so many other issues--but it does provide insights and raise useful questions. Parnell died a commonly acknowledged Great Man. The first journalists and historians to assess his career took his stature for granted. More recently, however, revisionist historians have been asking just what he did accomplish and have attempted to answer this question in terms of such tangibles as legislation, net emigration, progress toward Home Rule, and the like. The Myth reminds us that Parnell's role as principal representative of the aspirations of his people must also be considered. His contemporaries considered him to be one of Europoe's great men for a reason: only one individual at a time can perform such a function for a nation, and, as the history of Ireland illustrates, the role often goes unfilled.

As with his career, the Myth offers insights into Parnell's influence on the years after his death without telling the full story. I have already discussed the importance of the Parnellite myth. Parnell's very disappearance from the scene also had a potent effect.

Not only did it deprive nationalist Ireland of a leader of the stature of O'Connell and de Valera, but it also removed the focussing instrument for much of Ireland's social, cultural and political energy. During his lifetime, Parnell had drawn tenant farmers, Fenians, laborers and others into his movement, harnessing their talent and enthusiasm and convincing them to subordinate their particular interests to the struggle for Home Rule. When he fell from power and Home Rule began to fade into the future, many of those who had followed him turned their energies to other concerns: the language movement, literary societies, Gaelic sports, agricultural cooperatives and separatist politics. By no means all of the activists in these areas were former Parnellites, but they had all been affected by Parnell's fall. Some were disillusioned and bitter, others actually relieved, but the lives of all of them were changed, and the years after Parnell were markedly different from those of his ascendancy.

What is the significance of the Parnell Myth in wider terms? It is important for what it tells us about the dynamics of nationalism. While each nation's history is in some respects unique, and, while Ireland, as a European nation, enjoyed certain advantages in its struggle to win an accepted place in the world community, at least some elements of its experience are shared by other small nations or other nations emerging from colonial status. The Myth demonstrates, first of all, the high values placed on independence, dignity and nationality and underlines the fundamental importance of the role that dignity and self-respect play in the question of independence. (It is so fundamental that, throughout my work on this study, it has been frustrating to not have had available a word which meant independence combined with dignity.) It clarifies the distinction between political independence and the independence of spirit, represented in the Myth by Parnell's <u>attitude</u>, that satisfies nationalist aspirations. It demonstrates the need that nations feel for psychological as well as de jure independence--and reminds us that, for small nations, the question of independence is never fully put to rest. The Myth reflects the extent to which a small or emerging nation may perceive all political problems involving a powerful neighbor or native/alien ascendancy class simply as conflicts of nationality. Finally, it demonstrates the crucial importance attached to the leader's role in representing the nation's aspirations, a role so vital that, should he disappear and not be fully succeeded in it by his erstwhile successor, it may be filled by stories about the man himself.

The idea behind this study is that the stories people tell about the past may reveal important things about their present condition and how they perceive it. The Parnell Myth does this, and more. It demonstrates that the national question remained a vital issue for Irishmen until the middle of this century and that the values of independence and dignity were, for them, inextricably linked. It also affords an insight into the relationship between Parnell and his people, allowing a fuller understanding of his role as leader. To many modern people, a myth is a story which distorts reality. The Parnell Myth, when carefully examined, comes closer to the ancients' idea of myth: a story that enables us to see reality more clearly and appreciate its meaning more fully.

## Notes to Chapter 9

[1]"The Week's Work," United Ireland (Dublin), 10 October 1891.

[2]Pall Mall Gazette, 10 October 1892, quoted in "The Parnell Legend," Weekly Freeman (Dublin), 15 October 1892.

[3]Leading article, Daily Express (Dublin), 8 October 1894.

[4]Leading article, Daily Express (Dublin), 9 October 1899.

[5]T. P. O'Connor, "Orators Who Have Influenced Me," p. 21.

[6]M. J. MacM., review of Parnell: The Last Five Years, by Alfred J. Robbins, and of The Parnell of Real Life, by William O'Brien, in Dublin Magazine, April-June 1926, p. 60.

[7]John J. Horgan, Parnell to Pearse, p. vii.

[8]Denis Ireland, "October Afternoon at Glasnevin," p. 35.

[9]So far as I can tell, Conor Cruise O'Brien coined the phrase "literary Parnellism." Conor Cruise O'Brien, "Parnellism of Séan O'Faoláin," Irish Writing, July 1948, pp. 59-75, reprinted in Conor Cruise O'Brien, Maria Cross: Imaginative Patterns in a Group of Modern Catholic Writers, 2nd ed. (London: Burns & Oates, 1963), pp. 87-105.

[10]Conor Cruise O'Brien, States of Ireland, p. 23.

[11]Emmet Larkin, The Roman Catholic Church and the Creation of the Modern Irish State, 1878-86 (Philadelphia: American Philosophical Society, 1975); Emmet Larkin, The Roman Catholic Church and the Plan of Campaign in Ireland 1886-88 (Cork: Cork University Press, 1978); Emmet Larkin, The Roman Catholic Church in Ireland and the Fall of Parnell 1888-91 (Chapel Hill: University of North Carolina Press, 1979); Emmet Larkin, The Historical Dimensions of Irish Catholicism (New York: Arno Press, 1976); William L. Feingold, The Revolt of the Tenantry: The Transformation of Local Government in Ireland, 1872-1886, with a foreword by Emmet Larkin (Boston: Northeastern University Press, 1984); Michael V. Hazel, "Charles Stewart Parnell and the Creation of the Modern Irish State, 1874-86," Ph.D. thesis, University of Chicago, 1974; Lawrence W. McBride, "The Administrative and Judicial Elite in Ireland, 1892-1922," Ph.D. thesis, University of Chicago, 1978; David W. Miller, Church, State and Nation in Ireland 1898-1921 (Pittsburgh: University of Pittsburgh Press, 1973).

[12]I first advanced this argument in "The Parnellian Tradition."

## BIBLIOGRAPHY

### Chronological Bibliography of Sources for the Parnell Myth

Note: Sources marked with an asterisk (*) were not indexed.


Annual Register for 1891

Dutton, G. H. J. A Delineation of the Character and Talents of the Late C. S. Parnell, M.P. and the Right Hon. W. H. Smith, M.P. Skegness: G. H. J. Dutton, [1891].

The Last Home-coming: A Parable. Dublin: C. W. Gibbs, [1891].

McCarthy, Michael J. F. Mr. Balfour's Rule in Ireland. Dublin: Hodges, Figgis & Co., 1891.

McWade, Robert M. The Uncrowned King: The Life and Public Services of Hon. Charles Stewart Parnell. N.p.: Edgewood Publishing Co., 1891.

O'Connor, T. P. Charles Stewart Parnell: A Memory. London: Ward, Lock, Bowden & Co., 1891.

Sullivan, Donal. The Story of "Room 15". Collection of a series of articles from National Press (Dublin), 21 November-5 December 1891. Dublin: National Press Co., 1891.

"Dead!" Evening Press (Dublin), 7 October 1891. Reprinted in Dublin Evening Mail, 7 October 1891.

Clancy, John. Speech at National Club, Dublin, 7 October 1891. "Meeting at the National Club." National Press (Dublin), 8 October 1891.

Primrose. "Charles Stewart Parnell." Dublin Evening Mail, 8 October 1891.

"Sketch of His Life and Career." Daily Express (Dublin), 8 October 1891.

[Tuohy, J. M.]. Reminiscences of Charles Stewart Parnell. Freeman's Journal (Dublin), 8 October 1891. Reprinted in Dublin Evening Mail, 8 October 1891, in Evening Telegraph (Dublin), 8, 9 October 1891, in Weekly Freeman (Dublin), 17 October 1891.

Tynan, Andrew. Speech at National Club, Dublin, 7 October 1891. "Meeting at the National Club." National Press (Dublin), 8 October 1891.

Butterly, J. Speech at Irish National Federation, Inchicore, 8 October 1891. Quoted in National Press (Dublin), 9 October 1891.

"Charles Stewart Parnell." England and Primrose Record (London), 10 October 1891.

"Charles Stewart Parnell." Irish Catholic and Nation (Dublin), 10 October 1891.

"The Dead Chief." United Ireland (Dublin), 10 October 1891.

[McGrath, John]. "Done to Death." United Ireland (Dublin), 10 October 1891.

"Mr. Parnell As I Knew Him (By a Physical Force Man)." United Ireland (Dublin), 10 October 1891.

"News of the Week." Spectator, 10 October 1891, p. 481.

"The Reptile Press of Ireland." United Ireland (Dublin), 10 October 1891.

"Some Personal Recollections of Mr. Parnell (By One of His Parliamentary Followers)." United Ireland (Dublin), 10 October 1891.

"Topics of the Day: The Death of Mr. Parnell." Spectator, 10 October 1891, pp. 484-85.

"The Week's Work." United Ireland (Dublin), 10 October 1891.

Whitehall Review, n.d. Reprinted as "Some False Impressions of Mr. Parnell (By an Irish M.P. in the Whitehall Review)." Irish Times (Dublin), 13 October 1891.

[Godkin, E. L.]. "Parnell." Nation (New York), 15 October 1891, p. 289.

[Labouchere, Henry]. "Charles Stewart Parnell: Obiit October 6, 1891." Truth, 15 October 1891, p. 772.

"Funeral of Charles Stewart Parnell, M.P." Irish Ecclesiastical Gazette (Dublin), 16 October 1891.

Healy, Timothy M. Speech at Cavan, 15 October 1891. Quoted in Daily Express (Dublin), 16 October 1891.
Parnell, Delia T. S. Interview. Daily News (London), n.d. Reprinted in Dublin Evening Mail, 16 October 1891, in National Press (Dublin), 16 October 1891.
Buchanan, Robert. Untitled poem. Echo (London), n.d. Quoted in "Englishmen Reproach Irish Ingratitude." United Ireland (Dublin), 17 October 1891.
Burnett, W. H. Letter. United Ireland (Dublin), 17 October 1891.
"A Fallen Leader." Punch, 17 October 1891. Quoted in Dublin Evening Mail, 19 October 1891.
"Continental Opinion on Mr. Parnell." Irish Catholic and Nation (Dublin), 17 October 1891.
H. H. J. Untitled poem. United Ireland (Dublin), 17 October 1891.
"The 'King' Is Dead." Harper's Weekly, 17 October 1891, p. 795.
Mary. Untitled tribute to Charles Stewart Parnell. United Ireland (Dublin), 17 October 1891.
"The Memory of the Dead: By a Suir Priest." Tipperary News (Neenagh, Co. Tipperary), n.d. Reprinted in United Ireland (Dublin), 17 October 1891.
"Parnell." Harper's Weekly, 17 October 1891, p. 791.
Redmond, William. "The Price." United Ireland (Dublin), 17 October 1891.
"The Spirit of Parnellism." Irish Catholic and Nation (Dublin), 17 October 1891.
Tynan, Katharine. "A Wandering Star." United Ireland (Dublin), 17 October 1891.
"A Ludicrous Story." Daily Express (Dublin), 19 October 1891.
"Dead Caesar's Brutus (From a Correspondent)." Dublin Evening Mail, 21 October 1891.
Review of Charles Stewart Parnell: A Memory, by T. P. O'Connor. Dublin Evening Mail, 21 October 1891.
"The Duty of a Catholic Journalist: A Word to Our Assailants." Irish Catholic and Nation (Dublin), 24 October 1891.
"Liberal Opinion on Leader-killers." United Ireland (Dublin), 24 October 1891.
"Too Late." United Ireland (Dublin), 24 October 1891.
Cahill, Richard Staunton. "In Memoriam." United Ireland (Dublin), 24 October 1891.
Morley, John. Speech at Manchester Reform Club, Manchester, 26 October 1891. Quoted in "Mr. Morley at Manchester." Times (London), 27 October 1891.
Bryce, James [O. D.] "Charles Stewart Parnell." Nation (New York), 29 October 1891, pp. 330-33. Reprinted in James Bryce. Studies in Contemporary Biography. London: Macmillan & Co., 1903. Pp. 227-49.
Taylor, U. Ashworth. Untitled poem. United Ireland (Dublin), 31 October 1891.
W. I. P. "Ireland's Leader." United Ireland (Dublin), 31 October 1891.
McCarthy, Justin. "Charles Stewart Parnell." Contemporary Review, November 1891, pp. 625-36. Reprinted in Living Age, 12 December 1891, pp. 669-76. Excerpted in Freeman's Journal (Dublin), 30 October 1891.
"The Progress of the World: Irish Politics." American Review of Reviews November 1891, p. 372.
[Shaw, Albert]. "Three Fallen Leaders: I. Parnell--'The Uncrowned King of Ireland.' " American Review of Reviews, November 1891, pp. 417-20.
[Shaw, Albert]. "Three Fallen Leaders: II. Boulanger--An Episode in French History." American Review of Reviews, November 1891, pp. 421-26.
[Stead, W. T. ] "The Progress of the World." Review of Reviews, November 1891, pp. 437-39.
Healy, Timothy M. Speech at Longford, 1 November 1891. Quoted in Dublin Evening Mail, 2 November 1891.
Chicago Figaro, n.d. Reprinted as "Parnell and the Ghouls." United Ireland (Dublin), 7 November 1891.
"De Mortuis Nil Nisi Bonum." Catholic Union and Times (Buffalo, N. Y.), n.d. Reprinted in United Ireland (Dublin), 7 November 1891.

Farnham, T. H. "Parnell." New England Magazine, December 1891, p. 469.
Lister, Thomas [Baron Ribblesdale]. "A Railway Journey with Mr. Parnell." Nineteenth Century, December 1891, pp. 969-74.
St. John, Ralph D. "Charles Stewart Parnell." Chautauquan, December 1891, pp. 321-25.
Beach, Thomas [Major Henri Le Caron]. Twenty-five Years in the Secret Service: The Recollections of a Spy. 2d ed. London: William Heinemann, 1892.
Denvir, John. The Irish in Britain: From the Earliest Times to the Fall and Death of Parnell. London: Kegan Paul, Trench, Trübner & Co., 1892.
Lucy, Henry. A Diary of the Salisbury Parliament. London: Cassell & Co., 1892.
Mac and O'. The Parnell Leadership and Home Rule: From an Historical, Ethical and Ethnological Point of View. Dublin: Gill & Son, 1892.
Traill, H. D. "Parnell and Butt: A Dialogue in the Shades." Fortnightly Review, 1 January 1892, pp. 115-26.
"1891." Weekly Freeman (Dublin), 9 January 1892.
"Mr. Parnell's Fundamental Principle." Weekly Freeman (Dublin), 25 June 1892.
"Ivy Day" [advertisement]. Irish Daily Independent (Dublin), 4, 5 October 1892.
"Ivy Day" [advertisement]. Irish Daily Independent (Dublin), 6 October 1892.
Tynan, Katharine. "The Green Ivy." Irish Daily Independent (Dublin), 7 October 1892.
"What He Was to the Irish Exile." United Ireland (Dublin), 8 October 1892.
Curtis, William O'Leary. "The Commemoration." United Ireland (Dublin), 15 October 1892.
Pall Mall Gazette, 10 October 1892. Quoted in "The Parnell Legend." Weekly Freeman (Dublin), 15 October 1892.
Curtain, Jeremiah C.; Luby, Thomas C.; and Walsh, Robert F. The Story of Ireland's Struggle for Self-government: With the Lives and Times of Her Great Leaders. New York: Gay Bros. & Co., 1893.
O'Brien, William. Irish Ideas. London: Longmans, Green & Co., 1893.
[Elliot, Arthur R.] "The Great Irish Conspiracy." Review of Twenty-five Years in the Secret Service, by Thomas Beach. Edinburgh Review, January 1893, pp. 247-81.
"Topics of the Day: Banquo's Ghost." Spectator, 15 April 1893, pp. 473-74.
"Letters to the Editor: Mr. Gladstone and Mr. Parnell." Spectator, 29 April 1893, pp. 570-71.
[Ormsby-Gore, Seymour F.] "Priest-ridden Ireland." Blackwood's Magazine, August 1893, pp. 264-71.
Carew, James L. "My Captain and Friend." Irish Weekly Independent (Dublin), 7 October 1893.
Graves, Percival. " A Lament." Irish Songs and Ballads. Manchester: A. Ireland & Co., 1880. Reprinted in United Ireland (Dublin), 7 October 1893.
Leamy, Edmund. Speech at National Club, Dublin, 6 October 1893. Daily Express (Dublin), 7 October 1893.
"Parnell the Irishman." United Ireland (Dublin), 14 October 1893.
[Frederick, Harold]. "The Ireland of To-day." Fortnightly Review, 1 November 1893, pp. 686-706.
Healy, Timothy M. "A Great Man's Fancies." Westminster Gazette, 3 November 1893. Reprinted in Dublin Evening Mail, 3 November 1893; Daily Express (Dublin), 3 November 1893; Evening Telegraph (Dublin), 3 November 1893; Weekly Freeman (Dublin) 11 November 1893; R. Barry O'Brien, The Life of Charles Stewart Parnell 1846-1891. 3rd ed. 2 vols. London: Smith, Elder & Co., 1899. 1: 361-63.
X. "The Rhetoricians of Ireland." Fortnightly Review, 1 December 1893, pp. 713-27.
O'Grady, Standish. The Story of Ireland. London: Methuen & Co., 1894.
Tynan, Patrick J. P. The Irish National Invincibles and Their Times. London: Chatham & Co., 1894.
[Milman, Archibald]. "The Peril of Parliament." Quarterly Review, January 1894, pp. 263-88.

Lex. "The Story of the Parnell Commission." Green Bag, August 1894, pp. 362-70.
"The Courage of Parnell." United Ireland (Dublin), 6 October 1894.
The Century Cyclopedia of Names (1895 ed.) S.v. "Parnell, Charles Stewart."
Dictionary of National Biography (1895 ed.) S.v. "Parnell, Charles Stewart."
"Books: Mr. Parnell." Review of Dictionary of National Biography, s.v. "Parnell, Charles Stewart." Spectator, 6 July 1895, pp. 19-20.
Fitzgerald, T. D. "The Genesis of Parnell's Leadership." United Ireland (Dublin), 5 October 1895.
J. M'G. "A Day at Carlow." United Ireland (Dublin), 5 October 1895.
Meade, P. H. Speech at Cork, 4 October 1895. Quoted in Irish Daily Independent (Dublin), 5 October 1895.
J. B. K. "American Opinions on Mr. Parnell." United Ireland (Dublin), 12 October 1895.
"Parnell and Our Policy." United Ireland (Dublin), 12 October 1895.
"Reminiscences of Parnell's Visit to America: By an Exile." United Ireland (Dublin), 12 October 1895.
Hopkins, Tighe. Kilmainham Memories. London: Ward, Lock, Bowden & Co., 1896.
O'Leary, John. Recollections of Fenians and Fenianism. 2 vols. London: Downey & Co., 1896; reprint ed., Shannon: Irish University Press, 1969.
O'Brien, William. "London Revisited: Some Reminiscences." Contemporary Review, June 1896, pp. 805-12.
O'Connor, T. P. "Home Rule and the Irish Party." Contemporary Review, August 1896, pp. 179-90.
"Ivy Day in Dublin." Irish Daily Independent (Dublin), 7 October 1896.
"The Last Days of Charles Stewart Parnell." United Ireland (Dublin), 10 October 1896.
"Our Fealty to the Dead: By Our Special Correspondent in England." United Ireland (Dublin), 10 October 1896.
"Parnell Anniversary Supplement." Irish Daily Independent (Dublin), 12 October 1896.
O'Brien, William. "Was Mr. Parnell Badly Treated?" Contemporary Review, November 1896, pp. 678-94.
McCarthy, Justin. A History of Our Own Times. Vol. 5: From 1880 to the Diamond Jubilee. London: Chatto & Windus, 1897.
[Elliot, Arthur R.] "Our Own Times and Oxford Liberals." Review of A History of Our Own Times, by Justin McCarthy. Edinburgh Review, October 1897, pp. 483-504.
"Mr. Dillon, Mr. Redmond, Mr. Parnell: Disclosures by Mr. W. O'Brien." American Review of Reviews, January 1897, pp. 77-78.
"The Dead Lion." Irish Weekly Independent (Dublin), 2 October 1897.
"After Death." Irish Daily Independent (Dublin), 6 October 1897.
Leading article. Dublin Evening Mail, 11 October 1897. Reprinted in Daily Express (Dublin), 12 October 1897.
"Parnell and Cork." Irish Daily Independent (Dublin), 12 October 1897.
Healy, Timothy M. Why Ireland Is Not Free: A Study of Twenty Years in Irish Politics. Dublin: Nation Co., 1898.
McCarthy, Justin. The Story of Gladstone's Life. London: Adam & Charles Black, 1898.
Morris, William O'Connor. Ireland 1798-1898. London: A. D. Innes, 1898.
Redmond, John E. "Fifteen Years in the House of Commons." Speech at New York, 29 November 1896; in Ireland, as part of "Irish Popular Leaders from Swift to Parnell," 1898. Published in Historical and Political Addresses 1883-1897, by John E. Redmond. Dublin: Sealy, Bryers & Walker, 1898; London: Simpkin, Marshall, Hamilton, Kent, & Co., 1898. Pp. 1-30.
Redmond, John E. "Ireland since '98." North American Review, April 1898, pp. 385-97.
MacDonagh, Michael. "Great Men: Their Simplicity and Ignorance." Cornhill Magazine, October 1898, pp. 498-509.
Johnson, Lionel. "The Man Who Would Be King." Review of The Life of Charles Stewart Parnell 1846-1891, by R. Barry O'Brien. Academy, 19 November 1898, pp. 293-94.

"The Life of Parnell." Review of The Life of Charles Stewart Parnell 1846-1891, by R. Barry O'Brien. Spectator, 19 November 1898, pp. 740-42, 26 November 1898, pp. 776-78.

[Stead, W. T.] "The Book of the Month: Parnell the Avenger." Review of The Life of Charles Stewart Parnell 1846-1891, by R. Barry O'Brien. Review of Reviews, December 1898, pp. 599-606.

Garvin, J. Louis. "Parnell and His Power." Review of The Life of Charles Stewart Parnell 1846-1891, by R. Barry O'Brien. Fortnightly Review, 1 December 1898, pp. 872-83. Excerpted as "Parnell As an Inter-racial Type." American Review of Reviews, January 1899, p. 94.

McCarthy, Justin. "Charles Stewart Parnell." Reminiscences. 2 vols. London: Chatto & Windus, 1899. 2: 89-116.

O'Brien, R. Barry. The Life of Charles Stewart Parnell 1846-1891. 3d ed. 2 vols. London: Smith, Elder & Co., 1899.

"Charles Stewart Parnell." Review of The Life of Charles Stewart Parnell 1846-1891, by R. Barry O'Brien. Westminster Review, January 1899, pp. 1-12.

[Millar, J. H.] "The Rebel King." Review of The Life of Charles Stewart Parnell 1846-1891, by R. Barry O'Brien. Blackwood's Magazine, January 1899, pp. 138-50.

E. G. J. "Parnell, Irish Patriot and Nationalist." Review of The Life of Charles Stewart Parnell 1846-1891, by R. Barry O'Brien. Dial, 1 February 1899, pp. 74-76.

[Webb, Alfred]. "Parnell." Review of The Life of Charles Stewart Parnell 1846-1891, by R. Barry O'Brien. Nation (New York), 9 February 1899, pp. 106-7, 16 February 1899, pp. 123-24.

[Elliot, Arthur R.] "Parnell and His Work." Review of The Life of Charles Stewart Parnell 1846-1891, by R. Barry O'Brien. Edinburgh Review, April 1899, pp. 543-72.

O'Shea, John J. Review of The Life of Charles Stewart Parnell 1846-1891, by R. Barry O'Brien, and of "Parnell the Avenger," by W. T. Stead. American Catholic Quarterly Review, April 1899, pp. 40-57.

Courtney, Leonard. "Parnell and Ireland." Review of The Life of Charles Stewart Parnell 1846-1891, by R. Barry O'Brien. Nineteenth Century, June 1899, pp. 880-90. Excerpted as "Mr. Courtney on the Secret of Parnell." Review of Reviews, June 1899, p. 548.

de Kay, Charles. "An Intellectual Phenomenon." Review of The Life of Charles Stewart Parnell 1846-1891, by R. Barry O'Brien. Critic, August 1899, pp. 729-32.

Hannigan, D. F. "Parnell and Cromwell: A Dialogue between Two Ghosts." Westminster Review, September 1899, pp. 244-48.

Vindex. Cecil Rhodes: His Political Life and Speeches 1881-1900. London: Chapman & Hall, 1900.

"Parnell Day." Irish Daily Independent (Dublin), 8 October 1900.

Redmond, John E. "Irish National Reunion." Arena, April 1900, pp. 353-57.

Leading article. Weekly Freeman and National Press (Dublin), 13 October 1900.

McCarthy, Justin. Ireland and Her Story. New York: Funk & Wagnalls, 1903.

Morley, John. The Life of William Ewart Gladstone. 3 vols. New York: Macmillan Co., 1903.

Davitt, Michael. The Fall of Feudalism in Ireland: Or the Story of the Land League Revolution. London: Harper & Bros., 1904.

Cobbe, Frances Power. Life of Frances Power Cobbe As Told by Herself. London: Swan Sonnenschein, 1904.

Plunkett, Horace. Ireland in the New Century. London: John Murray, 1904.

Adams, Richard. "Men I Have Met: Parnell." Irish Packet, 12 March 1904, pp. 563-64.

An Old Reporter. "Leaves from My Private Notebook: A Day with Parnell." Irish Packet, 26 March 1904, p. 653.

Parker, Gilbert. "The New Ireland." Review of Ireland in the New Century, by Horace Plunkett. National Review, June 1904, pp. 579-609.

Cunninghame-Graham, R. B. "An Tighearna: A Memory of Parnell." Dana: A Magazine of Independent Thought, November 1904, pp. 193-99.

Fox, James. "Mr. Davitt's History of the Land League." Review of The Fall of Feudalism in Ireland, by Michael Davitt. Catholic World, December 1904, pp. 300-12.

"Mr. Parnell's Superstition." Irish Packet, 17 December 1904, p. 295.

"The Late Mr. Leamy." Irish Packet, 31 December 1904, p. 343.

Dickinson, Emily Monroe. A Patriot's Mistake: Being Personal Recollections of the Parnell Family by a Daughter of the House. Dublin: Hodges, Figgis & Co., 1905; London: Simpkin, Marshall & Co., 1905.

McCarthy, Justin. An Irishman's Story. New York: Macmillan Co., 1905.

O'Brien, William. Recollections. London: Macmillan & Co., 1905.

Sullivan, T. D. Recollections of Troubled Times in Irish Politics. Dublin: Gill & Son, 1905.

Anderson, Robert. Sidelights on the Home Rule Movement. London: John Murray, 1906.

Hubbard, Elbert. Little Journeys to the Homes of Great Lovers: Charles Parnell and Kitty O'Shea. East Aurora, N. Y.: Roycrofters, 1906.

An Irish Nationalist. "Home Rule, Rome Ruin." National Review, February 1906, pp. 1031-39.

"The Three Tragic Loves of Charles Stewart Parnell." Review of A Patriot's Mistake, by Emily Monroe Dickinson. Current Literature, May 1906, pp. 494-96.

Sheehy-Skeffington, Francis. Michael Davitt: Revolutionary Agitator and Labour Leader. London: T. Fisher Unwin, 1908; reprint ed., London: MacGibbon & Kee, 1967.

Butler, William. "Parnell." Lecture, n.p., 1908. Published in The Light of the West with Some Other Wayside Thoughts 1865-1908. Dublin: Gill & Son, 1909. Pp. 52-91.

D'Alton, E. A. History of Ireland. 3 vols. London: Gresham Publishing Co., 1910.

Denvir, John. The Life Story of an Old Rebel. Dublin: Sealy, Bryers & Walker, 1910; reprint ed., Shannon: Irish University Press, 1972.

St. Helier, Mary Jeune. Memories of Fifty Years. London: Edward Arnold, 1910.

O'Brien, R. Barry. The Life of Charles Stewart Parnell. Preface by John E. Redmond. 1 vol. ed. London: Thomas Nelson & Sons, [1910].

O'Brien, William. An Olive Branch in Ireland and Its History. London: Macmillan & Co., 1910.

O'Donnell, F[rank] Hugh. A History of the Irish Parliamentary Party. 2 vols. Vol 1: Butt and Parnell: Nationhood and Anarchy: The Curse of the American Money. Vol. 2: Parnell and the Lieutenants: Complicity and Betrayal: With an Epilogue to the Present Day. London: Longmans, Green & Co., 1910.

McDermot, George. "Sir Robert Anderson's 'Parnellism and Crime.'" Review of "The Lighter Side of My Official Life," [Blackwood's Magazine, October 1909-June 1910], by Robert Anderson. American Catholic Quarterly Review, April 1910, pp. 320-35.

Holland, Bernard. The Life of Spencer Compton, Eighth Duke of Devonshire. 2 vols. London: Longmans, Green, & Co., 1911.

Redmond, John E. "Where Parnell Stood." Reprinted from T. P.'s Magazine, February 1911. Westminster: Irish Press Agency, [1911].

An Philbin. "In Memoriam: Charles Stewart Parnell." Sinn Féin (Dublin), 30 September 1911.

Leading article. Irish Times (Dublin), 2 October 1911.

Morning Post (London), n.d., quoted in Irish Daily Independent (Dublin), 2 October 1911.

"Parnell Monument." Irish Daily Independent (Dublin), 2 October 1911.

"The Parnell Statue." Dublin Evening Mail, 2 October 1911.

"Parnell's Memory: The Statue Unveiled." Irish Daily Independent (Dublin), 2 October 1911.

Neil, Crawford. "Parnell," Sinn Féin (Dublin), 7 October 1911.

"Parnell." Sinn Féin (Dublin), 7 October 1911.

Praed, Rosa C. [Mrs. Campbell Praed], ed. Our Book of Memories: Letters of Justin McCarthy to Mrs. Campbell Praed. London: Chatto & Windus, 1912.

Lucy, Henry. "Sixty Years in the Wilderness: More Passages by the Way XXII: Poles Apart: William Henry Smith, Charles Stewart Parnell." Cornhill Magazine, August 1912, pp. 249-56.

O'Connnor, T. P. "Orators Who Have Influenced Me." Harper's Weekly, 30 August 1913, pp. 21-22.

O'Brien, William. "Two Pages of Secret History." Cork Free Press, 6 September 1913.

Parnell, Katharine O'Shea. Charles Stewart Parnell: His Love Story and Political Life. 2 vols. New York: George H. Doran Co., 1914.

O'Donnell, Frank Hugh. The Lost Hat: The Clergy, the Collection, the Hidden Life. [London: Murray & Co., 1914].

Parnell, Katharine O'Shea. "The Love Story of Charles Stewart Parnell." Daily Sketch (London), 5-30 May (except 10, 17, 24 May) 1914.

"Books: Charles Stewart Parnell (Communicated)." Review of Charles Stewart Parnell, by Katharine Parnell. Spectator, 30 May 1914, pp. 912-14, 6 June 1914, pp. 953-54.

Review of Charles Stewart Parnell, by Katharine Parnell. English Review, June 1914, pp. 421-22.

MacNeill, J. G. Swift. "The Tory-Parnell Home Rule Alliance, 1885." Fortnightly Review, 1 June 1914, pp. 999-1008.

Figgis, Darrell. "Charles Stewart Parnell." Review of Charles Stewart Parnell, by Katharine Parnell. Nineteenth Century and After, July 1914, pp. 217-27. Reprinted in Living Age, 22 August 1914, pp. 495-503. Reprinted with revisions, in Bye-ways of Study. Dublin: Talbot Press, 1918. Pp. 1-24.

"Parnell and Mrs. O'Shea." Review of Charles Stewart Parnell, by Katharine Parnell. Nation (New York), 5 November 1914, pp. 551-52.

Larson, Laurence M. "New Memories of Charles Stewart Parnell." Review of Charles Stewart Parnell, by Katharine Parnell. Dial, 16 December 1914, pp. 498-500.

Kettle, Thomas M. Irish Orators and Oratory. Dublin: Gresham Publishing Co., 1915.

Boyce, Neith. "Books and Men." Review of Charles Stewart Parnell, by Katharine Parnell. Harper's Weekly, 20 February 1915, p. 187.

Parnell, John Howard. Charles Stewart Parnell: A Memoir. London: Constable & Co., 1916.

Pearse, Padraic. Ghosts. Dublin: Whelan & Son, 1916.

Russell, George W. E. "Four Demagogues." Portraits of the Seventies. New York: Charles Scribner's Sons, [1916]. Pp. 171-226.

MacNeill, J. G. Swift. "Rhodes and Parnell on Imperial Federation." Fortnightly Review, 1 July 1916, pp. 89-99.

"Parnell Anniversary." Weekly Independent (Dublin), 14 October 1916.

Barker, Ernest. Ireland in the Last Fifty Years (1866-1916). Oxford: Clarendon Press, 1917.

R. L. "The Historical Basis of Irish Nationalism IV." New Statesman, 3 March 1917, pp. 511-13.

Connolly, Nora. The Unbroken Tradition. New York: Boni & Liveright, 1918.

Hughes, Katherine. Ireland. New York: Friends of Irish Freedom, 1918.

O'Brien, William. "Parnell and His Liberal Allies." Review of Recollections, by John Morley. Nineteenth Century and After, January 1918, pp. 170-83. Reprinted in William O'Brien, The Parnell of Real Life. London: T. Fisher Unwin, 1926. Pp. 150-79.

Barker, Ernest. Ireland in the Last Fifty Years. New & enl. ed. Oxford: Clarendon Press, 1919.

O'Hara, M. M. Chief and Tribune: Parnell and Davitt. Dublin: Maunsel & Co., 1919.

O'Loughran, Robert. Redmond's Vindication. Dublin: Talbot Press, 1919.

Horgan, John J. Review of Chief and Tribune, by M. M. O'Hara. Studies 8 (June 1919): 315-17.

Henry, R. M. The Evolution of Sinn Fein. New York: B. W. Heubsch, 1920.

Hutchinson, Horace G. "Charles Stewart Parnell." Portraits of the Eighties. London: T. Fisher Unwin, 1920. Pp. 27-44.

Keating, Joseph. "Parnell." In Great Irishmen in War and Politics. Edited by Felix Lavery. London: Andrew Melrose, 1920. Pp. 44-59.

MacDonagh, Michael. The Home Rule Movement. Dublin: Talbot Press, 1920.

O'Brien, William. Evening Memories. Dublin: Maunsel & Co., 1920.

Stone, Melville E. "Things Seen." Collier's: The National Weekly, 26 June 1920, pp. 8-9, 36, 38.

Gwynn, Stephen. The Irish Situation. London: Jonathan Cape, 1921.

Sheehan, D. D. Ireland since Parnell. London: Daniel O'Connor, 1921.

O'Connor, T. P. "The Life Drama of the Parnells." Daily Telegraph (London), n.d. Reprinted in Living Age, 26 March 1921, pp. 776-85, 2 April 1921, pp. 56-61.

"Illustrations of Topical Interest." Irish Independent (Dublin), 7 October 1921.

Ireland. Dhail Éireann. Debate on the Treaty between Great Britain and Ireland (1921).

Wilson, P. W. "Ireland As a Free State." American Review of Reviews, January 1922, pp. 52-58.

Stewart, Herbert L. "The Last Fifty Years of Irish Agitation." Independent, 28 January 1922, pp. 67-69.

"Republican Election Campaign." Irish Times (Dublin), 13 February 1922.

Leading article. Republic of Ireland/Poblacht na hEireann (Dublin), 14 February 1922.

"Editorial." Catholic Bulletin and Book Review, October 1923, pp. 657-58.

O'Brien, William. "A Missing Page of Irish History." Review of The Life of Sir William Harcourt, by A. G. Gardiner. Catholic Bulletin and Book Review, October 1923, pp. 690-706.

Ervine, St. John. Parnell. London: Ernest Benn, 1925.

*"A Portrait of Parnell." Review of Parnell, by St. John Ervine. Times Literary Supplement, 2 July 1925, p. 441.

Malone, Conor. "Mr. Ervine's 'Jab' Painting of Parnell." Review of Parnell, by St. John Ervine. Catholic Bulletin and Book Review, August 1925, pp. 821-26.

Hayden, Mary T. Review of Parnell, by St. John Ervine. Studies 14 (September 1925): 488-89.

"Parnell and Afterwards." Review of Parnell, by St. John Ervine. Irish Book Lover, October 1925, p. 60.

O'Brien, William. "Parnell and Afterwards." Review of Parnell, by St. John Ervine. English Review, October 1925, pp. 506-23. Reprinted, with minor alterations, in The Parnell of Real Life. London: T. Fisher Unwin, 1926. Pp. 180-213.

Boyd, Ernest. "Readers and Writers." Review of Parnell, by St. John Ervine. Independent, 17 October 1925, p. 449.

O'Brien, William. The Parnell of Real Life. London: T. Fisher Unwin, 1926.

Phillips, W. Allison. The Revolution in Ireland 1906-1923. London: Longmans, Green & Co., 1926.

Robbins, Alfred. Parnell: The Last Five Years. London: Thornton Butterworth, 1926.

*"New Light on Parnell." Review of The Parnell of Real Life, by William O'Brien, and of Parnell: The Last Five Years, by Alfred Robbins. Times Literary Supplement, 4 March 1926, p. 151.

Inis Cealtra. "Mr. William O'Brien and the Real Parnell." Review of The Parnell of Real Life, by William O'Brien. Catholic Bulletin and Book Review, April 1926, pp. 406-12.

Rylett, Harold. "Parnell." Review of Parnell: The Last Five Years, by Alfred Robbins, and of The Parnell of Real Life, by William O'Brien. Contemporary Review, April 1926, pp. 475-81.

M. J. MacM. Review of Parnell: The Last Five Years, by Alfred Robbins, and of The Parnell of Real Life, by William O'Brien. Dublin Magazine, April-June 1926, pp. 60-64.

Inis Cealtra. " 'Oiling the Axle' at Westminster." Review of Parnell: The Last Five Years, by Alfred Robbins. Catholic Bulletin and Book Review, May 1926, pp. 513-21.

"Items of Interest: The Memory of Parnell." Irish Independent (Dublin), 7 October 1926.

Baumann, Arthur A. "Charles Stewart Parnell" and "The Statesman's End." The Last Victorians. Philadelphia: J. B. Lippincott Co., 1927. Pp. 267-74 and 307-15.

Cournos, John. "Charles Stewart Parnell--Ireland's Uncrowned King" and "The Comparison of Lassalle with Parnell and Balzac." A Modern Plutarch: Being an Account of Some Great Lives in the Nineteenth Century, Together with Some Comparisons between the Latin and the Anglo-Saxon Genius. Indianapolis: Bobbs-Merrill Co., 1928. Pp. 156-78 and 200-06.

Healy, Timothy M. Letters and Leaders of My Day. 2 vols. London: Thornton Butterworth, [1928].

*"Mr. Healy's Reminiscences." Review of Letters and Leaders of My Day, by Timothy Healy. Times Literary Supplement, 29 November 1928, p. 926.

Devoy, John. Recollections of an Irish Rebel. New York: n.p., 1929; reprint ed. Shannon: Irish University Press, 1969.

O'Connor, T. P. Memoirs of an Old Parliamentarian. 2 vols. London: Ernest Benn, 1929.

*"Mr. T. P. O'Connor's Memoirs." Review of Memoirs of an Old Parliamentarian, by T. P. O'Connor. Times Literary Supplement, 4 April 1929, p. 266.

Creel, George. "Love of the Leader." Mentor, September 1929, pp. 24-27, 58, 60-61.

Harrison, Henry. Parnell Vindicated: The Lifting of the Veil. London: Constable & Co., 1931.

"Annual Parnell Pilgrimage." Irish Independent (Dublin), 7 October 1931.

Leslie, Shane. "Charles Stewart Parnell 1846-1891. Studies in Sublime Failure. London: Ernest Benn, 1932; reprint ed., Freeport, N. Y.: Books for Libraries Press, 1970. Pp. 59-112.

O'Neill, Brian. The War for the Land in Ireland. London: Martin Lawrence, 1933.

Higginbottom, Frederick J. The Vivid Life: A Journalist's Career. London: Simpkin Marshall, 1934.

Erskine of Marr, Ruaraidh. "Charles Stewart Parnell." King Edward VII and Some Other Figures. London: J. M. Dent & Sons, 1936. Pp. 93-108.

Haslip, Joan. Parnell: A Biography. London: Cobden-Sanderson, 1936; New York: Frederick A. Stokes Co., 1937.

Leamy, Margaret. Parnell's Faithful Few. Preface by Thomas F. Woodlock. New York: MacMillan Co., 1936.

"Lost Leader." Review of Parnell's Faithful Few, by Margaret Leamy. Time, 8 June 1936, pp. 86-87.

S. F. Review of Parnell, by Joan Haslip. Ireland To-day, September 1936, pp. 72-73.

Pritchett, V. S. "Portrait of Parnell." Review of Parnell, by Joan Haslip. Christian Science Monitor Magazine, 2 September 1936, p. 11.

Colum, Padraic. "Ireland and Parnell." Review of Parnell's Faithful Few, by Margaret Leamy. Commonweal, 11 September 1936, pp. 459-61.

*Churchill, Winston S. "The Tragic Story of Parnell." Strand, October 1936, pp. 600-09. Reprinted, with minor alterations, as "Charles Stewart Parnell." Great Contemporaries. Rev. ed. London: Thornton Butterworth, [1938]; reprint ed., Chicago: University of Chicago Press, 1973. Pp. 343-59. "Charles Stewart Parnell" appears only in the revised edition of Great Contemporaries.

"Interesting Items: 'In Memory of the Chief.' " Irish Independent (Dublin), 7 October 1936.

Macardle, Dorothy. The Irish Republic. Preface by Éamon de Valéra. Corgi ed.

London: Victor Gollancz, 1937; paperback ed., London: Transworld Publishers, 1968.

"Screen: Parnell: Paradox in Mutton-chops." Literary Digest, 5 June 1937, pp. 26-29.

de Blacam, Aodh. "Parnell, Moore and the Nation." Review of Parnell, by Léon OBroin, and of The Minstrel Boy, by L. A. G. Strong. Irish Monthly: A Journal of Catholic Action, September 1937, pp. 630-41.

Gibbons, John. Ireland--The New Ally. London: Robert Hale, 1938.

Harrison, Henry. Parnell, Joseph Chamberlain and Mr. Garvin. London: Robert Hale, 1938.

MacBride, Maud Gonne. A Servant of the Queen: Reminiscences. London: Victor Gollancz, 1938; Dublin: Golden Eagle Books, 1950.

MacAodha, Ruaidhre, and ÓhÉagceartaigh, Séan. Parnell. Dublin: Craobh na hAiseirghe and Dublin Wicklowmen's Association, 1941.

MacDonagh, Michael. "Parnell: Once the Most Talked-of Man in Ireland." Irish Weekly Independent (Dublin), 4 October 1941.

"Memory of Parnell Honoured." Irish Independent (Dublin), 7 October 1941.

Bannard, H. E. "Fifty Years Ago: Parnell's Tragedy." Spectator, 10 October 1941, pp. 351-52.

MacDonagh, Michael. "With Parnell at Avondale." Irish Weekly Independent (Dublin), 11 October 1941.

"Parade Pictures." Irish Independent (Dublin), 13 October 1941.

*"Great Tribute to 'The Chief.' " Irish Weekly Independent (Dublin), 18 October 1941.

*MacDonagh, Michael. "Parnell Found the House of Commons Tiresome." Irish Weekly Independent (Dublin), 18 October 1941.

Marshall, David. "Parnell after Fifty Years." Commonweal, 24 October 1941, pp. 6-9.

*MacDonagh, Michael. "Michael MacDonagh Tells How Parnell Disliked Having His Picture Taken." Irish Weekly Independent (Dublin), 25 October 1941.

*Sheehan, Patrick A. "Irish M.P.s Caused Uproar in the Commons." Edited by H. Gaffney. Irish Weekly Independent (Dublin), 1 November 1941. "A hitherto unpublished article by Canon Sheehan, and edited by Rev. Father H. Gaffney, O.P., of Parnell in action."

Ireland, Tom. Ireland Past and Present. New York: G. P. Putnam's Sons, 1942.

Marshall, David. "The Fenians after Seventy-five Years." Catholic World, December 1942, pp. 276-86.

Sullivan, Maev. No Man's Man. Dublin: Browne & Nolan, 1943.

"Parnell's Superstitions." Ireland's Own, 8 June 1946, p. 1.

Gwynn, Stephen. "Parnell." Time and Tide, 22 June 1946, pp. 584-85.

Colum, Padraic. "Heroes of Democracy." Catholic World, November 1946, pp. 122-30.

Horgan, John J. Parnell to Pearse. Dublin: Browne & Nolan, 1948.

P. McK. Review of Parnell to Pearse, by John J. Horgan. Irish Ecclesiastical Record: A Monthly Journal under Episcopal Sanction, June 1949, pp. 564-65.

Ussher, Arland. The Face and Mind of Ireland. New York: Devin-Adair, 1950.

Harrison, Henry. "Memories of an Irish Hero." Listener, 22 March 1951, pp. 455-56.

O'Hegarty, P. S. A History of Ireland under the Union 1801-1922. London: Methuen & Co., 1952.

Moore, Mary. "Those Were the Days! When Parnell Came to Meath." Ireland's Own, 20 September 1952, p. 6.

Harrison, Henry. Parnell, Joseph Chamberlain and "The Times": A Documentary Record, Tempora Mutantur. Dublin: Browne and Nolan, 1953.

F. M. J. Review of Parnell, Joseph Chamberlain and "The Times," by Henry Harrison. Irish Ecclesiastical Record: A Monthly Journal under Episcopal Sanction, December 1953, p. 447.

## Secondary Sources


Archer, J. R. "Necessary Ambiguity: Nationalism and Myth in Ireland." Éire-Ireland 19 (Summer 1984): 23-37.

Arlen, Michael J. "The Air: Waiting for the Storyteller." New Yorker, 21 April 1975, pp. 105-11.

"Blue-shirts and the I. R. A." Quarterly Review, October 1933, pp. 292-305.

Bromage, Mary C. DeValera and the March of a Nation. London: Hutchinson & Co., 1956; Four Square Books, 1967.

Carroll, Joseph T. Ireland in the War Years. Newton Abbot: David & Charles, 1975; New York: Crane, Russak & Co., 1975.

Burch, Vacher. Myth and Constantine the Great. London: Oxford University Press, 1927.

Churchill, Winston S. Speech on BBC Radio, London, 13 May 1945. Reprinted in New York Times, 13 May 1945, and in "Review of War, Pledge for Future: DeValera Denounced." Vital Speeches of the Day, 1 June 1945, pp. 482-83.

Connolly, Thomas L. The Marble Man: Robert E. Lee and His Image in American Society. New York: Alfred A. Knopf, Borzoi Books, 1977.

Cruise O'Brien, Conor. "Ireland in International Affairs." In Conor Cruise O'Brien Introduces Ireland. Edited by Owen Dudley Edwards. London: Andre Deutsch, 1969. Pp. 104-34.

______. Parnell and His Party 1880-90. Oxford: Clarendon Press, 1957.

______. Donat O'Donnell . "Parnell's Monument." Bell, October 1945, pp. 566-73.

______. ed. The Shaping of Modern Ireland. Foreword by Conor Cruise O'Brien. Thomas Davis Lectures, Radio Éireann, Dublin, 1955-56. London: Routledge & Kegan Paul, 1960; Routledge Paperback, 1970.

______. States of Ireland. London: Hutchinson & Co., 1972; New York: Random House, Pantheon Books, 1972; Vintage Books, 1973.

______. Writers and Politics. New York: Random House, Pantheon Books, 1965.

de Valera, Eamon. Speech on Radio Éireann, Dublin, 16 May 1945. Reprinted in "International Morality: Answer to Churchill." Vital Speeches of the Day, 1 June 1945, pp. 485-86.

Dictionary of the History of Ideas. S.v. "Myth in the Nineteenth and Twentieth Centuries," by Mircea Eliade.

Edel, Leon. "Walden: The Myth and the Mystery." American Scholar 44 (Spring 1975): 272-81.

Farrell, Brian. Chairman or Chief? The Role of Taoiseach in Irish Government. Studies in Irish Political Culture, no. 1. Dublin: Gill & Macmillan, 1971.

Fussell, Paul. The Great War and Modern Memory. Oxford: Oxford University Press, 1975; paperback ed., 1977.

Gaster, Theodor H. "The Dimensions of Myth." American Council of Learned Societies Lectures in the History of Religions for 1976-77. Divinity School of the University of Chicago, Chicago, Illinois, 25-29 April 1977.

Grene, David. "Ireland and the War." University of Chicago Magazine, April 1941, pp. 14-16.

Hamer, D. A. "Gladstone: The Making of a Political Myth." Victorian Studies 22 (Autumn 1978): 29-50.

Hazel, Michael V. "Charles Stewart Parnell and the Creation of the Modern Irish State, 1874-86." Ph.D. thesis, University of Chicago, 1974.

International Encyclopedia of the Social Sciences, 1968 ed. S.v. "Myth and Symbol," by Victor W. Turner.

Ireland, Denis. "October Afternoon at Glasnevin." Threshold 3 (Winter 1959-60): 33-35.

Ireland-East Tourism and Parnell Commemoration Committee. Avondale Avondale, Rathdrum, Co. Wicklow : Ireland-East Tourism, n.d.

Kirk, G. S. Myth: Its Meaning and Functions in Ancient and Other Cultures. Sather Classical Lectures, vol. 40. Cambridge: Cambridge University Press, 1970; Berkeley: University of California Press, 1970; Ann Arbor: Campus, 1973.

Kroll, Jack. "Behind the Front Page." Review of All the President's Men, directed by Alan J. Pakula. Newsweek, 5 April 1976, p. 85.

Larkin, Emmet. The Historical Dimensions of Irish Catholicism. The Irish Americans. New York: Arno Press, 1976.

______. The Roman Catholic Church and the Creation of the Modern Irish State 1878-1886. Memoirs of the American Philosophical Society, vol. 108. Philadelphia: American Philosophical Society, 1975.

Lyons, F. S. L. Charles Stewart Parnell. New York: Oxford University Press, 1977.

______. The Fall of Parnell 1890-91. London: Routledge & Kegan Paul, 1960.

______. Ireland since the Famine. Revised ed. London: Collins/Fontana, 1973.

______. John Dillon: A Biography. Chicago: University of Chicago Press, 1968.

______. Parnell. Irish History Series, no. 3. Dublin: Dublin Historical Association, 1970.

McBride, Lawrence W. "The Administrative and Judicial Elite in Ireland, 1892-1922." Ph.D. thesis, University of Chicago, 1978.

McCaffrey, Lawrence J. Daniel O'Connell and the Repeal Year. [Lexington]: University of Kentucky Press, 1966.

______. The Irish Question 1800-1922. [Lexington]: University of Kentucky Press, Kentucky Paperbacks, 1968.

McGuirk, Tom. "Ivy Day in the E.E.C." Irish Times (Dublin), 12 October 1973.

McManus, Francis, ed. The Years of the Great Test. Thomas Davis Lectures, Radio Telefís Éireann, 1962. Cork: Mercier Press, 1967.

Mann, Thomas. "Freud and the Future." In Essays. Translated by H. T. Lowe-Porter. New York: Vintage Books, n.d. Pp. 303-24.

Miller, David W. Church, State and Nation in Ireland 1898-1921. Dublin: Gill & Macmillan, 1973; Pittsburgh: University of Pittsburgh Press, 1973.

Moss, Howard. "Great Themes and Connections." Review of Cavafy, by Robert Liddell. New Yorker, 1 August 1977, pp. 63-68.

Munger, Frank. The Legitimacy of Opposition: The Change of Government in Ireland in 1932. Contemporary Political Sociology Series, vol. 1. Beverly Hills: SAGE Publications, 1975.

Murphy, John A. Ireland in the Twentieth Century. The Gill History of Ireland, no. 11, general editors James Lydon and Margaret MacCurtain. Dublin: Gill & Macmillan, 1975.

Murphy, William Michael. "The Parnellian Tradition." Paper presented at the 17th annual meeting of the American Committee for Irish Studies, James Madison University, Harrisonburg, Virginia, 26 April 1979.

______. "Symbol and the Meaning of the Parnell Myth." Paper presented at a joint session of the American Committee for Irish Studies and the American Historical Association, Chicago, Illinois, 28 December 1974.

O'Carroll, John P. and Murphy, John A., eds. DeValera and His Times. Cork: Cork University Press, 1983.

O'Connor, T. P. The Parnell Movement: With a Sketch of Irish Parties from 1843. London: Kegan Paul & Co., 1886.

O'Farrell, Patrick. England and Ireland since 1900. Oxford: Oxford University Press, 1975; paperback ed., 1975.

O'Keefe, Timothy J. "The Art and Politics of the Parnell Monument." Éire-Ireland 19 (Spring 1984): 6-25.

O'Kennedy, Michael. "No Wish for 'Constant Mendicant' Role," interview by John Cooney. Irish Times (Dublin), 1-2 August 1977.

O'Mahony, Peter T., ed. Eamon de Valera 1882-1975: The Controversial Giant of Modern

Ireland. Dublin: Irish Times, 1976.

"Ourselves Alone: Parnell Fought the Battle from Ireland." Irish Weekly Independent (Dublin), 7 October 1893.

Pakenham, Frank [Earl of Longford] and O'Neill, Thomas P. Eamon de Valera. Boston: Houghton Mifflin Co., 1971.

Redfield, Robert. Tepoztlan: A Mexican Village: A Study of Folk Life. Chicago: University of Chicago Press, 1930; Midway Reprint, 1973.

Redmond, John E. "What Has Become of Home Rule?" Nineteenth Century, November 1894, pp. 665-77.

______. "What Next?" Nineteenth Century, November 1893, pp. 688-97.

Sargeant, Winthrop. "Books: Plus Ca Change." Review of The Mythic Image, by Joseph Campbell. New Yorker, 21 July 1975, pp. 86-88.

Sherlock, Thomas. The Life of Charles Stewart Parnell: With an Account of His Ancestry. Boston: Murphy & McCarthy, 1881.

Slotkin, Richard. Regeneration through Violence: The Mythology of the American Frontier, 1600-1860. Middletown, Conn.: Wesleyan University Press, 1973; paperback ed., 1974.

Steinman, Michael A. "Yeats's Parnell: Sources of His Myth." Éire-Ireland 18 (Spring 1983): 46-60.

[Tannler, Albert M.]. One in Spirit. Chicago: University of Chicago Libraries, 1973.

Warren, Maude Redford. "Again a New Ireland." Saturday Evening Post, 19 November 1932, pp. 16-17, 81-82, 84-86.

Wilson, P. W. "Ireland As a Free State." American Review of Reviews, January 1922, pp. 52-58.

Woolf, Virginia. The Years. London: Hogarth Press, 1937; Penguin Books, 1968.

# INDEX

Abbreviations:

PM: Parnell Myth

RBOB: The Life of Charles Stewart Parnell, by R. Barry O'Brien

KOSP: Charles Stewart Parnell: His Love Story and Political Life, by Katharine O'Shea Parnell

TPOC: Charles Stewart Parnell: A Memory, by T. P. O'Connor

Virginia E. Glandon

# Arthur Griffith and the Advanced-Nationalist Press Ireland, 1900–1922

American University Studies, IX (History), vol. 2
339 pages hardcover $ 33.–
ISBN 0-8204-0041-6

This book focuses upon the role of Arthur Griffith, Ireland's controversial journalist-statesman, and his fellow journalists in the context of the advanced-nationalist press, during the Irish Renaissance: 1900–1922. It evaluates the contributions to the national cause of Griffith and others and contrasts their goals for Ireland, as seen in their newspapers. It reveals the great diversity of opinion among advanced nationalists – a diversity which precluded a united front as they sought to win freedom from English rule. It assesses Griffith's long struggle, first as a journalist and later as a statesman, to unite the Irish behind his plan for an independent Irish state – and why he failed to hold the new nation together as head of its Provisional Gouvernment in 1922. An index of Irish newspapers which circulated in Ireland during the period surveyed is included.

PETER LANG PUBLISHING, INC.
62 West 45th Street
USA – New York, NY 10036

Donald P. Doumitt

# Conflict in Northern Ireland

The History, the Problem, and the Challenge

New York, Berne, Frankfurt/M. 1985. 247 pp.
American University Studies, Series 9: History, Vol. 5
ISBN 0-8204-0102-1 Hardcover US $ 14.–

This study has three objectives: 1) to analyze the intellectual influence on the rise of Ireland's national consciousness from 1890 to 1981, 2) to clarify the social and psychological tensions in Northern Ireland, and 3) to explore the means of a possible resolution of the present civil war.
The importance of the study is that it identifies Northern Ireland's present multi-faceted political character and social polarization which stunted her political development. It focuses on the attitudes of prejudice, religious bigotry, and exaggerated fears and social paranoia endemic to that area. These character traits contribute to the enmity found between Protestant and Catholic and perpetuate the present societal divisions.
The study analyzes the problem of violence, the use of power tactics of competitive groups to manipulate the working class and explores the behavior on the part of Ulster's populace in spite of the information available to them. Probing these problems allows the researcher to explore new ideas in search of a peaceful solution.

PETER LANG PUBLISHING, INC.
62 West 45th Street
USA – New York, NY 10036